TRINITY COLLEGE DUBLIN
THE FIRST 400 YEARS

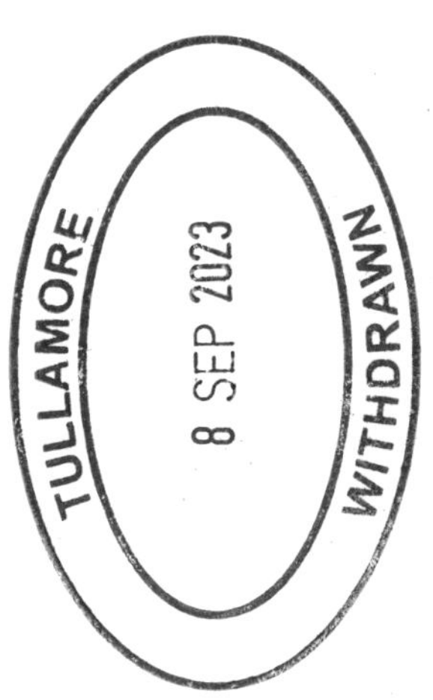

To colleagues and friends in every part of the College

Number 7 in the Trinity College Dublin Quatercentenary Series

TRINITY COLLEGE DUBLIN

THE FIRST 400 YEARS

by J.V. Luce
Fellow Emeritus of Trinity College Dublin
and Public Orator in the University of Dublin

With a foreword by
T.N. Mitchell
Provost of the College

Trinity College Dublin Press

Published in 1992 by
Trinity College Dublin Press
Trinity College
Dublin 2
Ireland

British Library Cataloguing in Publication Data
Luce, J. V.
Trinity College Dublin: First 400 Years. —
(Trinity College Dublin Quatercentenary Series; No. 7)
I. Title II. Series
378.418

ISBN: 1-871408-06-7

Acknowledgements
The illustrations, except those noted below, come from the College's own collection. All were taken by Brendan Dempsey, photographer in the Centre for Language and Communication Studies. I wish also to thank him for his assistance in their selection and reproduction.

I wish to thank the following for supplying photographs and granting permission for their reproduction: The National Portrait Gallery, London (no. 1); The National Library of Ireland (no. 4); the College Historical Society (no. 27); John Minihan (no. 38); Mrs Jennifer Lyons (no. 40); Mrs Lynn Mitchell and *The Irish Times* (no 41); *The Irish Times* (no. 54).

For further information about the portraits and busts, the reader is referred to *Paintings and Sculptures in Trinity College Dublin* by Anne Crookshank and David Webb (Dublin, 1990).

Front Cover: *The Front Square during a quarterly examination,* c. *1819.*
Back Cover: *A perspective drawing of the proposed College, sent to Lord Burghley in 1691 and now in Hatfield House. The plain qaudrangle of brick buildings, with their tall chimney stacks, is viewed from the west. The Liffey is on the north side, and the Provost's lodgings and garden at the south-west corner. The steeple in the north range is a relic of the monastery of All Hallows.*

Produced for Trinity College by
Town House
Dublin 4

Text and cover design: Bill Murphy
Colour origination by The Kulor Centre
Black and white origination by Accu-Plate Ltd
Printed by Criterion Press, Dublin

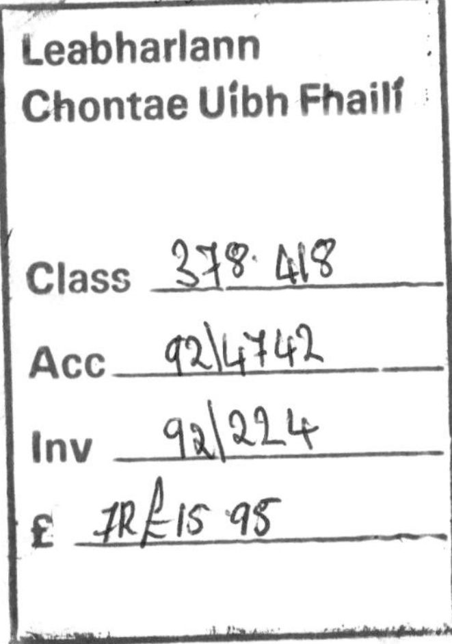

Contents

List of colour plates

List of black and white photographs

Foreword

This is the story, concisely and lucidly told, of one of Ireland's oldest and most famous institutions, and one of the great centres of European education and learning. It seemed fitting, on the eve of the College's four-hundredth anniversary, that the story should be updated and presented in a fresh and readable manner to make more accessible to the Irish public and to the growing numbers of overseas visitors the essential facts about the College's history and its distinguished record of educational achievement and innovation. In 1989 the Quatercentenary Committee decided to commission a new history in this mould, and, as its chairman, I was given the task of finding a suitable author. It proved an easy assignment. I had to look no further than my own School of Classics and Professor J.V. Luce, who as Scholar and Fellow had an association with Trinity extending over more than fifty years, and who knew all facets of the College intimately from long and distinguished service in a variety of posts, including those of Senior Tutor, Public Orator, Senior Dean, and Vice-Provost. He was, besides, a well known Hellenist, a scholar of international reputation, a splendid stylist, famed teacher, and articulate interpreter of many aspects of classical antiquity. He had all the necessary attributes of ability and experience to produce an engrossing new exposition of the College's eventful and sometimes colourful past.

John Luce readily accepted the commission and has fulfilled all our expectations. He has written an account that is eminently readable, packed with information, but laced with valuable insights and made concise by the experienced historian's eye for the significant people and events. He divides the work largely by provostships, which provide a convenient chronological framework helpful to the reader, but at critical points he departs from them to give a panoramic view of the trends, developments and conflicts of a particular era. He has also succeeded admirably in presenting the course of events in College against the historical backdrop that often crucially affected them, and he gives a particularly useful account of the College's adjustment to Irish independence and of its relationship with the Irish government, especially during the critical years of the McConnell provostship.

I am honoured to be associated with the production of this new history, which will add greatly to the public understanding of the College and its past and will stand as a worthy memorial of the quatercentenary.

T.N. Mitchell
Provost
24 September 1991

Preface

The annals of Trinity College, Dublin, tend to arouse mixed feelings in Irish hearts. Respect for the academic achievements of the place is likely to be tempered by regret that the stubborn crosscurrents of religion and politics so long delayed its full acceptance as a national institution. I have tried to tell the story of Trinity in a fair and factual way; the reader is asked to make due allowance for the pride and prejudice of a third-generation graduate.

My indebtedness to previous historians of the College, and especially to the magisterial work of Brendan McDowell and David Webb, will be clear and is hereby gratefully acknowledged. If I have broken new ground in bringing the story down to the eve of the quatercentenary, the attempt has made me even more aware of the truth of Horace's remark that writing about the recent past is a 'risk-filled enterprise'.

Many friends and colleagues helped me in a multitude of ways, and I ask them to accept the dedication as my 'thank-you'. Here I have space only to mention by name some of those who gave me particularly valued assistance. Aidan Clarke, Erasmus Smith's Professor of Modern History, cast a constructive and professional eye over the final draft and saved me from a number of errors, particularly in the earlier period. Any that remain are my own responsibility. Frank Mitchell, who was Registrar for the first fourteen years of Dr McConnell's provostship, commented on a draft of chapter 13. Ian Howie, Registrar at the time of the 'merger', vetted chapter 14, and helped me to a more balanced view of the whole affair. A younger colleague, David McConnell, kindly gave me his perspective on the student unrest of the late 1960s and 70s, as did Patrick Smyth, a student at the time. Both of them made a number of suggestions which I was happy to incorporate in chapter 15. Trevor West generously put a pre-publication draft of his history of College sport at my disposal, and my account of that aspect of College life owes much to his researches.

In the administration, I have to thank Dermot Sherlock for his ready response to numerous queries on student statistics. The Treasurer, Franz Winkelmann, and the former Secretary, Gerry Giltrap, who have played key roles in the modernisation of Trinity over the last thirty years, were most helpful with information and advice. I should also like to express my appreciation of the courtesy of the present Secretary, Michael Gleeson, and his staff, particularly Daphne Siggins and Monica Alcock, in facilitating my access to recent College records.

The present Provost, Dr Tom Mitchell, and I were close colleagues for a decade in the School of Classics, and I am very grateful to him for commissioning the work in his capacity as chairman of the Quatercentenary Committee and also for contributing the Foreword.

The writing, done in the first two years of my retirement, has been a 'labour of love', both arduous and stimulating, and sustained as always by the understanding support of my wife. I feel greatly honoured to be able to offer the book as my personal contribution to the celebration of Trinity's four-hundredth birthday.

John V. Luce
Trinity College Dublin
9 December 1991

CHAPTER 1

The foundation and early years of the College

As the sixteenth century entered its last decade, Ireland was still without a university, a fact all the more surprising when one considers that three of Scotland's universities date from before 1500. The leading citizens of Dublin were anxious to remedy this situation, and the provision of a university for the now rapidly growing city had long been under active discussion. As early as 1547, George Browne, Archbishop of Dublin, had sent Edward VI a well-considered proposal for the establishment of a 'fair and large Colledge' on the site of St Patrick's Cathedral 'beside Dublin'.[1] The Cathedral had recently been suppressed, and the Archbishop proposed to use its buildings and endowments for the new foundation. When the Cathedral was re-established under Queen Mary, the proposal was temporarily shelved, but was revived again with enthusiasm by the Lord Deputy, Sir John Perrot, in 1584.

Perrot was well aware that strong representations on Ireland's need for a university had already been made to Elizabeth I by James Stanihurst, the Speaker of the Irish House of Commons, and by the Irish Council. He reckoned that the Cathedral revenues would suffice to found two new colleges, but he met strong opposition from Adam Loftus, now Archbishop of Dublin. In 1563 Loftus, as Primate in Armagh, had been willing to support the St Patrick's scheme, but now that he was in Dublin he saw things differently. He has been accused of selfish concern for his diocesan revenues, and doubtless these were an important consideration, but he may well have come to the honest belief that Dublin's interests would best be served by retaining St Patrick's as a cathedral, and finding a different site for the College.

At this juncture, the problem of the site was decisively solved by a resolution of Dublin Corporation, passed under Lord Mayor Edward Devenish in January 1591.[2] It was agreed and ordered 'that the scite of All

Hallowes and the parkes thereof shalbe wholly given for the erecon of a Colledge there.'[3] In earlier times All Hallows had been an Augustinian monastery of considerable wealth and importance, but it had suffered dissolution under Henry VIII, and the site, lying about half-a-mile to the east of the city walls, had been made over to the city in 1538. The precinct amounted to about twenty-eight acres, and consisted of the monastic buildings, now in a derelict state, with surrounding fields and orchards rented out to local proprietors.[4] It was a generous gesture to make it available for educational purposes freely and in perpetuity, and the College has always remembered the Lord Mayor and Corporation as major benefactors.

The gift of the site formed part of a well-orchestrated campaign, probably masterminded by Loftus. As Archbishop of Dublin, he was in a good position to influence the Corporation and had delivered a well-calculated address to them in July 1590, in which he had stressed the economic benefits that a university would bring to the city. Loftus also had the ear of Lord Burghley, and was ably supported in his plans by two prominent Dublin citizens, Henry Ussher, Archdeacon of Dublin, and Luke Challoner, who, as one of the first Fellows, was to work longer and more effectively for the early College than any of his peers.[5]

With the site secured, the Mayor and Corporation next requested the Lord Deputy and Council to make representations to Queen Elizabeth I for a charter. Henry Ussher travelled to London in November 1591 to act in person as petitioner on behalf of the city. He carried letters of recommendation for the Privy Council in which the Dublin authorities gave it as their opinion that a university in the city would be a good means 'to plant religion, civilitie, and true obedience in the hearts of this people'. Burghley had doubtless been well briefed by Loftus, and the Queen's warrant (dated 29 December 1591) signifying her willingness to licence 'a College for learning', was sent by him to Dublin in a letter received there in January 1592. The charter itself may have been drawn up in Dublin in accordance with the royal wishes. It bears the date 3 March 1591 (1592, new-style), which must therefore be regarded as the day when Trinity College formally came into existence.

The charter speaks of the Queen's general goodwill towards studies and those engaged in them, notes her special interest in providing better education for her Irish subjects, and signifies her gracious assent to the petition of Henry Ussher, presented in the name of the City of Dublin. The College was to be named *Collegium Sanctae et Individuae Trinitatis juxta Dublin a Serenissima Regina Elizabetha fundatum* (The College of the

Holy and Undivided Trinity near Dublin founded by the Most Serene Queen Elizabeth), and its purpose was to provide 'for the education, formation, and instruction of youths and students in the arts and faculties', a purpose that the College has succeeded in carrying out for close on four hundred years.

The charter twice refers to the College as *mater Universitatis* (mother of a university), and this has generated protracted argument about the relationship between the two. But much of the discussion relates to the legal and constitutional position after the formal incorporation of the Senate in 1857, and is not relevant to the early College. The phrase first appears in the opening summary of Ussher's petition, and may well have been a Dublin formulation which the Queen simply adopted without any hidden or long-term purposes in mind. If so, Loftus and his friends will have used the phrase as a suitably modest way of conveying their proposal to the royal ear. By 'College' they will have meant the staff and buildings necessary for the provision of education at university level. Conscious of their lack of resources, they had only one College in mind, so Trinity, initially at least, would not have been seen as a university comparable in structure to multi-collegiate Oxford or Cambridge (though it might expand in that way). But Loftus and his associates also wanted their Dublin college to have university status in the sense that it would be an independent, self-perpetuating academic institution, empowered to confer degrees.

This was exactly what Elizabeth I granted them. She constituted the College with Loftus as its first Provost, Henry Ussher, Luke Challoner and Launcelot Moine (Money) as its first Fellows, and Henry Lee, William Daniel[6] and Stephen White as its first Scholars. The names were listed *nomine plurium* and it was envisaged that the body of Fellows and Scholars would grow from the start. Provost, Fellows and Scholars were to constitute the corporate body, and the Fellows were given the right (later revoked by the charter of Charles I) to elect a new Provost by majority vote within three months of a vacancy. The Provost and Fellows were also empowered to make laws, statutes and ordinances for the decent and loyal government of the College, and were advised to adopt whatever fit laws they might see in operation in Oxford or Cambridge. The College authorities were authorised to advance their students to the degrees of Bachelor, Master, and Doctor in all arts and faculties, at a suitable time. William Cecil, Lord Burghley, was nominated as the first Chancellor[7], but the Provost and Fellows were empowered to elect future Chancellors. They were also authorised to appoint a Pro-Chancellor and Proctors, and such other persons as might be required for the due performance of scholastic exercises. Provision was also made for a Court of seven Visitors (including the Archbishops of Dublin and of Meath, the Chief Justice, and the Lord Mayor of Dublin) to deal with disputes that the Provost and a majority of the Fellows could not settle. Trinity College was thus incorporated as a university from its very inception, a fact well summarised by James I when he allowed it parliamentary representation in 1613 on the grounds that 'it is called a College and considered to be a University'.

Elizabeth I is rightly remembered as Trinity's founder, in the sense that she gave the necessary royal assent to Dublin's proposal; but she made no provision, initially at least, for an endowment for the 'House', though this was clearly requested in the petition. However, she did specify that the body corporate had the right to acquire and hold property in perpetuity, with exemption from all forms of taxes and exactions. So the Lord Deputy Fitzwilliam and the Irish Privy Council at once set about raising money for the new foundation by sending an appeal for subscriptions to leading citizens in every county in Ireland.[8] Fitzwilliam himself set a good example with a gift of £200, and Loftus gave £100. The list of donors contains some interesting names: Sir Turlough O'Neill (the uncle of the Earl of Tyrone) gave £100, and Sir Hugh Magennis, with the gentlemen of County Down, donated £140. The total comes to £2047, but the list is unfortunately incomplete. The money was applied to the building and furnishing of the new College.

Work was far enough advanced for the College to receive its first students early in 1594, and Trinity began its academic work on 9 January of that year. We have a description of its appearance from Walter Travers in a letter he wrote to Burghley in August 1594 soon after he arrived in Dublin to take up his appointment as the second Provost:

> Beinge a quadrant of bricks of 3 storeys, and on every side within the court, it is 120 feet broad, the west side which is of chambers, and the north side wherein are the Chapell, hall, buttery and kitchen, are orderly fynished. The other two sides are only walles, saving some little beginninge of chambers, which for want of further meanes, is yet unperfect.

The Elizabethan quadrangle was completed with a galleried library along the top of its south range and more chambers in its east range. It continued to form the nucleus of the College buildings until well into the Georgian period, and its last vestiges were not removed until the final decade of the eighteenth century. Plans and views from that time show it situated in what is now the area of Front Square between the Campanile and the 1937 Reading Room. Its northern range, with Chapel (rebuilt in 1683) and Hall (rebuilt in 1697), lay on the axis that links the Front Gate and the Campanile, and its southern range extended between the Old Library and the Examination Hall.

Walter Travers (*c.* 1548–1634) came from a fellowship at Trinity College, Cambridge. He was chosen by the Fellows on the strong recommendation of one of their number, Matthias Holmes, and had the support of Burghley (who failed to secure him preferment in England). He was sworn in on 5 December 1594. Travers planned accommodation for 220 students, but the build-up was slow, and in 1597 there were only ten scholars in residence. They included James Ussher, a nephew of Henry, later destined to achieve great eminence in scholarship and the Church. Of the three original Fellows, only Challoner remained. The numbers were made up by Lee and Daniel who had soon advanced to fellowship (in 1593), and two outsiders are also said to have been elected in 1593. These were James Fullerton, who had been Master of the Free School, Dublin since 1588, and his assistant, James Hamilton. Both were Scotsmen and laymen, and the two men were later knighted by James I. There are indications that they were acting as political agents for James in Ireland, helping to prepare the ground for his accession to the English throne. They certainly added a new dimension to the early fellowship body, being men of the world rather that academics, and they did valuable work in securing and managing the estates that the College was now beginning to acquire after persistent lobbying by Travers.

The first grant of estates was made by the Queen in May 1597, and consisted of consfiscated land in Kerry and Limerick, amounting to some 3000 acres. The College had been pressing for some years for an annual endowment of at least £100, and the grant was calculated to yield more than this sum. But the great Irish uprising, led by the Earl of Tyrone, which raged during the closing years of Elizabeth's reign, disrupted the collection of rents. Between 1598 and 1603 the College had to rely on ad hoc grants from the Lords Justices, which were given on a generous scale.

Trinity was allowed a surprisingly large measure of independence from the start. Its constitution gave it the right to make its own laws and appoint its own officers, including the Provost, without dictation (though not, admittedly, without pressure) from church or state. No tests for entry or office-holding were prescribed initially, no ecclesiastical observances enjoined. Until the Laudian revision of the Statutes in 1637, there was no obligation on Fellows to take holy orders, and eight remained as laymen. Its founders planned it in a farsighted and liberal spirit, confident that it would provide a good and much-needed higher education for the sons of Dubliners, and hoping that it would develop into a civilising and unifying institution for the whole country. It was not their fault, and it was Trinity's misfortune, that the educational balance was distorted, and the high hopes frustrated, by ever-intensifying religious and political animosities in the first half of the seventeenth century.

The training of churchmen was still an important function of all universities at this time, Catholic as well as Protestant. Trinity was cast in this mould, and its initial ethos tended towards the Puritan wing of Anglicanism. The cause is to be sought in the Cambridge influence, which was strong in the early College. Trinity's first five Provosts (as well as Luke Challoner and Henry Ussher) were Cambridge men, and Cambridge at the time was a great nursery of Puritanism. The scholars it produced formed the intellectual cutting edge of the Reformation in England. They were marked by a great zeal for learning, especially for the linguistic and historical expertise needed for biblical exegesis. They were suspicious of episcopal authority, whether displayed in the Church of Rome or of England. Pious and devout, and very conscious of the individual's responsibility for his own character and actions, they took seriously the improvement of mind and morals, both in themselves, and in any young men placed in their charge.[9]

Provost Travers exemplified the type. He had been employed by Burghley, who was sympathetic to the Puritan movement, as tutor to his second son Robert. Burghley was a prime mover in the creation of the College, and Robert was its Chancellor from 1601 until his death in 1612. J. P. Mahaffy calls Travers a 'turbulent Presbyterian'. He was certainly a very argumentative Protestant, who controverted the Church of England in its discipline as vigorously as he opposed the Church of Rome in its doctrine. Burghley died on 4 August 1598, and his protégé left for England a little over two months later. The College then had to survive three very difficult years without a head, because the next Provost, Henry Alvey, was not admitted until 8 October 1601.

In assessing the early growth of the College, we are handicapped by the fact that year-by-year records of entrants go back only to 1637. The earlier admission books have not survived. Fortunately, however, some lists of names are preserved in the *Particular Book*,[10] and these indicate that eighty-nine students were admitted in the first fifteen years, and that by the early 1620s the annual intake was running at about sixteen. Students were normally admitted in their early teens, so the four-year course up to BA was being taken by what we would regard as schoolboys. Most would then stay on for a further three years, studying for their MA. It is these candidate masters who equate in age with the modern undergraduate. On gaining their MA, the pick of these students could expect election to fellowship, which they might thus attain (as James Ussher did) by the age of twenty-one. In the Elizabethan charter, the tenure of fellowship is limited to seven years, a provision not repealed until the 1637 revision. So the early Fellows were more like postgraduates, continuing their studies until a permanent position in the outside world should become available. It is hardly surprising that Provost Temple decided to confine participation in the government of the College to the seven most senior of them. He was therefore responsible for introducing the distinction between Senior and Junior Fellows, which is still a significant feature of Trinity's constitution.

What sort of course did those early students study? The undergraduates, then as now, were divided into four classes by year, with separate lectures for each class. The Junior Freshmen were initiated into the traditional disciplines of rhetoric and logic. The Senior Freshmen went deeper into problems about the nature and methods of logical reasoning. Natural science was the staple for the Junior Sophisters (third-year students), while the Senior Sophisters (fourth-year) were lectured in psychology and ethics.[11] As a test of their comprehension, all students were required to present to their lecturer a weekly commentary (in Latin) on the subject-matter of the course. There was also provision for regular practice in public declamation in the College Hall, without notes, on a social, moral, or political theme. Sophisters had to take part in formal weekly disputations on logical themes or scientific questions.

James Ussher's first biographer, the Reverend Nicholas Bernard, gives some details of the teaching, presumably based on the great man's recollections of his student days before 1600:

> The education which that College then gave was very eminent. At the first foundation there were but four Fellows, and yet the tongues (i.e. Latin, Greek, Hebrew) and arts (i.e. the above syllabus) were very exactly taught to all the students, being divided into several classes. Aristotle's text was read in Greek by each tutor to his pupils: three lectures a day every Fellow read, at each of which there was a disputation on what had been then read, or the lecture before, and among other ways, they were sometimes ordered to dispute *more Socratico*. On Saturday in the afternoon each tutor read in Latin a

> Divinity lecture to his pupils, and dictated it so deliberately that they easily took it in writing, and so were their other lectures also.

The course constituted an introduction to 'Science' (*Scientia* = Knowledge) as it was then understood. The content of the logic lectures was basically Aristotelian, but there was some concession to modernity if, as seems very probable, Willam Temple's 1584 edition of Ramus's *Dialectica* was used as the main textbook.[12] As at Oxford or Cambridge, those not destined for the Church or academic life would leave with their BA after four years, but they were in a minority. Intending ordinands would work on for a further three years towards their MA. At Trinity this was far from being a formality. They had to attend lectures in political science and mathematics, take part in disputations on mathematical and physical topics, and deliver prelections on their course subjects, as well as keeping up their Greek and Hebrew.

In framing this curriculum, the authorities looked to Cambridge as their model, but also took account of the fact that the students came to university younger, and less well prepared, from Irish schools. Dublin also differed in making the formal lecture, rather than the disputation, the main fulcrum of student training. Even by the end of the sixteenth century, Ireland had been little affected by the literary enthusiasms of the Renaissance. The issues of the Reformation, on the other hand, were of central importance to the country. Not surprisingly, the first fruits of Trinity scholarship were seen in biblical and theological studies, and in ecclesiastical history, fields in which James Ussher gained an impressive reputation as the leading scholar of the British Isles. Although he resigned his Trinity fellowship about 1605, he continued to be associated with the College as its principal lecturer in Divinity from 1607 to 1621, with the title of Professor of Theological Controversies — a significant indication of the intellectual climate of the day. Theology completed the range of student study at this time. The Elizabethan charter had envisaged teaching in all the faculties, which included Law and Medicine as well as Divinity, but these other subjects did not develop until after the Restoration.

Notes

1. The Cathedral precincts had briefly been the site of a seminary with university status established by Alexander de Bicknor, Archbishop of Dublin, in 1320. Lectures in divinity and civil and canonical law seem to have continued until at least 1358, and some degrees were conferred, but the enterprise then petered out. A parliament held at Drogheda in 1465 passed a statue to found a university on the lines of Oxford, but again nothing came of it. In general, as McDowell and Webb (*History*, 1) indicate, the native Irish did not like the idea of a university in Dublin, the heart of the Pale, and the inhabitants of the Pale lacked the security and resources required for a successful foundation.
2. Murphy (*History*, 18) shows that Mahaffy (*Epoch*, 62) made a mistake about this date. Much confusion has been generated about this and other early dates in College history by the fact that contemporary documents use the old-style dating, under which the (legal) new year was not reckoned to begin until 25 March. The date on the College charter is 3 March 1591, which must be rewritten 1592 to get the *year* right by our reckoning. One should also add on ten days to get the date into *strict* new style, but I have followed the convention of altering only the year when quoting such dates.
3. The legal document making the grant is dated 21 July 1592, under Mayor Thomas Smith, who also, according to Mahaffy, laid the foundation stone on 13 March 1593. But this latter date cannot be correct since Smith's term of office ended in the autumn of 1592. Murphy (*History*, 18–20) argues convincingly that the ceremony took place on 13 March 1592 (as Stubbs also held). There is evidence that building was under way by the summer of 1592, and was well advanced by the spring of 1593. This dating puts the stone-laying only ten days after the charter date, which may seem implausible, but has the advantage of allowing twenty-two months for the building of the College, which we know opened its doors to students on 9 January 1594.
4. The 1991 campus, 40.9 acres in total, is not a great deal larger. The additional ground seems to have been acquired mainly in the north-east segment of the site.
5. The Ussher family was one of the oldest and most respected in Dublin. Arland Ussher had been Mayor in 1469, and one of his grandsons, John Ussher, had also been Mayor (in 1561), and had pressed the case for a university, first with Burghley in 1571, and ten years later with Sir Francis Walsingham, Queen Elizabeth's Secretary of State. Ussher was connected to Loftus through the marriage of his only son to Loftus's daughter, Isabella. Sad to say, he died in 1590, just before the scheme for a new university came to fruition. Henry Ussher, the Archdeacon, was his cousin once-removed. Luke Challoner was connected to the Ussher family through his wife, Elinor, and rented a farm near Finglas from Loftus. So Loftus, Henry Ussher and Challoner formed a closely knit group, connected by ties of marriage and business and united in purpose by a long continued interest in the development of higher education in Ireland. A great-great-great-great grandson of Loftus, another Henry Ussher, was elected to fellowship in 1764, designed the main building of Dunsink Observatory, and became the first Andrews' Professor of Astronomy in 1783.
6. Daniel went on to become a Fellow, and translated the New Testament and Book of Common Prayer into Irish, publishing his versions in 1603 and 1608 respectively.
7. Burghley, Chancellor of Cambridge since 1559, was a statesman who respected learning. His biographer, Edward Nares, credits him with the first suggestion of the foundation of Trinity (i.e. on its present site), and he probably played a major part in securing the charter. A letter to him from the Lord Deputy and Council, dated 26 May 1594, describes the college as 'by your especial means next under God, first founded in this distressed country' (TCD MS. Mun/P/1/6).
8. Sir James Ware (*Antiquities*, 248) gives the text of the circular letter issued on 11 March 1592. It sets out the purpose of founding a College 'whereby knowledge, learning and civility may be increased, to the banishing of barbarism, tumults, and disorderd living from among them, and whereby their children and childrens' children, especially those that be poor, may have their learning and education given them with much more ease and lesser

charges that in other universities they can obtain it.'

9. W. Macneile Dixon (*Trinity*, 30) makes an interesting judgment: 'The spirit of sturdy independence and devotion to literary and scientific freedom of thought which have from the first been the distinction of Dublin among British Universities owes not a little to the Puritan atmosphere of the College in its early career.'
10. The *Particular Book* comprises a miscellaneous collection of records, accounts and memoranda, covering the period from the earliest days of the College down to 1641. Shortly before the latter date, a separate Registry, Matriculation Book and Bursar's Book were instituted, and it seems probable that such earlier documents as were available were then assembled and bound up in a single volume. The *Book* was edited and published in facsimile by J. P. Mahaffy in 1904.
11. In the 1940s, medical and engineering students still had to take a modified arts course in addition to their professional subjects, and the author when holding studentship (a temporary junior lectureship) can recall lecturing them in logic, psychology, and ethics.
12. Pierre de la Ramée, or Petrus Ramus (1515–72), was a French humanist who met his death in the massacre of St Bartholomew's Eve. He reacted strongly against scholastic Aristotelianism, and worked successfully to present the elements of logic in a more up-to-date way. Milton approved of him, and wrote a treatise on logic, following his method. Popular among the Protestant intelligentsia, de la Ramée was valued for having introduced a note of Puritan practicality into the syllogistic methods of reasoning still used in the disputations of the day.

CHAPTER 2

Growth and reorganisation 1601–1641

The far from pacific annals of the Old Testament occasionally record that 'the land had rest for forty years', and the same could be said of Ireland in the first half of the seventeenth century. Mountjoy's victory at Kinsale in 1601 ensured the completion of the Tudor conquest, and from then to the great insurrection of 1641 the country remained comparatively peaceful. This lull in the military struggle between the English state and the Irish nation gave the young College a much-needed chance to put down its roots and grow in numbers, confidence and prosperity.

With the submission of Hugh O'Neill in 1603, English administration became effective throughout the whole of Ireland, and anglicisation went steadily ahead in law and language, but not in religion. In Elizabeth's time the Catholic religious orders had spearheaded the Counter-Reformation in Ireland with notable energy and fervour, and, under the Stuarts, Old English and native Irish alike remained staunchly Catholic. Outside the towns, Protestantism was confined to the more recent English settlers, and spread only where they spread, as in Ulster after the plantations. Catholic families who wanted a university education for their sons were under pressure to send them abroad to study in Spain, France or the Netherlands. This created a dilemma for the Old English element in the population which remained generally loyal to the Crown, and there are indications that the new University in Dublin, which offered a good education nearer home, had some limited success in attracting entrants across the religious divide. Unlike Oxford, where students at matriculation had to declare assent to the Thirty-nine Articles, no conformity tests were in force for admission to the College, and before 1641 quite a number of Catholic laymen were educated there, some admittedly under compulsion as wards of court. In 1615 the student body included Thomas, son of Maurice Fitzgerald, and Fergal O'Gara, the patron of the 'Four Masters'. In an admission list of 1621, a Bryen O Bryen rubs shoulders with a Robert Ogden and a George Cottingham.

Some useful insights into the social composition of the student body can be gleaned from the accounts of the time, especially those for Commons. From entries that probably date from the first decade of the new century, we can infer that there were scholars supported by the College, scholars sponsored by well-to-do patrons, pensioners (who paid for their Commons plus a wear and tear charge of 2½d a week), and fellow commoners (who also paid for their commons plus 4½d a week). The last class had the privilege of dining at the Fellows' table. They were the sons of the nobility and gentry, who were now beginning to support the Dublin college rather than sending their offspring to Oxford or Cambridge. Their early presence in the College is confirmed by a list of student misdemeanours recorded from 1609 and 1610, which includes: striking a fellow commoner, going into Desmond's orchard, lodging in the town without leave, and offering violence to the partition doors of the library. The offences were variously punished by censure, fines, and deprival of dining rights for one to six weeks.[1]

James I was a learned man with a penchant for scholarship, and he proved a generous supporter of the College. Between 1610 and 1613 he endowed it with five separate grants of land in various parts of the country, the largest being in the north, and amounting to some 20,000 acres. He also gifted the patronage of nineteen livings, all in northern dioceses.[2] The hand of the former Fellows Fullerton and Hamilton is detectable in these Ulster benefactions. The King also confirmed in perpetuity an annual subsidy of £388.15s which the College had been receiving from the Crown, and this grant, known as the Concordatum Fund, was in fact continued down to the reign of Queen Victoria. This royal largesse helped to transform the poor college of Elizabeth into a reasonably well-endowed foundation.

In the first decade of the new century the College library was also put on a sound footing. A list of its holdings in 1600 shows a mere forty-six entries, but some years later the collection ran into several thousands. From 1601 on, the authorities succeeded in collecting from the Exchequer about £700 in instalments. This sum represented a donation which army officers serving in Ireland at the time of the foundation had promised from their pay. The benefaction had been designated for books, and in 1603, and again in 1609, the College gave effect to the donors' wishes by sending Luke Challoner and James Ussher to England to make extensive purchases for the library.[3]

Robert Devereux, second Earl of Essex, had succeeded Burghley as Chancellor in 1598. His tenure of the post coincided with the three-year vacancy in the provostship that occurred after Travers's retirement. Essex's approval for any new appointment was obviously desirable, but would have been difficult to obtain during his ill-starred Irish campaign in 1599, and impossible after his subsequent disgrace and imprisonment in the Tower of London. His execution early in 1601, and the appointment of Robert Cecil as his successor, opened the way for a new attempt to fill the post, and with the approval of the Irish Council an invitation was sent to Henry Alvey, a Fellow of St John's College, Cambridge. Alvey arrived in Dublin on 7 October, and the Fellows headed by Challoner duly appointed him Provost the following day. The election was approved by the Lecturers and Masters in Arts, a significant indication of the democratic nature of the early constitution. In March 1602 Alvey went back to England, and did not return until October 1603. An outbreak of plague in June 1604 caused a temporary closure of the College, and he again retired to England until June 1605.

Alvey was a conscientious Puritan who kept meticulous accounts. From these one can recover the surnames of some thirty-five students resident in the College in 1605/06 (including three Pelhams and three Kavanaghs), and it is possible to estimate that the Society numbered about seventy at the close of his tenure. Though Alvey was Provost for eight years, he resided for not much over five, and left little or no mark on Trinity. During his absences, the College effectively was administered by Luke Challoner and James Ussher.

Alvey's successor, William (later Sir William) Temple was elected on 14 November 1609 at a salary of £100 a year. He came of an old Warwickshire family, and had held a fellowship at King's College, Cambridge. Eminent as a scholar and logician, he was also experienced in public affairs, having been secretary to Sir Philip Sidney (who died in his arms at Arnheim), and then to the second Earl of Essex. The first layman to hold the provostship, Temple was also a married man, and may have had his wife and family with him in his College lodgings, though there is no direct evidence of this.

Temple was active in securing the King's support for the College. He also improved its internal administration by bringing the current statutes into a well codified form. The version produced early in his term of office survives only in part, but clearly formed the basis of the later revision by Provost Bedell in 1628/29, which in turn was largely incorporated in the Laudian reform of 1637. Temple defined the duties of various College officers, including the Bursar and the Deans, on the Cambridge model. Under his rule, the number of Fellows was increased from four to sixteen, and the number of Scholars (in the sense of students maintained at the expense of the College) from twenty-eight to seventy.

Rising numbers led to the opening of the College's first extra-mural hall of residence in 1617. Named Trinity Hall, it lay to the west of Hoggen Green (now College Green), near the present Trinity Street. Challoner, with some other leading citizens, had acquired the one-acre site from the Corporation in 1604 in order to build a bridewell for vagrants. The Corporation had stipulated at the time that if this project failed (which it did), the land should be used for a College hall or free school. The site was now transferred to College ownership, buildings were erected, a resident Master appointed, and students resided there until 1641.

Temple had his share of difficulties. There were protracted quarrels with the Fellows over the terms of new leases for the College lands. He also came under pressure from the Archbishop of Canterbury, George Abbot, to conform more strictly to Anglican ritual. Abbot had been elected Chancellor in 1612 in succession to Robert Cecil, and wanted to change the constitution of the College in ways that would have strengthened the role of the Chancellor and diminished the autonomy of the Fellows. He also criticised Temple and the Fellows for not wearing surplices in Chapel. This was far from being a minor point. It was symptomatic of the Church of England's increasing dismay about the nonconformist path being followed by the College. Temple fought back, arguing that, as a layman, he had no obligation to wear a surplice. He also made a special journey to London to lobby the authorities on the constitutional issues, and succeeded in having the matter deferred. But the issue of reform was soon to be taken up by Laud.

Temple was the first Provost to die in office, on 15 January 1627, at the age of seventy-two. The Fellows immediately showed their independent spirit, not to say factionalism, by selecting two successors. The choice of the Seniors was Joseph Mede, a Cambridge divine, but he refused to accept the position. The Juniors, asserting their right under the charter to a voice in the election, chose Robert Ussher, the Vice-Provost, and proceeded to swear him in. Meanwhile, the Chancellor and Vice-Chancellor (James Ussher) were proposing William Bedell, a more eminent man than either of the Fellows' candidates. Thanks to the firm, not to say dictatorial, intervention of Charles I, Bedell's candidature finally prevailed, and he was formally sworn in on 16 August 1627.

William Bedell (1571–1642) was a graduate of Cambridge, and had held

cont. p15

1 *William Cecil, Lord Burghley (1521–98), chief minister of Queen Elizabeth I, and a prime mover in the foundation of the College.*

2 (Bust) *James Ussher (1581–1656), Fellow (1599–1605), Professor of Divinity (1607–21), Vice-Chancellor (1615–c.1641), Bishop of Meath (1620–24), Archbishop of Armagh (1624–56). Ussher matriculated with the first group of students in 1594 and later became one of the leading biblical scholars of Europe.*

3 *George Berkeley (1685–1753), philosopher and churchman, Fellow (1707–24), Bishop of Cloyne (1734–53), author of* A Treatise concerning the Principles of Human Knowledge *(1710), and other celebrated works.*

4 *A sketch of the College, viewed from the west, made by an English visitor, Thomas Dinely, in 1680. The original quadrangle lies in the centre, with some additional ranges extending north and west from it, notably Sir Jerome Alexander's Building (fronting College Green). The steeple of the chapel is visible, with the College pump in the court behind, that was later to become Library Square.*

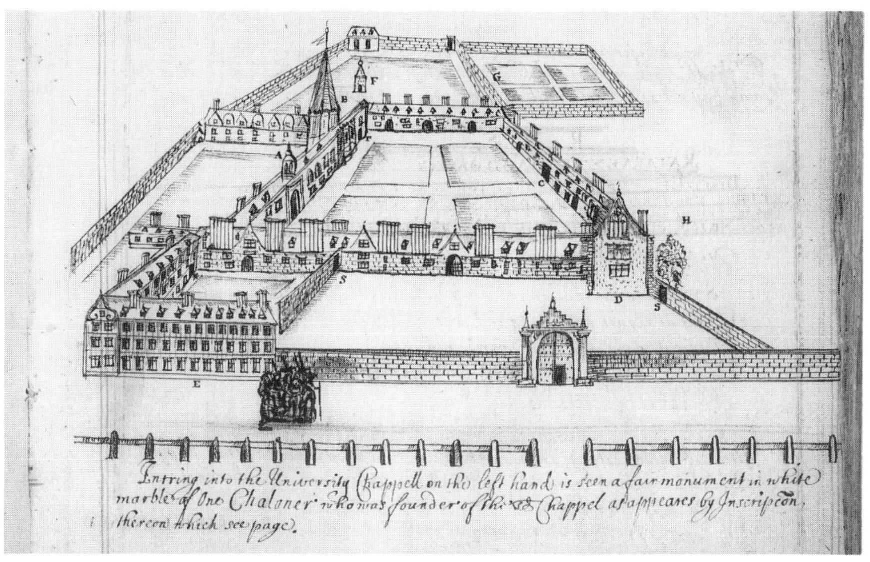

5 *A recent aerial view of Trinity College, taken from the west.*

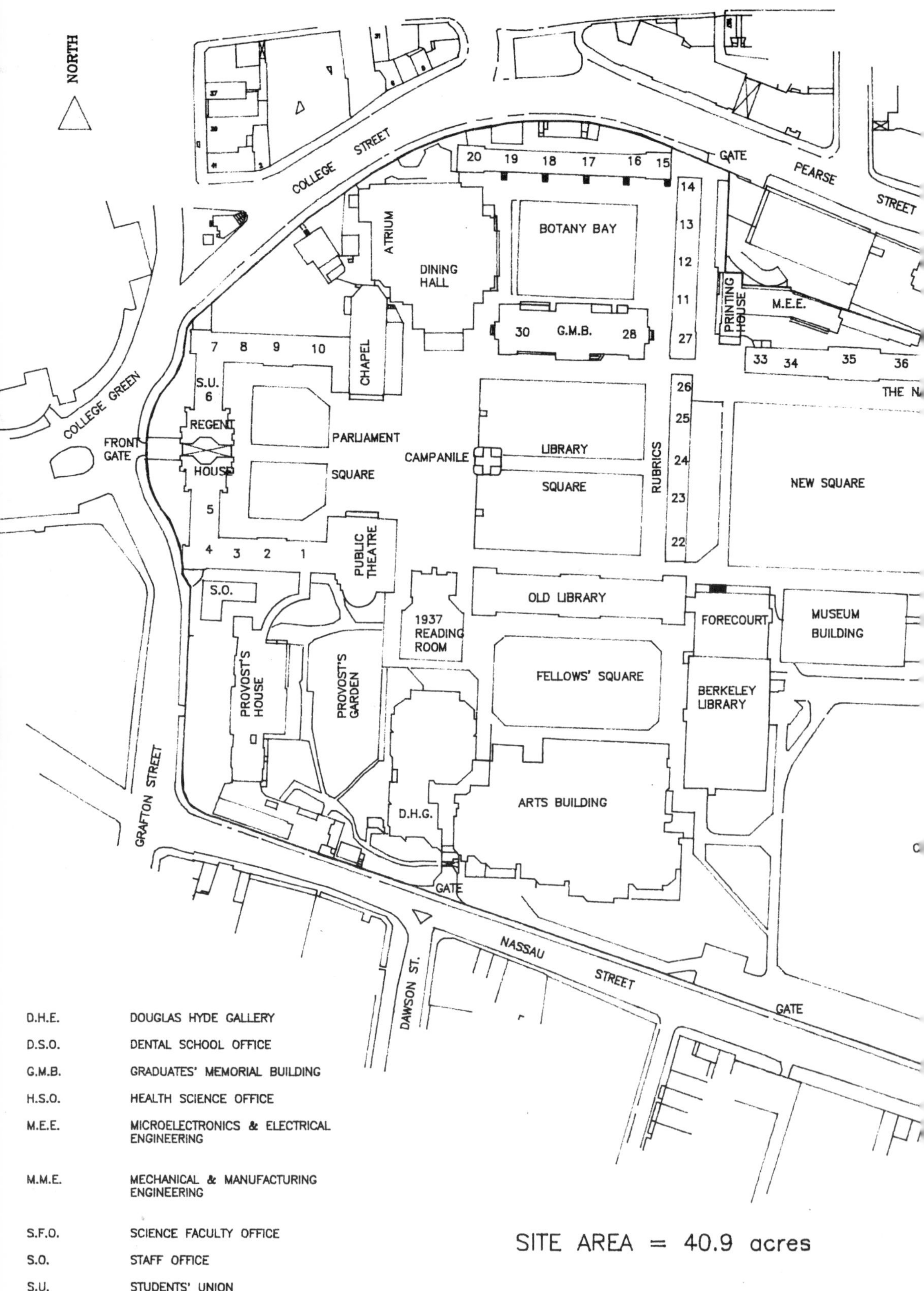
NORTH
COLLEGE STREET
PEARSE STREET
GATE
20 19 18 17 16 15
14
13
12
11
27
ATRIUM
DINING HALL
BOTANY BAY
30 G.M.B. 28
PRINTING HOUSE
M.E.E.
33 34 35 36
THE N
COLLEGE GREEN
FRONT GATE
7 8 9 10
CHAPEL
S.U. 6
REGENT HOUSE
5
4 3 2 1
PARLIAMENT SQUARE
CAMPANILE
LIBRARY SQUARE
RUBRICS
26
25
24
23
22
NEW SQUARE
PUBLIC THEATRE
S.O.
OLD LIBRARY
FORECOURT
MUSEUM BUILDING
1937 READING ROOM
FELLOWS' SQUARE
BERKELEY LIBRARY
PROVOST'S HOUSE
PROVOST'S GARDEN
D.H.G.
ARTS BUILDING
GRAFTON STREET
GATE
NASSAU STREET
DAWSON ST.
GATE
D.H.E. DOUGLAS HYDE GALLERY
D.S.O. DENTAL SCHOOL OFFICE
G.M.B. GRADUATES' MEMORIAL BUILDING
H.S.O. HEALTH SCIENCE OFFICE
M.E.E. MICROELECTRONICS & ELECTRICAL ENGINEERING
M.M.E. MECHANICAL & MANUFACTURING ENGINEERING
S.F.O. SCIENCE FACULTY OFFICE
S.O. STAFF OFFICE
S.U. STUDENTS' UNION
SITE AREA = 40.9 acres

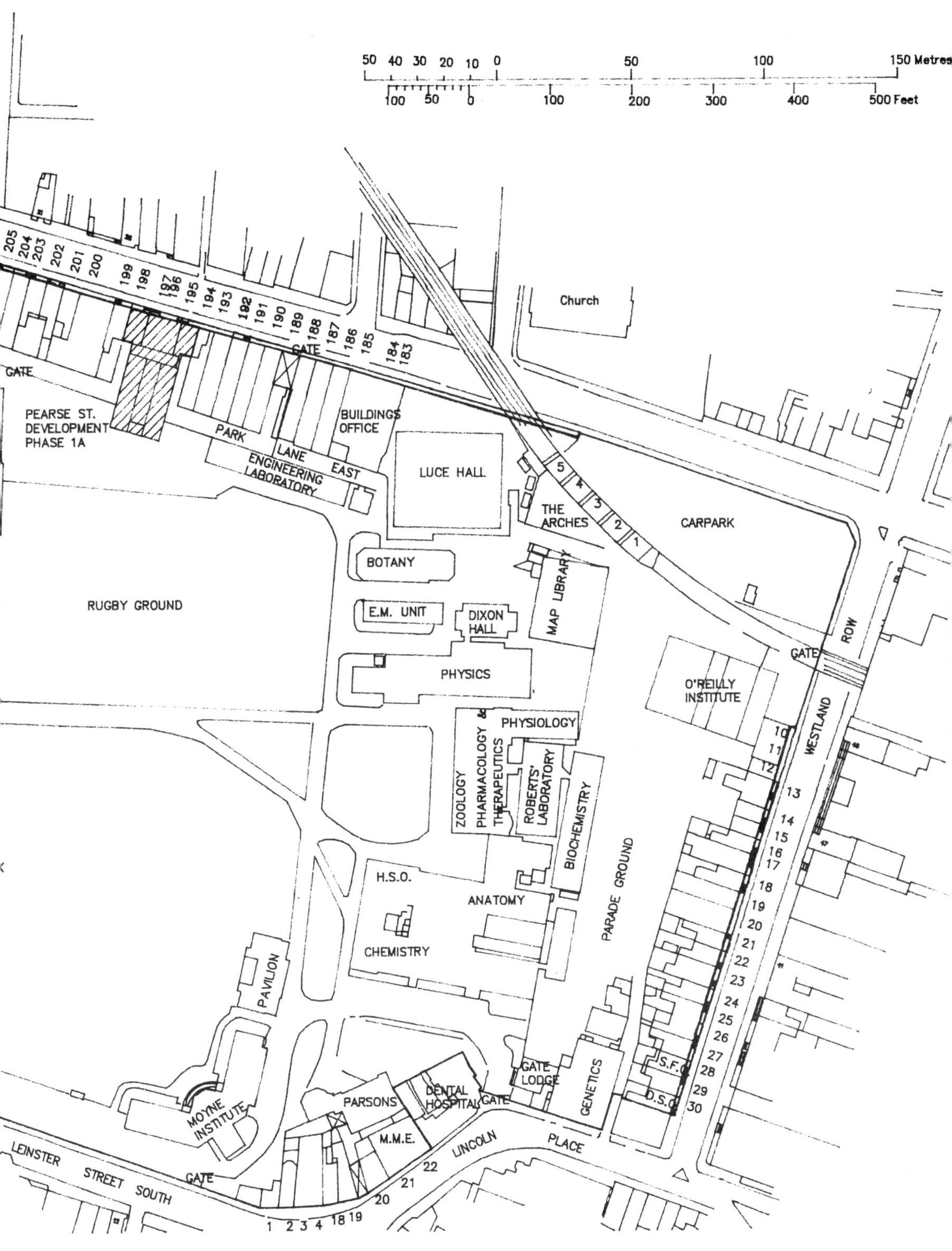

6 *A plan of the campus.*

1990

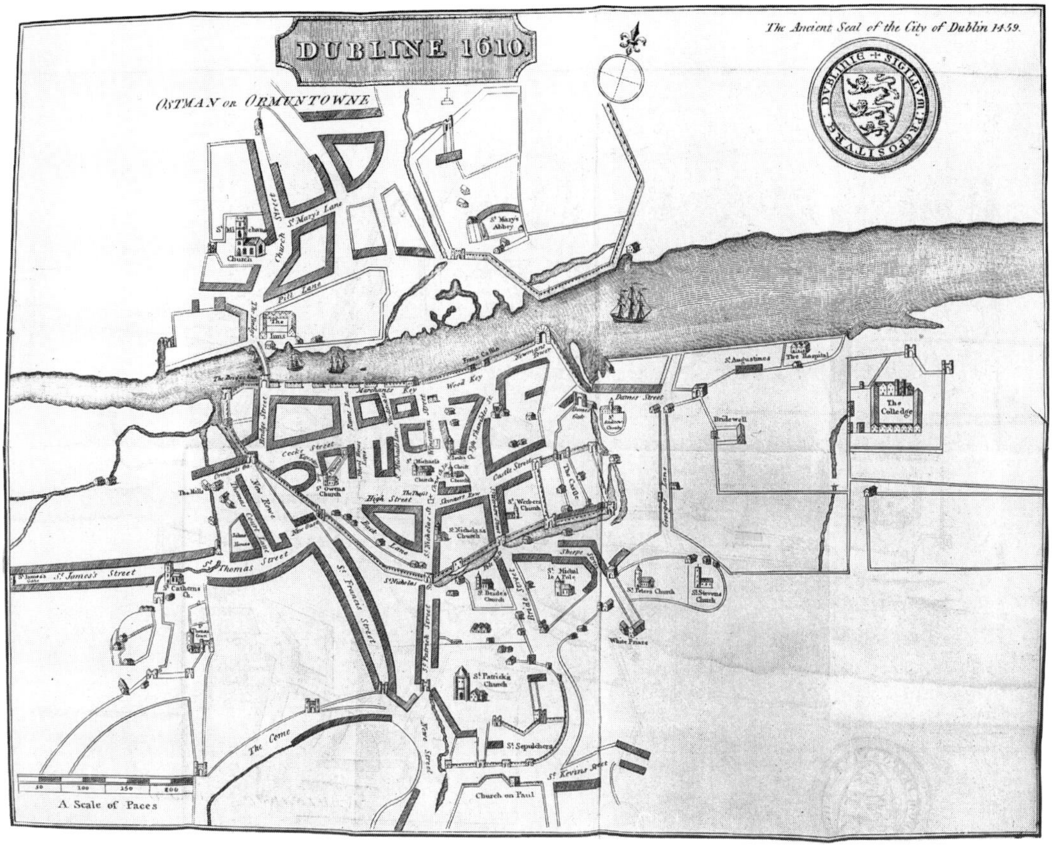

7 *Map of Dublin by John Speed (1610). The College lies by the Liffey, well to the east of the city wall.*

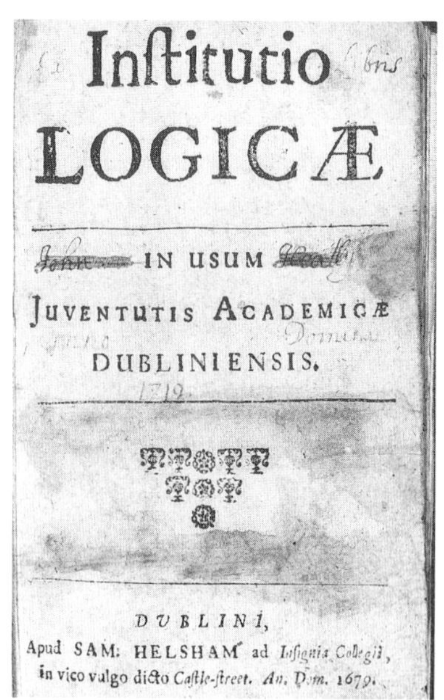

Inſtitutio

LOGICÆ

IN USUM

JUVENTUTIS ACADEMICÆ

DUBLINIENSIS.

DUBLINI,

Apud SAM: HELSHAM ad *Inſignia Collegii*, in vico vulgo dicto *Caſtle-ſtreet*. *An. Dom.* 1679.

8 *The title page of Narcissus Marsh's introduction to logic, printed in Dublin in 1679 and believed to be the first textbook written especially for Trinity students. An intermediate owner, John Heatly, has inscribed his name, dated 1719.*

9 *The memorial tablet to the Reverend Dr Michael Moore in the 1937 Reading Room. Moore was 'head of the College' for a brief period in 1689/90 (in the absence of Provost Huntington).*

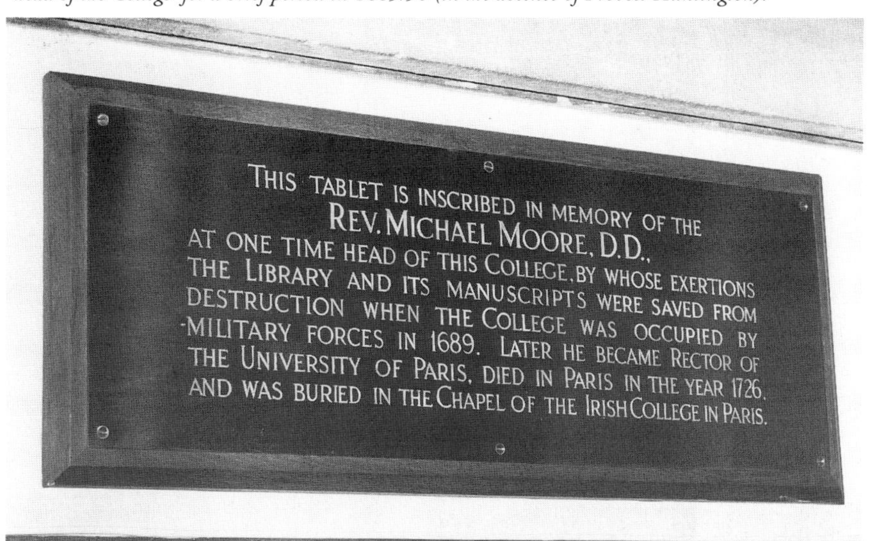

10 *The Printing House, by Richard Castle (1734).*

11 *'Challoner's corner', the small cemetery between the Chapel and the Dining Hall. Besides the tomb of Luke Challoner, it contains the memorial tablets or grave slabs of six Provosts, from Sir William Temple to Leland Lyons.*

12 *Wet cobbles on a winter evening: houses 2 to 5 in Front Square.*

cont. from p14

a fellowship at Emmanuel College. From 1607 to 1610 he had been chaplain to Sir Henry Wotton, the British ambassador to Venice, where he had acted as theological mentor to the leader of the anti-papal party. He was a highly cultured and scholarly man, totally devoid of worldly ambition, who came somewhat reluctantly to the provostship from a country rectory in Suffolk. Bedell was also a man of courage and resolution, with a zeal for ordered living and a strong sense of duty to God and man. In Temple's declining years, the College seems to have drifted into laxity in religious observances, and there had been some rather scandalous irregularities in the conduct of its finances. Bedell's first action was to initiate steps for the recovery of debts and the proper auditing of the accounts. He then set about restoring discipline among the Fellows and students, especially in regard to Chapel observances. The Holy Communion was again administered regularly — under Temple the rite seems to have lapsed for over a decade.

Bedell next turned his attention to producing a complete and orderly version of the statutes, which seem to have fallen into a chaotic condition, 'part Latin, part English, and in sheets of paper without order', as he wrote in his journal. He built largely on Temple's work, adding an elegant preface on the value of higher education, and laying more stress on the orderly conduct of divine worship. He instituted the reading of a chapter from the Bible during Commons, prescribed that no married man should be admitted Fellow or Scholar, and formalised Temple's distinction between Senior and Junior Fellows by explicitly excluding Juniors from the government of the College and the election of a Provost. By early September 1627, less than a month after his arrival in Dublin, he had gained the assent of the Fellows to his revised version, which had been formally published by a reading in College Chapel.

Posterity has tended to regard Bedell's fostering of Irish studies as his most forward-looking measure. He instituted an Irish lecture in Hall, and Irish prayers in the Chapel on holy days. Sir William Ussher, the Clerk of the Council, presented twelve Irish testaments for the use of the scholars, and the Provost himself set a good example by taking up the study of the language, which he described as 'learned, exact, and full of difficulty.' Bedell was later to commission an Irish version of the Old Testament, but this was not published until 1685.

One must understand that this enthusiasm for Irish was not primarily motivated by literary or historical considerations, but by a desire to give ordinands the ability to preach to the native Irish in their own language. The desirability of such communication had been recognised earlier by

James I, and in Temple's time he had urged the College to train some native speakers for this purpose, but nothing had been done. Charles I was now delighted by 'the Irish lecture begun by Mr Bedell', as Laud reported to Ussher.

Bedell's short but effective tenure of the provostship ended in September 1629, when he was appointed Bishop of Kilmore. Over the next twelve years he gained the respect of all in his diocese, including the native Irish. His death from fever on 7 February 1642 was brought on by hardships suffered during the early months of the 1641 insurrection, when he was confined for three weeks as a prisoner in a ruinous castle in midwinter on an island in Lough Oughter in County Cavan. He was a man of great talent and vision, and has left an enduring legacy in the College's Latin graces, which were his composition.

His successor, Robert Ussher, had been a Fellow since 1611, and was the first 'son of the House' to become Provost.[4] He was the choice of the Fellows, and both Laud and the King concurred in his election, which took place on 13 January 1630. Trinity for some time had been attracting students from England as well as all parts of Ireland, and the new Provost had to tackle the problem of providing accommodation for the increasing numbers. In December 1629 the Lords Justices had moved to suppress mass-houses in the city, and early the following year the College petitioned for the use of one of them. The Register soon records that 'the possession and custodium of two mass houses in Bridge Street, and soon after one in ye Back lane was granted us'. The Bridge Street house adjoined another in Cook Street, and they were knocked into one and became St Stephen's Hall. The Back Lane premises (now Tailors' Hall) were called Kildare Hall after their owner, the Dowager Countess of Kildare. Kildare Hall was also known as New College (or New House), a significant designation, probably indicating a sense that Trinity was about to develop a multi-collegiate structure.

This interesting development (which was not destined to last) was handled by Ussher with energy and imagination, but he was not a success as Provost. He seems to have been unduly hard on the students, banning the comedy which they had been accustomed to perform at Christmas, and he also lost the confidence of the Fellows. The English authorities decided that a change was needed, and his resignation was secured in 1634 by the offer of ecclesiastical preferment as Archdeacon of Meath.

Laud and Wentworth engineered the change in the provostship. Wentworth had arrived in Dublin as Lord Deputy in 1633. Laud became Archbishop of Canterbury in the same year; he also succeeded Abbot as

Chancellor on the invitation of Primate Ussher, but against the wishes of the Provost and Fellows.[5] Together they formed a powerful axis devoted to a policy of centralised state control, enforced loyalty to the English Crown, and strict conformity to Anglicanism. The College naturally figured in these plans, and Laud had a chosen instrument in mind to further their policy.

This was the redoubtable William Chappell (1582–1649), a good scholar and a keen controversialist in the High Anglican cause. Chappell's appointment restored the almost unbroken pattern of Cambridge men as early heads of the College. He had been a Fellow of Christ's College since 1607, where he had tutored John Milton, perhaps gaining consequential immortality as the 'old Damoetas' of 'Lycidas'. Through Laud's influence, he had been promoted to the deanery of Cashel in August 1633, and he was offered the provostship in the following year. The Fellows were against the appointment, and only reluctantly elected him on the direct orders of Wentworth, that 'great but bad man' as W.E.H. Lecky called him. We have a vivid account of what happened from Wentworth's own pen:

> I went to the College myself, recommended the Dean to the place, told them I must direct them to choose the Dean, or else to stay until they should understand his Majesty's pleasure, and in no case to choose any other. They are all willing, so as on Thursday next he will be Provost, and your Grace [Laud] shall not need to trouble the King about it.[6]

So Chappell entered on his duties in September 1634, although he was not formally sworn in until the promulgation of the new Statutes three years later. J.P. Mahaffy comments that 'the appointment of a High Church and an English Provost was a great move against the Evangelical and national cause in Ireland'. Soon after taking office, Chappell discontinued the teaching of Irish and enforced the wearing of surplices and hoods in the Chapel. This latter measure was in line with Laud's drive against the spread of Puritanism.[7] The outside halls of residence were let go. The Fellows had not been enthusiastic about that development because it tended to reduce the income they derived from their tutorial chambers. Wentworth wanted to placate the Catholic interest by returning the mass-houses, and Laudian discipline preferred the centralisation of the flock in one fold. Money for expansion on site was provided partly from government funds and partly by private subscription. New ranges of residential accommodation (of which no trace now remains) were put up near the present Dining Hall and Chapel.

Laud had drawn up new statutes for Oxford in 1636, and now as Chancellor, and with the full co-operation of the Provost, he did the same for Trinity. For the most part the Laudian Statutes simply reiterate what Bedell, following Temple, had codified. But in some crucial respects they also represent a revision of the original charter. The two most fundamental changes were the removal from the College of its right to elect to the provostship, and the removal from the Provost and Fellows of their absolute right to make statutes and ordinances for the due government of the College. The right of appointment to the provostship was now formally vested in the Crown, and the right to make statutes and ordinances was similarly reserved to the Crown, though the College was given some power to make decrees to meet new situations, provided such decrees were not repugnant to the existing statutes and had received the assent of the Visitors. The number of Fellows was fixed at sixteen, and the Visitors were reduced to two — the Chancellor and the Archbishop of Dublin. This had the regrettable effect of excluding the Lord Mayor of Dublin from any further direct part in College affairs.

The government of the College by the Provost and seven most senior Fellows was confirmed. However, in keeping with Laud's monarchical views, the powers of the Provost in regard to discipline and College elections were considerably strengthened. The Provost could now expel any member of the College for a grave offence on his own authority, and could carry the election of his nominee on a third vote.

The original provision that tenure of fellowship be limited to seven years was repealed by the new charter as 'inimical not only to scholars and the College, but also to the kingdom and the Church'. This seems to have been a concession to the Fellows in return for their agreement to surrender the College's power to make its own statutes. Since, however, tenure of fellowship was made conditional on not holding an ecclesiastical benefice, Church preferment continued to ensure the resignation of most Fellows at a comparatively early age. Bedell, like Temple, had been a married man, but now the Provost and all the Fellows, with the exception of the Jurist and Medicus (Fellows appointed to lecture in law and medicine), were bound to celibacy, and were also required to be in holy orders. The number of Scholars 'on the Foundation' was fixed at seventy, a feature of Trinity's constitution that still survives unchanged.[8]

The revised statutes were formally promulgated by charter of Charles I, and took effect on 5 June 1637, which was Trinity Monday. On that day, in the Chapel and before the newly appointed Visitors, the Provost and all the existing Fellows and Scholars individually pledged themselves to obey the new statutes. The College did not surrender the Elizabethan charter, which it still holds, but it had to accept that some of that charter's more liberal provisions had been repealed by the Caroline charter. Trinity Monday was also appointed as the day when all future elections to fellowship and scholarship would be made, and this too has proved an enduring feature of Trinity life, though Trinity Monday is now secularly defined as the Monday of 'Trinity Week', rather than the day after the Feast of the Holy Trinity.

Chappell was appointed Bishop of Cork and Ross in June 1638, but Wentworth and Laud insisted on his remaining in the provostship, even though this was in clear violation of the statutes he had sworn to uphold the year before. However, he was anxious to resign, and did so. on 20 July 1640, when arrangements for the induction of his successor had been completed.

Notes

1. See Mahaffy, *Epoch*, 132; also *Particular Book*, 40v, 214v.
2. The place-names and dioceses are listed in Stubbs, *History*, 50. When the College lost its advowsons after Disestablishment in 1869, it received £140,000 in compensation.
3. It has often been stated that the amount was £1800, and that it was donated in a lump sum by the officers and commanders of the British army soon after the battle of Kinsale. This story goes back to Bernard's *Life of Ussher* (1656), but was vigorously controverted by Mahaffy (*Epoch*, 70–71 and 116–17). The version given in the text is now generally accepted.
4. He was the son of the Henry Ussher, 'at whose instance, charge, and travel, the Charter of the Foundation of the College was first obtained'. The phrase comes from a letter of James Ussher, who as Vice-Chancellor was writing to Laud (then Bishop of London) in August 1629 to advance his cousin's candidature. The letter continues: 'I know he sincerely intendeth the good of his country, meaneth to go on where Dr Bedell has left, and in his proceedings will order himself wholly according as your lordship shall be pleased to direct him'. He did indeed continue Bedell's policy of promoting Irish studies, directing that ' a chapter of the Irish Testament should be read by a native each day during dinner'.
5. Ussher may have come to regret his support of Laud for the chancellorship. He was always a man for the 'middle way'. The articles he had drafted for a convocation of the Church of Ireland in 1613–15 may have been 'firmly Anglican', as a recent Irish historian says (R.F. Foster, *History of Ireland*, 48–49), but in 1634 he typically championed his Church's independence against an attempt to make it adopt the Thirty-nine Articles.
6. *Letters* I, 255, quoted by Murphy, *History*, 90.
7. Bedell watched approvingly from Kilmore, and wrote to a friend: 'I do much approve his reformation of the manners of the College.... In the service of God many account he hath brought in too much ceremony: others esteem the condition of this country and time do require it: and I think it may do more good here than in England'. Bedell also comments favourably on Chappell's measures to improve the rents and enlarge and beautify the buildings.

8. Laud also introduced some changes in the curriculum, but more in emphasis than substance. Porphyry's *Introduction* to Aristotle's logic was prescribed for first-year students, and important texts of Aristotle himself were listed for the other years. The changes represented a reversion to traditionalism, especially in the handling of logic, where Aristotle's authority was reasserted against the too 'protestant' methodology of Ramus. The teaching of Greek was upgraded by a provision that two of the Fellows should lecture in it. Otherwise, the existing scheme as set out in Bedell's Statutes was left unchanged.

CHAPTER 3

Rebellion and revolution 1641–1660

Chappell's successor, Richard Washington, a Fellow of University College, Oxford, was sworn in on 1 August 1640, but his reign was destined to be short and inglorious. He took up office on the eve of a major shift in political power that resulted in the downfall and execution of Wentworth the following May. In England, tension between Crown and Parliament grew towards breaking point; in Ireland, a resurgent House of Commons began to reassert its authority over the College. In February 1641 a committee of the House was appointed to investigate academic grievances, and this led to the arraignment of ex-Provost Chappell before the Lords in the following June. The House's main objective was to halt and reverse the anglicisation of the College that had been steadily pursued during his provostship. This explains the order for the postponement of the elections to fellowship and scholarship due to be held in mid-June. During previous years, fellowship elections had undoubtedly been manipulated in the English interest, and by now all the Fellows except Thomas Seele (later to become Provost) were English by birth. It was also one of the charges against Chappell that he had discriminated against native Irish students in the election of Scholars.

The case against Chappell was never pressed to a conclusion, being overtaken by larger and more violent events. The great Irish rebellion broke out in Ulster on the night of 22 October 1641, and a week later Provost Washington and most of the Fellows fled to England. A notable exception was Nathaniel Hoyle, who remained on as Vice-Provost and helped to steer the College through the turmoil of the next few years.

The rebellion was marked by widespread pillage, murderous atrocities and savage reprisals. An initial attempt to seize Dublin Castle was foiled at the last moment, and for some weeks the outbreak was confined to the North, but by the end of 1641 it had spread to most of the country, including the Pale. The Lords Justices inflamed the situation by alienating the Catholic gentry of Leinster and proroguing the Irish Parliament, and the religious divide was further deepened in December when Westminster decided that in future no toleration should be extended to Catholicism in Ireland. In the following February the same Parliament, the famous 'Long Parliament', designated two and a half million Irish acres as subject to confiscation and allocation to any adventurers prepared to invest in financing the war against the rebels.

When the rebellion broke out, Trinity's income from its estates in the North and elsewhere was cut off, and its position rapidly became precarious through lack of funds, students, and staff. Matriculations fell drastically, and no new entrants were recorded between 1645 and 1652. There were no elections to fellowship in 1641 or the two following years. The provostship was vacant from 1641 to 1645, and the chancellorship too became vacant with the execution of William Laud on 10 January 1645.

Immediately after Washington's hasty departure, the Irish Council licensed a nonconformist minister, Dr Faithful Teate (or Tate), to reside in the Provost's lodging and take charge of the College, pending the appointment of a new Provost. Teate was an Irishman, a graduate of the College, and a Doctor of Divinity. His authority was shared with Dr Dudley Loftus, a judge of the Prerogative, both being jointly designated 'temporary sub-rectors'. The Council also requested the Bishop of Meath and the Master of the Rolls to assess the state of the finances, and to convey the plate and other money to the Castle for safekeeping. Teate was not a success as pro-Provost. He soon lost the confidence of the Council and the College because of his excessively Puritan and anti-royalist outlook, and in April 1643 he was removed from office.

Teate's successor was the Bishop of Meath, Anthony Martin, a native of Galway, who had been a Fellow in the College between 1611 and 1615. Martin proved a better choice, and on 18 February 1645 he was formally appointed to the vacant provostship. He had been educated in Emmanuel College, the main focus of Cambridge Puritanism, but like most of his Trinity colleagues he was a man of moderate views who tried to steer a middle course between the more extreme claims of Royalists and Roundheads. The career of his Vice-Chancellor, Henry Jones, showed that the problem of divided loyalties could be overcome. Jones, who was a nephew of Archbishop Ussher, became Bishop of Clogher in 1645, functioned as Scout Master General during the Commonwealth, and after the Restoration was elevated to the see of Meath.

In 1646 the King empowered Martin to appoint four Junior Fellows.

One of these, Richard Coghlan, can hardly be judged a success, for there is a record of his expulsion in October 1647 for various offences, including that he 'called the Provost fool and knave and swore he would kick him'. The Register perhaps bears mute witness to his violent propensities, for large parts of three of the pages detailing his misdemeanours have been torn away.

The College needed all the help it could get to weather the unsettling violence of the times. James Butler, the Marquis of Ormonde, had been appointed Lord Lieutenant in November 1643 and, thanks to his good offices, various small financial grants were made to the College to tide it over the next few years But the financial position remained very bad. A petition to Ormonde spoke of the College's 'likely ruin', and almost all the silver plate that had been acquired or donated earlier in the century was pawned between 1642 and 1649.

After Laud's execution, the College was glad to secure Ormonde, a good King's man, as its new Chancellor. When Ormonde withdrew to England in 1647, Martin received some help and support from the new Governor of Dublin, Colonel Michael Jones, brother of the Vice-Chancellor, who proved to be well disposed to the College. Relief subscriptions were also collected in London and sent to Dublin. Martin had to face a new horror when a serious outbreak of plague afflicted Dublin towards the end of 1649, and he himself was carried off by the infection in the summer of 1650.[1] The College was probably closed at this time; it was one of the lowest points in its history.

When the dark days of the rebellion and the Cromwellian conquest finally came to an end, the College began a slow revival under the Commonwealth. Reconstruction started in September 1651 when the Parliamentary Commissioners installed as Provost their household chaplain, the Reverend Dr Samuel Winter. The Register contains a copy of the confirmatory order for his appointment, signed by Oliver Cromwell, and dated 3 June 1652. Joseph Travers and Nathaniel Hoyle, distinguished ex-Fellows, were recalled from England, and the library was sumptuously refurnished with the aid of a grant of £400 from the Vice-Chancellor.[2]

Winter, like Bedell and Martin, was a product of Emmanuel College, Cambridge. Mahaffy characterises him as 'not only a zealous Christian and a learned man, but a thorough gentleman'. He showed these qualities in his opposition to Anabaptists, his reluctance to antagonise Episcopalians, and his fondness for horses.[3] In Dublin, Winter preached regularly and confined his teaching to theology. In the best Puritan tradition, he insisted on the importance of a sound knowledge of scripture in the original tongue, and this led him to prescribe compulsory Greek and Hebrew for all students up to MA level.

We can trace the gradual renewal of normal College activities under Winter's rule. The first Register entry of his provostship is a Board order that 'the porter suffer not the clothes of any person whatsoever to be dried within the quadrangle', that no woman was to be allowed enter the College 'unless such as are approved of by the Provost', and that no scholar is to be allowed out to the town 'except such as are licensed by a ticket from the Provost or some of the Fellows'. The emergency was over, and a Puritan sense of order and sobriety had returned to the courts of the College. The rhythm of teaching and examination was resumed, with twelve students graduating BA, and seven MA, in May 1654. The following May saw fourteen BAs and one BD conferred, and in 1657 matriculations, which had been running at an average of six a year, rose to twenty-six.

Winter showed conspicuous generosity in financing scholarships for poor students, and in giving a large sum for the purchase of books for the library. He also strengthened the College staff by bringing over noted preachers, such as Samuel Mather, and making them Fellows. The wide evangelical horizons of the College at this time can be seen in the admission between 1657 and 1659 of two boys, one born in New England, and the other in the East Indies. As Mahaffy notes, they were 'the sons of pious ministers, whose missionary zeal had carried them first abroad and then to Ireland'.

Winter's provostship also witnessed a move to develop the secular side of the College's teaching with appointments, in 1652, to 'professorships' in law (Joseph Travers) and mathematics (Miles Symner). Travers was returning to the fellowship he had formerly held under Temple; Symner, a new Fellow, had been a Scholar and then a major in the parliamentary forces. He was much in advance of his time in being a strong supporter of the new philosophy of Francis Bacon. Their professorial assignments were more in the nature of ad hoc 'lectureships' than full 'chairs'. Symner's post had a distinctly vocational bias. His job was to train students (and also serving soldiers, who were admitted to his lectures) in the techniques of land surveying, an expertise then much in demand in the country. The first creation by the Crown of permanent professorships did not come until after the Restoration, Law being established by letters patent in 1668, and Divinity in 1674.

Henry Cromwell visited Ireland in March 1654, and an entry in the

Register (dated 16 March 1653 O.S.) indicates that Winter and his Senior Fellows met to elect him to the chancellorship, ignoring the claims of Ormonde who was still the legal incumbent. Cromwell may have delayed accepting the appointment, but he was certainly in office by August 1655, when a contemporary report describes his formal reception into the College. It was an occasion of much ceremonial, with doctors processing in scarlet and the presentation of a 'congratulatory salutation'. The new Chancellor then presided at a Commencements ceremony at which a number of degrees, including one in law *ad eundem gradum* (the first mention of such) were conferred.[4] Henry (who became Lord Deputy in 1657) proved a good friend to the College, increasing the state grant, and helping to protect the College estates from being subsumed under the widespread confiscations of the time. In the late 1650s he began actively pursuing a scheme for a new College to be built on a site between St Stephen's Green and Baggot Street and including part of the present Merrion Square. As an indication of the financial provision needed, the Parliamentary Commissioners produced a detailed schedule of the annual cost of salaries and Commons in Trinity. The total came to £1207, and they recommended various increases, particularly for Fellows and Scholars, amounting in all to £442.[5]

Henry Cromwell's design to promote learning and piety also included plans for a public library and schools. The nucleus of the library (which was also to serve the new College) was to be provided by the books of Primate Ussher, who had died in April 1656; he had been buried, with Oliver Cromwell's approval, in Westminster Abbey. Ussher originally had intended to leave the great collection, amounting to over ten thousand books and manuscripts, to his old college, but his income had been so depleted by the Irish wars that he felt obliged to bequeath them instead as his main legacy to his daughter Lady Tyrrell, the grand-daughter of Luke Challoner. When she put the collection on the market, Oliver Cromwell expressed interest, and delayed the sale by order of the Council of State, while appointing a committee of three divines to examine the catalogue, and to report on what items should be purchased by the state. Negotiations were carried on with Sir Timothy Tyrrell, and the purchase of the whole library for £2200 was eventually agreed. The purchase price was partly raised by contributions from the army in Ireland, with Henry setting a good example by a personal donation; the English Exchequer made up the balance. The books were then shipped to Dublin, but the purpose for which they had been acquired lapsed with the fall of the Commonwealth. They were in store in Dublin Castle when, in 1661, the Irish House of

Commons managed to persuade Charles II to assign them as his gracious 'gift' to Trinity College.[6] It used to be thought that the Book of Kells formed part of the collection, but this was not so. The great Gospel manuscripts of Kells and Durrow were separately presented to the College at about this time by Henry Jones, who may have taken custody of them on his appointment as Bishop of Meath.[7]

Notes

1. There is uncertainty about the date. Murphy (*History*, 111), after Borlase, says June; the *Trinity College Record Volume* (1951), following Ware, gives July.
2. A brass tablet recording the benefaction is preserved in the Long Room. It mentions a splendid staircase, windows, shelving, seats, and other ornaments.
3. He brought over a good breed from England, and used them on journeys to remote parts of Tyrone, Donegal and Kerry, to collect College rents. His accounts for these journeys detail items of expenditure such as fodder, shoeing, and the provision of frost nails. He apparently travelled without escort, returned carrying large sums of money, and suffered no mishap or molestation beyond the stealing of his horses on one occasion by the 'Irish army'. Mahaffy (*Epoch*, 307) rightly cites these details as an index of the country's pacification.
4. The report, which does not seem to have been noticed before, is in *The Clarke Papers* Vol. iii, Camden Society LXI (1899), 50. I owe the reference to my colleague Dr Aidan Clarke.
5. The existing salaries, with the proposed increases in brackets are: Provost: £100 (£50); seven Senior Fellows (total): £68 (£72); nine Junior Fellows (total): £27 (£81). The Fellows' salaries look small, but they would have been considerably increased by tutorial fees. They estimated for a total of seventy Scholars (including thirty 'natives'), and for what would now be called a wage-earning staff of a butler, a cook, a manciple, a gardener, a laundress, and a porter. They proposed that £1649 should therefore be earmarked for the new College, and revived the idea of using the expropriated revenues of the vicars choral and minor canons of St Patrick's Cathedral for this purpose.
6. This account of how Ussher's great Library came to Trinity differs somewhat from that given by Stubbs (*History*, 110). It is based on Urwick (*The Early History of Trinity College, Dublin*, 90–94), who sets out the evidence in detail. For details of the collection see Bernard Meehan in P. Fox (ed.), *Treasures of the Library*, 97–110.
7. See William O'Sullivan in *Irish Historical Studies* 11 (1958/59), 5–7.

CHAPTER 4

Restoration times 1660–1690

The Restoration of 1660 was as much a restoration of parliamentary government as of the monarchy. Charles II was welcomed back to London as King in late May, but for months beforehand Convention Parliaments in England and Ireland had been preparing the way for a return to pre-Commonwealth constitutionalism. There was general agreement that the spectres of anarchy and military dictatorship had loomed too ominously during the interregnum.

The College felt the first jolt of change on 29 March when the Irish Convention suspended Winter from the provostship. The reason given was that he had never taken the Provost's oath, but basically he was dismissed because he was a creature of the Protectorate, and the new authority was not prepared to recognise the legality of his appointment under that regime. Winter went quietly, retiring to his native England, where he died on 24 October 1666.

Ormonde, who was at court in London, was assumed to have resumed his duties as Chancellor of the University, and in June the members of the College sent him a loyal address.[1] He proceeded to choose the eminent Anglican theologian Jeremy Taylor, Bishop of Down and Connor, as his Vice-Chancellor in place of Henry Jones, instructing him to 'reform the disorders' of the College. There is no evidence of a major breakdown in discipline; in fact the College under Winter had been managed strictly enough. What concerned the authorities was its irregular constitution, a point sarcastically made by Bishop Taylor when he called it 'a heap of men and boys'.

The main issue to be tackled was the constitutional position of the Fellows. Only one of them, Nathaniel Hoyle, was regarded as having a proper title to his office, since his election went back to 1631 and he had taken his oath under the Laudian statutes. The places of the Provost and all other Fellows were declared vacant, but it was made clear to the Fellows that they would be reappointed if they were prepared to swear the necessary conformities to the new regime. Nine of them accepted these terms, and their position was regularised by a King's Letter of 29 December 1660 under which seven Senior Fellows were appointed and empowered to elect suitable juniors. This they duly did, electing eight Junior Fellows on 29 January 1661. Only four of these were new appointments; the others had been elected before 1660, and were confirmed in office. All except John Stearne, the Medicus, were in holy orders. This, with the exception also of an occasional lay Jurist, was to be the pattern for many years to come. 'The days of the ambiguous Puritanism of Temple were over; Trinity College was to be staunchly Anglican for the next two centuries.'[2]

At much the same time the hierarchy of the Church of Ireland was brought up to strength by the simultaneous consecration of twelve bishops at an impressive ceremony in St Patrick's Cathedral. The Dean wrote a special anthem for the occasion, whose refrain, though decidedly pedestrian, at least sums up the essence of the Restoration:

Angels look down, and joye to see
Like that above, a Monarchie;
Angels look down, and joye to see
Like that above, a Hierarchie.

There was perhaps more joy in heaven than in Ireland, but at least the country remained reasonably peaceful for close on thirty years. Dublin quadrupled in population during this period, and the quality of Trinity's academic life rose with the city's increasing prosperity.

The question of the provostship was settled by the formal admission of Thomas Seele (1611–75) on 19 January 1661. Seele was a Dubliner, educated at Trinity, where he obtained a fellowship in 1634. Born in the shadow of Christ Church Cathedral — his father was verger and sexton there — he remained staunchly Anglican all his life. He gained a considerable reputation as a preacher, so much so that Henry Cromwell and the Council banned him from the pulpit in 1658. In 1649, he had suffered imprisonment for attending an Anglican service in St Patrick's Cathedral, held in direct contravention of an order by the Parliamentary Commissioners. Seele's loyalty to the established Church ensured him ecclesiastical preferment at the Restoration, first as Chancellor of St

Patrick's Cathedral, and later as its Dean. He held this latter office, together with his provostship, from 1666 to his death on 2 February 1675.

The new Provost tightened discipline among the students, and also brought more order and colour into the Chapel services by appointing regular preachers and a College organist. A shortage of money in the early years of his rule prevented the appointment of any new Fellows from 1664 to 1666, and caused the postponement of scholarship elections in the latter year. But thereafter the financial situation gradually improved, and so did the intake of students. Matriculations were running at thirty-five in 1665, but nine years later had risen to fifty. Seele was not outstanding as a scholar, but he was clearly a competent administrator, and he deserves credit for stabilising the College after the political vicissitudes of the previous two decades, and for presiding sensibly over its return to modest prosperity.

The next Provost, Michael Ward (1643–81), was a notable and precocious careerist. Born in Shropshire, he had crossed to Ireland for a Trinity education, and had been elected a Fellow in 1662 and Professor of Divinity in 1670. He became the College's youngest ever Provost when he was admitted on 12 March 1675 at the age of thirty-one. Less than four years later he was elevated to the see of Ossory, and his meteoric career ended with his death in October 1681, soon after taking up his appointment as Bishop of Derry. Sir James Ware describes him as 'of great sagacity in dexterously managing proper conjunctions'. That this is a euphemism for jobbery, rather than a tribute to his logical powers, is rendered probable by the fact that from 1670 to 1678, while Fellow and then Provost, he also managed to hold the deanery of Lismore. There is nothing significant to record about his tenure of the provostship.

Having helped to appoint two Trinity men to the post, Ormonde now looked to Oxford to supply the next Provost, recommending to the Crown the Reverend Dr Narcissus Marsh. Marsh (1638–1713) took up his appointment on 24 January 1679. A former student at Magdalen, an ex-Fellow of Exeter College, and a Doctor of Divinity, he had been Principal of St Alban's Hall for the past six years. He was a very considerable scholar with special expertise in logic, mathematics, and oriental languages.

Marsh's encouragement of Irish was an interesting and unexpected aspect of his provostship. He acquired a good knowledge of the language, and encouraged the 'native' scholars to learn it, appointing a native speaker (Mr Higgins) as a lecturer to teach them. A contemporary source tells us that up to eighty people, including Fellows, attended the classes, and made good progress. Marsh also co-operated with Robert Boyle, the celebrated chemist in the production of an edition of the Bible in Irish (Boyle prepared the fount of type). The version of the Old Testament was that prepared for Bishop Bedell by Denis Sheridan fifty years before. The Irish lectureship lapsed under Marsh's successor, and was not revived until about 1708 when Charles Lynegar was appointed 'professor' with the support and encouragement of Dr Hall, the Vice-Provost, and Archbishop King.[3]

In 1681 Marsh produced an elementary work on logic for undergraduate use, probably the first textbook especially written for students of Trinity. The College under him was a busy and crowded place, and the original Chapel and Hall could no longer accommodate the increased numbers. Marsh made plans to replace them with larger structures on the same site. He also continued the construction of the residences that came to form the old Front Square. This was a larger square to the west of the original Quadrangle. Known as the 'great court', it had begun to take shape in the 1670s, thanks to a bequest from Sir Jerome Alexander. A range on the north side and a portion of the Jacobean West Front (completed in 1697) were the first to be built. The construction of the new Chapel was well advanced when Marsh resigned in September 1683 to become Bishop of Ferns and Leighlin. It was consecrated under his successor on 5 October 1684.

Marsh never settled well to life in Dublin, and his diary contains a famous *cri de coeur*, which will find an answering echo in many an academic heart:

> Finding this place very troublesome, partly by reason of the multitude of business and impertinent visits the Provost is obliged to, and partly by reason of the ill education that the young scholars have before they come to the College......I was quickly weary of 340 young men and boys in this lewd and debauch'd town; and the more so because I had no time to follow my always dearly beloved studies.

He probably exaggerated the numbers, but even at three hundred the student body was much larger than it had been before. Narcissus Marsh went on to become Archbishop of Cashel (1691–94), of Dublin (1694–1703), and finally of Armagh (1703–13). He is, or should be, well remembered in Dublin for establishing a splendid library in St Patrick's Close beside the Cathedral, at a personal a cost to himself of over £4000.[4]

The last Provost before the crisis of 1689–90 was Robert Huntington (1637–1701). He too was an Oxford man, and came reluctantly from a fellowship at Merton to take up office in September 1683. An early interest in oriental languages had brought him to the Near East where he spent ten years as chaplain to the Levant Company in Aleppo. This gave him the opportunity to visit Cyprus, Palestine, and Egypt, and to acquire a valuable collection of manuscripts, some of which he later presented to Trinity's library. His scholarship reflects the increasing interest of his age in the historical aspects of languages. So it is not surprising to find that in Dublin he took an interest in the completion of Marsh's Irish Bible project. In the course of a letter to an unnamed correspondent (probably Boyle), he expressed the surprisingly liberal view that 'the Nation should make their language triumphant, and the rather because there are Laws against it'.[5]

Any Irish studies in the College at this time were extracurricular. They had to be because the traditional curriculum, laid down in detail in the Laudian statutes, allowed no place to them. The course therein prescribed consisted of logic, physics, and ethics, taught in the scholastic way, with ancillary Latin and Greek, and with due deference to the authority of Aristotle. Such a course was impervious to the new spirit of Baconian science with its emphasis on observation, induction and experiment. The 'new philosophy', as it was called, was being propagated in London by the Royal Society, founded in 1660, which had no more than a tenuous and indirect connection with the universities of Oxford and Cambridge.

A similar Society began to take shape in Dublin in the autumn and winter of 1683, but here, by contrast, the links with Trinity College were close and striking. The prime mover was William Molyneux, a Dubliner of Huguenot extraction, who had graduated from the College in 1674, and had subsequently gone to London to study law. After his return to Dublin, he made and published the first English translation of Descartes' *Meditations* (1680). On conceiving his design for a philosophical society, he first sought the co-operation of a former fellow-student, St George Ashe, who had become a Fellow of the College. Ashe held the mathematics lectureship, founded and endowed by the Earl of Donegall at the Restoration, and was active in scientific research. He may well have introduced Molyneux to Provost Huntington, who had only recently arrived in Dublin, and who made his College lodgings available for the earliest recorded meeting of the group, held on 15 October 1683. At this meeting papers were read by Molyneux, Ashe, and former Provost Marsh. The earliest list of members of the Dublin Society contains fourteen names, of whom nine were either Fellows or graduates of the College.[6]

The Society soon acquired its own accommodation in Crow Street, but its early reception and recognition in the College testifies to a forward-looking and enlightened attitude among some at least of the academic staff. The library was currently acquiring a large number of contemporary works on science, and in 1685 an observatory was established, for which Ashe procured telescopes and other equipment. Looking back on his undergraduate days, Molyneux later expressed his disapproval of the 'Verbose Philosophy there professed and taught', but the same passage reveals that even as a student he had access to Descartes, Bacon, and the Proceedings of the Royal Society. We know that Molyneux's tutor, William Palliser, was interested in science as well as theology, and Palliser may well have helped him with his scientific reading.

In the last quarter of the seventeenth century, Trinity's teaching was probably less hidebound and less rigidly scholastic than Oxford's. In the early 1690s Molyneux himself was responsible for an extremely significant addition to the course when he recommended Locke's *Essay concerning Human Understanding* (published in 1690) to Ashe, who was now Provost. Ashe was so pleased with the *Essay* that he at once prescribed it for postgraduate study, and Molyneux was able to write to Locke to tell him that the Provost ' has ordered it to be read by the bachelors of the College, and strictly examines them in their progress therein'. Locke's ideas were thus well-known and canvassed within the College when Berkeley was a student in the opening decade of the next century, and he could hardly have developed his philosophy as he did without their stimulus. It is true that the *Essay* was not formally prescribed for *undergraduate* study until the mid-eighteenth century, but that only serves to confirm that the College had to make its innovations on the fringes of the traditional core curriculum.

The continuing problem of how to modernise a statute-entrenched course is also reflected in some caustic comments made in a student's letter in the early 1700s. He complains of having been taught 'conflicting hypotheses' in philosophy, but the detail of his complaint indicates that he was given at least a nodding acquaintance with Plato, Aristotle and Epicurus, among the ancients, and with Descartes, Colbert, Gassendi, Malebranche and Locke, among the moderns — not at all a bad mix of reading.[7]

By the middle of 1688 it was clear that James II had hopelessly antagonised opinion in England by his pro-Catholic policy. Given that a previous Stuart monarch had been executed, it was not hard to see that his days on the throne were numbered. Provost Huntington was in England for the long vacation. Forseeing trouble in Ireland too — there had already been some minor harassment of the College by the King — he decided to remain where he was, and in fact he did not return to Dublin until after the battle of the Boyne in July 1690.

James retreated to France in December 1688, but the greater part of Ireland remained loyal to him. Tyrconnell, his Catholic viceroy, organised an army and suppressed dissident Protestants. Early in 1689 the College found itself in a financial crisis. Student numbers had fallen, and the flow of rents had dried up. Measures agreed to meet the emergency included the reduction of meals in Hall to one a day, and the despatch of the library's manuscripts and the more important muniments to England. It was also decided to raise revenues by selling or pawning some of the College silver, even though the market was badly depressed.

On 25 February troops raided the College and took away horses and arms, though this was not so much an anti-Trinity move as a reflection of Tyrconnell's desperate need to re-equip his army. The raid was too much for the Fellows, and most of them left for England on 1 March. Only the Vice-Provost, Richard Acton, and four of his colleagues remained, of whom three (including Acton) died within the next fifteen months. James landed in Kinsale on the 12 March and reached Dublin twelve days later. The Vice-Chancellor, Anthony Dopping, Bishop of Meath, headed a delegation from the College which waited on the King, and was assured that he would respect their 'liberties and properties'. But early in September, on the King's orders, the College was commandeered for a barracks, and all the remaining Fellows and students were forced to leave.

During this occupation, the College was also used as a prison for the city's Protestants, and much damage was done to College rooms by the regiment quartered there. At one moment the soldiers were about to set fire to the Library, but they were prevented from doing so by the intervention of the Reverend Dr Michael Moore, Catholic chaplain to Tyrconnell, who had been installed as head of the College, and who was ably assisted by his librarian, Father Teigue McCarthy. A memorial tablet in the 1937 Reading Room commemorates Moore's timely exertions on behalf of the College's heritage of books. His tenure of office was short; he soon offended the King by preaching against the Jesuits, and was forced to leave the country. He ended up as Rector of the University of Paris, bequeathing his own library to the Irish College there, in whose chapel he is buried.

The Williamite victory at the Boyne and the subsequent flight of James in July 1690 restored the fortunes of the Protestant side in Dublin, if not immediately in the rest of the country. The Provost and the Fellows who had retreated to England returned, and the College breathed again.

Notes

1. In the late 1960s the text of the address was discovered in the Carte papers in the Bodleian Library. See T.C. Barnard 'Trinity at Charles II's Restoration: A Royal Address', in *Hermathena* 109 (1969), 44–49, who lists the names of those signing, presumably most of the members of the House still in residence.
2. McDowell and Webb, *History*, 23.
3. See M. Risk, 'Charles Lynegar, Professor of the Irish Language 1712', *Hermathena* 102 (1966), 16–25.
4. Marsh's Library has recently been renovated. It still functions as a public library and is much valued by visiting and local scholars. Its magnificent collection of books and manuscripts, still housed in their early eighteenth-century cases, is rightly regarded as one of Dublin's most unusual and precious treasures.
5. Quoted from *Analecta Hibernica* (1930), I, 163, by Maxwell, *History*, 76.
6. Molyneux's Dublin Society must be regarded as a direct forerunner of Dublin's famous *Royal Dublin Society* (the RDS). For details of the connection, see J. V. Luce, *Dublin Societies before the R.D.S.*, a pamphlet published by the RDS. The Dublin University Philosophical Society (the 'Phil'), formed in 1853 and in continuous existence since then, may also be regarded as a remoter offspring of Molyneux's original initiative. Marsh read a paper to the Society in which the term 'microphone' first appears in scientific literature. A graduate of a much later day, George Johnstone Stoney (1826–1911), coined the name 'electron' in 1891, an event suitably commemorated by a symposium organised by the science committee of the RDS on 20 November 1991.
7. John Shadwell's letter is discussed by A. A. Luce in his *Life of Berkeley* (London, 1949), 39, and by McDowell and Webb, *History*, 31–32.

CHAPTER 5

From the Boyne to the Georges 1690–1717

In the period covered by this chapter the military and religious turmoil of the seventeenth century subsided, but the passions generated by the 'Glorious Revolution' were slow to cool and continued to disturb College life from time to time. At first the College as a whole seemed thankfully content to accept the Williamite settlement. Later, as the struggle between Whig and Tory intensified, lines of division began to appear. One such rift tended to open between the authorities and the students. The Board generally thought it advisable to take a strong Whig line in enforcing discipline, while student sentiment tended to be Tory, particularly among the more aristocratic undergraduates. But the staff itself was also split along party lines with ardent Whigs in conflict with moderate and not so moderate Tories. The Whigs could be (and were) attacked for condoning a 'usurpation' as blatant as that of Cromwell, and even moderate Tories might be accused of disaffection to the regime, as Berkeley found to his cost. As a young Junior Fellow, he preached three sermons in College Chapel on the theme of 'passive obedience', and his treatment of this difficult and delicate topic brought on him the suspicion that he was a Jacobite. Rumours to this effect persisted, and delayed his ecclesiastical preferment; he was, for instance, denied a Dublin living in 1716.[1]

Any student professing Jacobite sympathies, whether out of conviction or cussedness, ran the risk of severe punishment. Grinling Gibbons's fine equestrian statue of William III in College Green tended to become a focus for demonstrations, and in 1710 three students were sent down for wrenching the baton out of the royal hand. In 1714 Theodore Barlow was expelled for drinking to the memory of Sorrel (the horse that threw and mortally injured King William). But by 1717 Queen Anne was three years dead, the Old Pretender had shot his bolt, and George I was firmly on the throne. This was the year when Richard Baldwin, a masterful and long-lived Whig, become Provost, a promotion that was in itself a factor making for stability. Under his firm rule anti-Jacobite paranoia abated, and the College eventually moved into a more settled and sedate era.

The College soon recovered from the trauma of its military occupation in 1689/90. Elections to fellowship and scholarship were resumed from 1692 on, and matriculations began to run at a level considerably higher than before the emergency. College finances also picked up quickly, helped by a royal subvention of £3000. Huntington had always been a reluctant incumbent of the provostship, and he retired as soon as he decently could, returning with relief to his native England in September 1692 to marry and take up a quiet benefice in the Essex countryside. He was succeeded by Molyneux's friend, St George Ashe. Ashe's appointment marked the end of the Crown's policy of appointing Cambridge or Oxford graduates. All subsequent Provosts down to 1991 were graduates of Trinity, and all except Hely-Hutchinson had also held fellowship.

Ashe (1658–1718) was born at Castle Strange in County Roscommon, and had been a Fellow since 1679. As a tutor he had numbered Jonathan Swift among his pupils, and they became and remained good friends.[2] He had a lively mind which led him into varied interests and enthusiasms of a mainly scientific nature. As a Fellow of the Royal Society, he had contributed astronomical observations to its *Transactions.* In January 1686 he read a paper to the Dublin Philosophical Society describing his invention of a new solid fuel consisting of a mixture of clay and coal dust. He put the Provost's lodgings at the disposal of the revived Dublin Society, which convened again on 26 April 1693, with Molyneux and Marsh (now Archbishop of Cashel) also present. The Society grew rapidly in numbers and forty-nine new members joined in the first year. These included five Fellows of Trinity — a good measure of the College's interest in the progress of the scientific enlightenment. They also included two archbishops and five bishops. A surprising number of the leaders of the established church took a lively interest in the science of the day and evidently found it in no way incompatible with their theology or piety. Ashe himself was soon to be elevated to the bench. He resigned the provostship on becoming Bishop of Cloyne in July 1695. By 1699 eight of the Irish bishops were ex-Fellows of Trinity. Their distinguished company also included William King, Bishop of Derry and soon to be Archbishop of Dublin. He had been a graduate of Trinity (but not a Fellow) and had read papers on land drainage and soil improvement to the Dublin Society.

The centenary of the first admission of students was celebrated on

9 January 1694. Ashe preached a commemorative sermon on Queen Elizabeth. The celebrations also included an expression of the College's gratitude for the support given it by the City of Dublin, and a nicely topical Latin debate on the question: Whether the Sciences and Arts are more indebted to the Ancients or the Moderns. An ode written by the Poet Laureate, Nahum Tate (who was a Trinity graduate), was sung in a setting by Henry Purcell, but words and music alike lacked inspiration.[3]

Ashe's successor was George Browne (1649–99), a native of Northumberland, who had been educated in the College, elected to Fellowship in 1673, and appointed Professor of Divinity in 1693. He continued to hold this chair during his provostship, which began on 22 July 1695 and came to an untimely end on Trinity Sunday (4 June) 1699. His death was due in part to an injury he had received the previous year. He had gone with his Senior Fellows to the Hall to deliver a public admonition to some students when a riot broke out and he was hit by a brickbat. Hely-Hutchinson says that he 'had the reputation of being the best president that ever filled this station', a judgment that seems to be based on a phrase in his memorial tablet (originally erected in the Chapel and now in the small cemetery beside it), for no particular achievement is on record to support it.

The decade of Ashe and Browne saw important additions to the College buildings. The enlarged Hall planned by Marsh, the Jacobean West Front, and the south range of the old Front Square were all completed in this period.

The next Provost, Peter Browne (*c.*1665–1735), had already made a name for himself when he was appointed on 19 August 1699 at the relatively youthful age of thirty-three.[4] He was born in County Dublin and entered Trinity College as a pensioner in June 1682 after attending the free school attached to St Patrick's Cathedral. Sixteen eighty-two was a vintage year: his fellow-students included Thomas Wilson, later Bishop of Sodor and Man, Edward Chandler, Bishop successively of Lichfield and Durham, and Jonathan Swift. Swift was an erratic scholar — a mark list for Easter term 1685 shows him with *bene* in Greek and Latin, *male* in physics, and *negligenter* in theme (Latin essay) — but Browne's career forged smoothly ahead. He was elected a Fellow in 1692, and was chosen to deliver the panegyric on Queen Elizabeth I at the centenary celebrations in 1694. John Toland's controversial *Christianity not mysterious* came out in 1696, and Archbishop Marsh encouraged Browne to publish a reply, which he did effectively enough the following year. Marsh is said to have thought so well of his rebuttal of Toland that he recommended him for the provostship.

Peter Browne had a high reputation as a preacher, and he proved an efficient Provost. By 1704 the number of students had risen to a peak of 472. This was the year in which George Berkeley obtained his BA and began to compose in elegant Latin some pieces on mathematical matters, including an algebraic game that he had invented. His *Arithmetical Miscellany*, published in 1707 when he was a candidate for fellowship, is little more than a trifle, but it affords some vivid glimpses of College life. We hear of the 'sad solitude' of 'those commonly called Pumps' (i.e. swots), and meet the idlers whiling away their time at chess, cards or dominoes while their friends look on and yawn. It also lets us see how the scope of College teaching could be broadened by private initiatives. Berkeley pays tribute to his tutor, the Vice-Provost Dr Hall, for introducing him to the pleasures of mathematics, a subject not officially on the undergraduate course. As a private tutor, Berkeley himself was no doubt also coaching others in the subject, including William Molyneux's son Samuel, to whom the book is dedicated.

There were no fellowship elections in 1705 or the following year, but a vacancy occurred in the autumn of 1706 when William Mullart resigned to take up appointment to a College living. Berkeley was the successful candidate in the subsequent election, and he was duly admitted on 9 June 1707. He was at work on his philosophical masterpieces when the celebrated case of Edward Forbes began to vex the College.

Forbes was a graduate of Aberdeen who had been allowed to proceed to his BA in Trinity in July 1705 on performing the required exercises. After the statutory period of three years, he obtained a grace for his MA on 10 July 1708, and the degree was conferred on him three days later. After a day or two, the Provost was informed that at the Proctors' dinner on the night before the ceremony, Forbes, a Jacobite, had shown scandalous disrespect to the memory of King William by proposing a toast in which the former sovereign was compared unfavourably with a highwayman called Balfe, who had been hanged in Dublin some years previously. After securing some sworn depositions on the incident, Browne summoned the Senior Fellows to a Board meeting on 21 July, and Forbes was suspended from his degree and permanently expelled from the College. A meeting of the Senate was then called for 2 August at which Forbes was formally stripped of his degrees. Seventy-six members of Congregation voted to confirm the Board's sentence, but eighteen members, including two Fellows (Walmesley and Helsham), voted against the degradation. More was at issue than just the suppression of Jacobitism in the College. The case also raised old and unresolved questions about the relations between College and University, and in particular whether, where graces for degrees were concerned, the Senate had power to go against the wishes of the Board. The Forbes case rumbled on for five or six years, with the Masters repeatedly attempting to have the Senate revoke his sentence, and the presiding Vice-Chancellor ruling such motions out of order.

Browne maintained a firm line against Forbes and his sympathisers, but he was not an extreme Whig. He quarrelled with one of his colleagues, Matthew French, who was much given to the witch-hunting of Jacobites in the College. But he would certainly not have condoned the conduct of another young Fellow, William Thomson (elected in 1713) if, as alleged, he drank to the health of 'all those that made no distinction between Oliver Cromwell that killed the father and King William that dethroned the son'.[5]

Browne resigned in April 1710 to take up appointment as Bishop of Cork, and later incurred odium for writing against the practice of drinking to the memory of the dead. His argument was developed on religious grounds, but its political import was clear enough. In the eyes of enthusiastic supporters of 'the glorious, pious, and immortal memory', his stance was worse than heresy, and it became customary to conclude the loyal toast with the phrase 'and a fig for the Bishop of Cork'. In the last decade of his life — he died in Cork in August 1735 — he published significant books on human understanding and divine analogy, ensuring himself a continuing reputation as a subtle and original thinker in the intellectual borderland between philosophy and theology.

Queen Anne had been impressed by Browne's abilities as a preacher and used her influence to secure him a bishopric. She also allowed him to suggest a successor, and he nominated his colleague Benjamin Pratt (1669–1721). Swift tells us that the provostship was 'one of the great employments of Ireland', and that the Queen reserved it for her personal dispensation, but would expect a recommendation from her viceroy. Pratt was well placed to secure this for he was domestic chaplain to the second Duke of Ormonde, who had recently succeeded Wharton as Lord Lieutenant, and who was also the Chancellor. Wharton himself favoured the claims of Dr Hall, who had been Vice-Provost since 1697, and used all his influence at Court to block Pratt's advancement, but he was unsuccessful.

Pratt was admitted to the provostship on 3 June 1710. He was a native of Garradice in County Meath and had been educated at Trinity where he gained a fellowship in 1693, the year after Peter Browne. Swift, who was quite a friend of Pratt, described him as 'a person of wit and learning'.[6] He had no qualms about absenting himself from the College for months at a time to move in London society. We meet him occasionally in the *Journal to Stella*, dining and playing cards with Swift, or walking with him to the city to purchase old books, or pictures, of which he was a 'great virtuoso'.

Pratt was away during the tense days of the Irish parliamentary election in the autumn of 1713 when a Tory supporter was killed after troops from Dublin Castle had fired on a riotous mob. The College electorate strongly favoured the Tory candidates — among the Scholars the balance was twelve to one in their favour — and one of the Fellows, Patrick Delany, a great friend of Swift, wrote an anonymous pamphlet satirising the ensuing Parliament. The Tories had expected to win, and were greatly disappointed when the Whigs secured a majority. But the result was gratifying to some of the Fellows, notably Richard Baldwin, the future Provost, who had recently taken over the vice-provostship from Hall.

Inside and outside the College, it was a time of unrelenting feud and faction. Pratt proved an ineffective head of the House as College seethed with current fears and anxieties about the succession. When the accession of George I in August 1714 had tipped the balance irrevocably in favour of the Whigs, the Castle expressed its disapproval of Trinity's disorders and disaffections by forbidding (by King's Letter) the holding of the usual elections to fellowship and scholarship on the following Trinity Monday.

Pratt must have realised that his days as Provost were numbered. Ormonde had been dismissed from his offices of state and driven into exile. Pratt's own fate was less abrupt and drastic, but his star sank with that of his former patron. He had proved too much of a Tory to be acceptable to the new Whig Ascendancy, and his provostship came to an end in June 1717 when he was appointed Dean of Derry.

Pratt's provostship saw work start on what is now the Old Library, the first of Trinity's great eighteenth-century buildings. Previously the books had been housed on an upper floor of the south range of the original quadrangle, and not in a separate building. The collections had been moved out when the area was temporarily used for Commons during the rebuilding of the Hall in the 1690s, and the whole library had subsequently been allowed to fall into neglect and disorder.[7] George Berkeley was appointed Librarian in 1709, and he at once began to complain about the inadequacy of the premises. He persuaded the Board to ask for public money to improve the situation, and a handsome initial grant of £5000 was secured, enabling plans to be made for a new building. Colonel Thomas Burgh, Chief Engineer and Surveyor General of Her Majesty's Fortifications in Ireland, was appointed architect. Though there is no direct evidence on the point, it is surely likely that he discussed the library's needs with the brilliant young Fellow who had initiated the project. The very ample scale on which the building was planned — its length was more than twice that of the original quadrangle — is consistent with the largeness of vision that Berkeley showed in all his work and writings. The foundation stone was laid on 12 May 1712, and two more government grants of £5000 each were needed (in 1717 and 1721) before the shell of the building was finished in 1724. The internal fittings and the positioning of the books took another eight years to complete, and the library was ready for use in 1732.

Burgh, a graduate of the College, was 'the first indisputably and unmistakably Irish architect', and his severely practical structure, more grand than plain, still dominates its surroundings. Well characterised as a 'power-house or warehouse of learning', it served all the College's library needs for over two hundred years. The original design had open arches instead of windows at ground level between the end pavilions, a feature copied from Wren's library at Trinity College, Cambridge, and intended to protect the books from rising damp by circulating air below them. One could not, however, walk through from Library Square to the Fellows' Garden because a wall divided the arcades down the centre. The area remained open until 1892, when the arches were glazed to provide more space for book storage and a reading-room.[8]

Readers were originally accommodated at tables in the Long Room on the first floor. This magnificent room, over two hundred feet long, was first roofed with a flat ceiling of plaster at a lower level than the present wooden barrel vaulting. The latter feature derives from a mid-Victorian alteration made under the gifted supervision of Messrs Deane and Woodward, and finished in 1862. They greatly increased shelf space by raising the roof and inserting another set of tall transverse bookstacks at gallery level. The horizontal lines of what had been a broad and well-lit upper section were thus transmuted into the shadowed verticality of a Gothic nave. The most recent historian of the College buildings has observed that 'even the projections of Burgh's Corinthian entablature and gallery balustrade assume new meaning in this extraordinary synthesis of Augustan classicism and Victorian Romanesque'.[9] It was a daring transformation that has undoubtedly enhanced the grandeur of what is still one of the largest single-chamber libraries in the world.

Notes

1. Berkeley later showed himself thoroughly loyal to the Protestant Succession, and in 1712 he published the sermons to dispel the misrepresentation he felt he had suffered. His political pamphlet entitled *Advice to the Tories who have taken the Oaths* (1715) showed his colours more clearly. It came out after the accession of George I (but before the Jacobite rebellion), when there were justified doubts about Tory loyalty to the Hanoverian succession. For a recent reassessment of his earlier position, see D. Berman, 'The Jacobitism of Berkeley's *Passive Obedience*, Journal of the History of Ideas 47 (1986), 309–19.
2. When Ashe died on 27 February 1718, Joseph Addison wrote to commiserate with Swift in the following terms: 'He has scarce left behind him his equal in humanity, agreeable conversation, and learning.'
3. Tate (1652–1715) is perhaps best known as the author of the popular Christmas carol 'While shepherds watched their flocks by night'. The list of well-loved hymns composed by Trinity graduates includes: 'Rock of ages' by Augustus M. Toplady (1740–78), 'Hark, ten thousand voices sounding' by Thomas Kelly (1769–1854), 'Abide with me' and 'Praise, my soul, the King of Heaven' by Henry F. Lyte (1793–1847), and 'Fight the good fight' by John S.B. Monsell (1811–75). See McDowell and Webb, *History*, 151 and n. 128.
4. Hely-Hutchinson, in his MS history of the College, says that he was a nephew of George Browne, but his biographer, A.R. Winnett (1974), thinks that this is doubtful.
5. The allegation was recorded by Matthew French, a Senior Fellow, in some personal memoranda about the events of the months from November 1713 to February 1714. The five leaves of jottings were found in the Singleton papers acquired by Columbia University in the 1930s, and kindly returned to the College. They provide new and valuable information about feelings and actions within and without the walls of Trinity at this time. See the annotated transcript by Dr E.H. Alton in *Hermathena* 57,58 (1941). The notes contain a brief for the incoming Lord Lieutenant, the Duke of Salisbury, on the history of the Forbes case, which enabled Alton to improve greatly on previous accounts of the incident.
6. This quotation and that of the previous paragraph are taken from Swift's 1711 pamphlet against Wharton, *Works* V,14.
7. See Peter Fox in *Treasures of the Library* (1986), 5–6.
8. The two quotations in the paragraph are from Maurice Craig's *Dublin 1660–1860* (1952).
9. E. McParland in *The Buildings of Trinity College, Dublin*, (Dublin, 1977), reprinted from *Country Life*, nos. 4114–16 and 4137–8 (1976).

CHAPTER 6

Trinity in the age of reason 1717–1794

For just over three-quarters of the eighteenth century Trinity was governed by only three Provosts, all of whom died in office. Richard Baldwin ruled from 1717 to 1758, Francis Andrews from 1758 to 1774, and John Hely-Hutchinson from 1774 to 1793. The record of the College in these years is one of steady progress and solid achievement, and it is dominated by the strong but sharply contrasted personalities of these three men. They presided at a time when Ireland remained untroubled by civil war or foreign invasion. The Catholic population lay prostrate under the Penal Laws. The Protestant Ascendancy was firm and assured. Only towards the end of the period did the ferment of the American and French Revolutions begin to disturb the imposed calm of the Pax Britannica.

Provosts' pedigrees are normally so impeccable that one is tempted to delve a little into the strange and somewhat conflicting evidence about Baldwin's childhood and youth. The record of his matriculation states that he was born at Athy in County Carlow, that his father (also Richard) was a gentleman of Athy, and that he was schooled by Mr Hinton at the famous grammar school in Kilkenny that also nurtured Swift, Berkeley and Congreve. But in his funeral tribute John Lawson, the Professor of Oratory and History, said that Baldwin was born in England and was brought to Ireland in infancy. More detail about an English origin is provided by a Mr Adamson, who was curate of Colne in Lancashire around 1800. Adamson recorded a local tradition that Baldwin was born in Colne of very humble parents, and that he had to leave the neighbourhood after mortally injuring one of his schoolfellows at the local grammar school. He was then said to have arrived destitute in Dublin at the age of twelve and to have been taken into service as a boy groom by Provost Huntington. Realising Baldwin's abilities, Huntington had arranged suitable schooling for him and had launched him on his successful College career.[1] His attendance at

Kilkenny (which could have come after earlier adventures) is certainly confirmed by the school register. He was there at the same time as Swift, and they were also up at Trinity together, although far from friends. They differed greatly in temperament and outlook. Baldwin was a model student, Swift a rebel who clashed with the Junior Dean. Baldwin used to say that the only talent Swift showed as a student was for lighting the fire in his rooms. Baldwin became a stern Whig, Swift a satirical Tory. Swift was a literary genius, while Baldwin never published anything.

All sources agree about the deep impression that the Jacobite occupation of the College in 1689–90 made upon Baldwin. He had just graduated, and was driven to take refuge in England, and the experience turned him into a very loyal and determined supporter of the Whig cause. Elected to fellowship in 1693, he had risen to be Vice-Provost by 1713, and took advantage of Pratt's absences in England to strengthen his grip on the affairs of the College. When Pratt was forced out by the Whig supremacy in the summer of 1717, Baldwin was duly rewarded with the provostship. He took up office at about the age of fifty, and ruled firmly, and indeed imperiously, for over forty years until his death on 30 September 1758. Celibate and in holy orders, he lived an austerely controlled life, keeping his faculties alert and unimpaired to the end.

His portrait, commissioned for the Dining Hall by the Scholars *c.*1745 (it is still there) shows a stern calm face, with strongly marked features.[2] The prominent monument in the Public Theatre, with its fine sculptured group by the Irish artist Christopher Hewetson, depicts him as a rugged figure, supported on his death-bed by his grieving *Alma Mater*, and casting his eyes heavenward to the crown of life for which he had indeed 'fought the good fight'. The roll in his left hand may represent his will. Baldwin died a wealthy man, bequeathing his whole estate (£24,000 with much property in land) to Trinity. The bequest was more than once disputed at law, and as late as 1820 reputed descendants in England were still litigating to try to recover it. Adamson's account of his early years was included in a legal brief that the descendants prepared at that time.

Baldwin took over a College where academic performance had become slack. We hear of neglected lectures, of poor Chapel attendance by the Fellows, and of 'Deans who never once attended dinner in the Hall during an entire year'.[3] He did his best to correct these shortcomings by example and by insistence on strict discipline among staff and students, and his autocratic manner of government led to many clashes with his Fellows, especially those with Tory sympathies.

Baldwin also had to preside over an unruly and turbulent student body.

The headstrong and ill-mannered behaviour of the sons of the nobility and gentry was a recurrent feature of the rowdyism that plagued the College in the first three decades of the eighteenth century. Fellows of middle-class origin were contemptuously treated as social inferiors. Riotous conduct associated with political differences had also become endemic. Seventeen thirty-four was a particularly bad year. The Junior Dean was stoned, and had his rooms wrecked, after publicly censuring a student who had insulted him. But there was worse to come.

Edward Ford, a son of the Archdeacon of Derry, had been elected a Fellow in 1730, and was living in No. 25 in the recently built east range of Library Square, known as the Rubrics. Stubbs describes him as 'an obstinate and ill-judging man'. He was not the Junior Dean (as is sometimes said), but he was not popular with the students, and his rooms had been vandalised some time before. They were situated over an arched passageway (now closed up) which led into what is now the New Square, but was then known as the Mall. On the night of 7 March 1734 Ford had retired to bed and was asleep when some students gathered in the Mall and smashed his windows with a volley of stones. He was so enraged that he rashly took a pistol which he kept by his bedside and fired it out of the window in their direction. They ran off, but were soon back with firearms (possession of which by students had recently been strictly forbidden under pain of expulsion). Ford again appeared at the window in his nightshirt, and pointed his pistol down at his tormentors through a broken pane of glass. A shot was then fired from below which wounded him so badly that he died later in the evening. His last words, recalled by a student who attended him were: 'I do not know [*sc*, who fired the shot], but God forgive them, I do.'

Baldwin immediately convened the Board to investigate the 'unfortunate murder of Mr Ford' as the Register not very happily styles it. Suspicion had fallen on a student named Cotter, who had rooms nearby; he had been entertaining three other students at a protracted drinking party, and the four were put on trial the following July. But a key witness absconded, identification could not be proved, and they were acquitted.[4] The Board, however, showed its opinion of the verdict by proceeding to expel Cotter and his associates. The prosecution was not well received in Dublin society. The high Tory reaction is well reflected in the heavy irony of a contemporary pamphlet: 'The ladies especially were astonished at the barbarity of the undertaking: so cruel a persecution against the sons of gentlemen, suspected only of a frolick, in which they intended no more than breaking a man's window, tho' it chanced indeed to end in his death.'[5]

It is a relief to be able to record that discipline gradually improved after about 1740, partly in reaction to the Ford case, and partly from better standards of conduct in society generally.

In 1700 the senior academic staff consisted of the Provost, seventeen Fellows, and the Regius Professor of Physic. There were also professorships in divinity and law, but these were always held by Fellows, as was the Donegall lectureship in mathematics. During the next fifty years the staff grew significantly. Ten new professorships were founded (of which only four were confined to Fellows) and the number of Fellows was increased to twenty. Annual matriculations were running at about sixty in 1700. They peaked at just over a hundred in 1725, but by 1750 they were back again to a little less than sixty. So the student population showed no permanent increase over the period, and the expansion in staff represented a real improvement in teaching strength, as well as a genuine broadening of its scope.

Perhaps the most important development came in the teaching of subjects related to medicine. The first medical 'chair' in effect had been established soon after the Restoration with the versatile and scholarly John Stearne as its first holder. Stearne was a grand-nephew of James Ussher on his mother's side. He entered Trinity in 1639 and gained scholarship in 1641, but then left the country to complete his education in England. His medicine seems to have been learnt at Cambridge. Stearne returned to a Trinity fellowship in 1651, combining medical practice in Dublin with College duties, including the teaching of Hebrew. He is the first recorded holder of a medical degree from the University (1658) and was one of the group of Fellows reappointed at the Restoration in the statutory post of Medicus, and he was also designated Public Professor of Physic from 1662 to his death in 1669. During this period he founded and presided over a Royal College of Physicians, designed as a daughter college of the University. It was first housed just west of Trinity in the former student residence of Trinity Hall, and received a royal charter in 1667. Its early history is well summarised by McDowell and Webb, who say that it was 'intended as a medical school subordinate to Trinity College, but after Stearne's death it drifted into a position of virtual independence, largely because the University was unable to supply qualified physicians to manage it.' They explain that the post of Medicus was usually held for short periods only by Junior Fellows who did not teach the subject consistently or effectively, while the Professor of Physic was normally a practising doctor with little contact with the University.

An important step towards remedying this situation was taken in June 1710 when the Board decided to construct an 'Elaboratory' on the western edge of College Park. The two-storey building (sited where the Berkeley Library now stands) was built by Thomas Burgh and was opened on 11 August 1711. It contained a chemical laboratory, a lecture-room, a dissecting room, and (upstairs) a museum. At the same time lectureships were established in anatomy, chemistry and botany. In this way Trinity provided a reasonable standard of 'pre-clinical' teaching within its walls, and so laid a solid foundation for the later development of its own distinguished Medical School. For the rest of his training, the student would depend on the 'clinics' of the Regius Professor in the city and on such lectures as he might give in the College of Physicians.[6]

Ad hoc benefactions also strengthened the teaching in arts and divinity. William King, the able and scholarly Archbishop of Dublin under Anne and George I, was Visitor to the College at this time, and kept a close eye on it for the Whigs. In 1718 he gifted a sum of money to establish a lectureship in divinity, an endowment further strengthened by a bequest under his will in 1729.

Increasing support was also forthcoming from the Erasmus Smith Trust. Erasmus Smith (1611–91) was a London merchant who 'adventured' money into the 'Irish wars' in the 1640s and secured large amounts of land under the Cromwellian settlement. He used his fortune to found and endow grammar schools in Ennis, Galway, Tipperary and Drogheda. From 1668 on, these schools were administered under a trust established by royal charter. Trinity College was closely associated with the development, for its Provost 'now and for the time being' was an *ex officio* member of the Board of Governors and so became a trustee. Provost Ward's name appears on an early committee appointed to look into the accounts, and Provost Marsh is recorded as certifying the suitability of a schoolmaster for Drogheda. From the 1680s, the Governors were supporting students at the College with exhibitions, and as early as 1687 were paying the salary of the lecturer in Hebrew. This lectureship had been established by the 1637 Statutes, but had tended to lapse when funds were short.[7]

Soon after 1720 the governors of the Trust found themselves with a substantial surplus of funds. After consultation with the Provost and Senior Fellows, they agreed a scheme for their disbursement, which included the endowment of three additional fellowships and two new professorships. In fact, this development was suggested by the College authorities, partly on the plea of increased numbers, and partly for its educational value. The benefaction took effect in 1724 after an empowering Act of Parliament had been passed. The professorships were in natural and experimental philosophy (mechanics and physics), and in oratory and history. The specific endowment of the subject of oratory was a pioneering development at the time, and in history also Trinity can claim a narrow priority over Oxford and Cambridge, for their chairs in the subject were not founded until later in the same year. Oratory and history remained linked at Trinity until 1762 when they were constituted as separate professorships.

By the terms of the 1724 Act, the professors were required to give appropriate teaching in their subject, and also to deliver four public lectures a year. Two of these lectures were to be furnished to the Erasmus Smith trustees and were to be printed and published if they thought fit. The stipulation was a modest stimulus to research, and probably helped to encourage the production of two respectable books by early holders of the chairs. The first Professor of Natural and Experimental Philosophy, Richard Helsham, held fellowship from 1704 to 1730. He was a medical doctor of some distinction, and his *Lectures on natural philosophy*, published in 1739 (the year after his death), became a popular textbook. John Lawson, elected a Junior Fellow in 1735, held the professorship of Oratory and History from 1750 until his comparatively early death in 1759. His *Lectures concerning oratory* (1758) went through four printings in two years, and in our day has been considered a sufficiently important landmark in the subject to deserve reprinting.[8] The book bears witness to the very thorough training in classics that Lawson had received as a student in the College.

Lawson was a firm believer in the value of ancient models, particularly those provided by the orators of Greece. He attributed the rise of oratory to the Greek love of liberty, praising Demosthenes as the supremely eloquent opponent of the tyrant Philip of Macedon. His successor but one in the professorship was a good Greek scholar, Thomas Leland, who held the post (in oratory alone after 1762) for twenty years from 1761. Leland followed Lawson's example by publishing his lectures on oratory in 1765, and he also made a considerable name for himself by scholarly work on Demosthenes. The two most celebrated Irish orators of the later eighteenth century were students in Trinity at the time when these scholars were active. Henry Flood attended the College from 1748 to 1751, and Henry Grattan from 1763 to 1767. It is not improbable that the talents of these 'patriot' orators were stimulated and their political attitudes to some extent moulded by their classical studies in Trinity.[9]

In 1724 the Erasmus Smith trustees also made a substantial grant of £940 to build and furnish two houses in the north range of Library Square. The benefaction was designed to provide rent-free rooms for holders of their exhibitions. Library Square was then nearing completion; it contained fourteen houses and enclosed an area more than three times as large as the original Elizabethan quadrangle. The Square was planned in the late 1690s to provide accommodation for the increasing student numbers, and soon after 1700 it had begun to take shape with the completion of its east range, which still survives as the Rubrics. The south side of the Square was formed by the Library, built between 1712 and 1724. Between September 1718 and January 1722, the Board put about £2600 into building the north range of the Square. Library Square was completed about 1725 by a west range situated on the line where the lawns now meet the cobbles of the Front Square. The grand vista that now can be enjoyed from Front Gate was not revealed until the demolition of this range in 1839. The Rubrics, which now close that view, constitute the oldest surviving portion of the College's fabric. They used to join up with the Library on one side and the north range on the other, but three bays at either end (including the portion of No. 22 where Oliver Goldsmith had his rooms) were demolished about 1860. In a rebuilding of the top floor in the 1890s the striking Dutch gables that now add interest to the roof-line replaced the plain dormers of the original.

When the Rubrics were first built, a tree-lined avenue — known as the Mall — ran along their eastern side on the line of the roadway that now links the Printing House to the podium of the Berkeley Library. The Mall extended as far as the Anatomy House, with a walled court to its east where students could take exercise. To the south of the Anatomy House, a long narrow 'physic garden' extended as far as the brick wall that then marked the southern boundary of the site along Patrick's Well Lane (now Nassau Street). The physical shaping of the College was taken a stage further in 1721–22 when elm trees were planted around the perimeter of the area now occupied by the cricket ground. College Park was further delimited by the building of a wall that ran diagonally across on a line from what is now the south-east corner of the New Square in the direction of the present Pavilion. A porter's lodge was constructed in the south-east corner of the Park, near where the wicket-gate now opens on to South Leinster Street behind the Moyne Institute.

In 1726 Dr Stearne, Bishop of Clogher and Vice-Chancellor, donated the princely sum of £1000 for the purpose of building a Printing House for the University. Richard Castle, formerly Cassell, a German immigrant who was to become the leading Dublin architect over the next two decades, was employed to design the building. Construction began in 1733 and was completed in 1734 at a cost of £1212. Castle's Printing House, with its elegant Doric portico, is now rather hemmed in by later buildings. Then it stood like a 'garden temple' in the north-west corner of the Park.

In 1731 the Board established a Premium Fund out of which the best answerers in the various classes at the termly examinations received a prize of £2. On 16 February 1732 the first prizes were awarded on the results of the Christmas examination. The Fund also provided substantial consolation prizes of £50, £40 and £30 for unsuccessful candidates in the fellowship examination.

The Board was inspired to make this move by a 'proposal for the general encouragement of learning in Dublin College', submitted to it the previous year by a distinguished graduate, the Reverend Samuel Madden.[10] The Fund was built up from benefactions, from annual contributions by the Fellows, and from a capitation charge of eight shillings on all students (except Sizars) when they first entered Trinity.[11]

One gets the impression that student exercises and examinations now began to be more systematically organised, perhaps as a result of the premium system. The earliest Senior Lecturer's Register to survive, dated 1731–49, gives details of the books prescribed for undergraduate study at about this time.[12] The book lists are the equivalent of a Calendar course, ante-dating the first printed calendar (1833) by about a century. They prescribe two complete courses, one in science, the other in classics. The science course may be set out as follows (annotations by the writer are given in parenthesis):

Junior Freshmen:	Burgersdicius (a systematic introduction to logic).
Senior Freshmen:	Clerk's Logic, Art of thinking, Smiglecius (selections). (There are probably only two books involved here, for the subtitle of Clerk's Logic was *Ars Ratiocinandi.* Smiglecius's book was a more advanced manual of logic.)
Junior Sophisters:	Colbert's General Physics, part of Clerk's Physics, Varenius's Geography, Wells's Astronomy. (Four books, presumably to cover the four terms.)

Senior Sophisters: Eustathius's Ethics, Small Puffendorf (probably the 1716 Dublin edition of Puffendorf's *The whole duty of man*, on ethics and jurisprudence), Sanderson's Prelections (an Anglican treatise on casuistry), Baronius's Metaphysics (selections).

This was a demanding schedule for students in their mid to late teens. It, or something very like it, would have been read by Edmund Burke (aged fifteen) and Oliver Goldsmith (two years older) who entered in 1744 and 1745 respectively. The reader will note the concentration on logic in the first two years. This traditional logic was not as purely formal as modern symbolic logic. It directed the student's attention to the grammatical structure of language, and attuned his mind to the study of philosophical problems. Then came a graduated progression from natural science through ethics to metaphysics. Aristotle's name has gone, but his systematic spirit is still much in evidence.[13]

In addition to the science course, the undergraduates also had an extensive list of Greek and Latin classical texts to cover, which would more than equate with a modern university course in classics. They were introduced to twenty-three authors from Homer to Justinus, and the prescription included the whole of the *Iliad*, the *Odyssey*, the *Aeneid*, and Livy. There were also weekly essays and exercises to be furnished to one's tutor, and periodic practice in declamation and disputation.

All in all, it was a good solid course, and one is not altogether surprised to find Lord Chesterfield, who was Viceroy in 1751, writing to a friend that 'The Irish schools and universities [*sic*] are indisputably better than ours.' At this period Oxford and Cambridge were little more than seminaries for the Church of England, and had become intellectually torpid. The sons of the English nobility tended to rely more on private tutors or the 'grand tour' to extend their education, and did not go to university in the same numbers as their Irish counterparts.

The provostship of Francis Andrews, which lasted from 1758 to 1774, was an exceptionally harmonious and successful period in the history of the College. The elegantly fronted building that still houses the Dining Hall and Staff Common Room was brought to completion early in his reign. Between 1763 and 1774 the matriculation rate doubled, bringing student numbers to well over five hundred. In scholarship, after a long fallow period, a number of the Fellows had begun to publish in classics (Thomas Leland and John Stokes), mathematics (Hugh Hamilton) and history

(Michael Kearney). And if Andrews himself was not particularly distinguished as a scholar, he was a man of wit and charm, who presided over the College with tact and tolerance, and made the new Provost's House (built for him and his successors) a resplendent focus of social life in the brilliant heyday of Georgian Dublin. The House is the only Dublin stone-built mansion of that period still in use as a private residence. Described as 'a masterpiece of the Indian summer of Palladian architecture in Ireland', it has remained almost unaltered in design and decoration and constitutes an appropriate memorial to Andrews's taste and accomplishments.[14]

Francis Andrews (1718–1774) was a native of Derry. He entered Trinity in 1733, graduated in 1737, and was elected a Fellow in 1740. There is no record of his having gained scholarship, but in 1738 he is listed as a recipient of the Berkeley medal for proficiency in Greek. As a young man he travelled in Italy, winning good opinions for his *savoir faire* and fluency in Latin. He was a fashionable and energetic figure who liked to be in the public eye. His main intellectual interests lay in the law and politics, rather than in academic scholarship. While holding his fellowship he also practised at the Bar, and during his provostship he sat in the House of Commons as MP for Midleton (1759–60) and Derry (1761–74), gaining a considerable reputation as a parliamentarian. He was the first lay Provost since Temple.

Andrews moved easily and agreeably in high society. His manners were described by a contemporary as 'frank and open, accompanied with so much good humour, good nature, and real benevolence that he had few if any personal enemies'.[15] He was like a second Horace in a new Augustan age, rising by talent and a good education from a comparatively humble provincial background, to become the valued companion of the great of the land. His appointment as Provost seems to have owed much to his friendship and interest with the Duke of Bedford. The Duke had gained popularity by his lavish entertaining at the Castle during his lord lieutenancy, and Andrews in a way returned the compliment when he secured Bedford's appointment as Trinity's Chancellor on the death of the previous incumbent (the Duke of Cumberland) in 1765.

At his formal installation, the College set new precedents in public ceremonial. The occasion was delayed to 1768, but no expense was then spared. The ceremonies included a solemn procession from Regent House to Hall, Commencements with the new Chancellor presiding, a Chapel service with *Te Deum* and *Jubilate* specially composed by the Earl of Mornington, and a banquet costing £250. Bedford was so pleased with his reception that he presented the University with the splendid portrait of himself by Gainsborough which still adorns the saloon in the Provost's House.

Andrews, the man of affairs, proved a sensible and capable administrator. Within a year of taking up office, he instituted a system of public entrance examinations held on stated days four times a year. Before 1759 the qualifications of candidates for entrance were tested privately and individually. We have an account of one such examination from the pen of Edmund Burke. The examination was conducted by his intended Tutor, Dr John Pellisier, and by the Senior Lecturer, Mr John Obins. Pellisier examined the candidate in Horace's *Odes*, Virgil's *Aeneid* and Homer's *Iliad* and called him a 'good scholar'. Obins gave him a further very strict examination in a wider range of Horace, including the *Satires* and *Epistles*. The examination naturally testifies to Burke's capabilities, but also to the scope and quality of his schooling at the Quaker school in Ballitore, County Kildare.

The new public system led to an educational exchange, the first on record, between the Dublin schools and the College. The headmasters naturally wanted to know where they stood, and wrote asking for advice on what classical authors they should be reading with their pupils. The Board prepared a list with the help of the Senior Lecturer, Dr Wilder, and sent it out with detailed advice on how the teaching of Latin and Greek should be carried out. The circular also included a recommendation that 'every young gentleman be completely instructed in the Common Rules of Arithmetic before he should think of entering the College'.

Another important academic development resulted from Andrews's influence with the Erasmus Smith Trust. In 1762 he persuaded the governors to endow three new professorships at an annual salary of £100 each. (Modern) history was split off from the existing professorship of oratory and history, and was constituted as a separate chair. Hebrew became a professorship on the same level, as did mathematics. Payments under this benefaction continued to be made down to 1847.

As a man of taste and refinement, Andrews also addressed himself to the cultivation of music in the College. In 1762 a regular choir was first established in the College Chapel and a Sunday choral service instituted. He also secured the assent of the Earl of Mornington (later to become the father of the first Duke of Wellington) to appointment as the University's first Professor of Music. The Earl seems to have been taking an interest in the Chapel music. He was a young man not long out of College, having graduated MA in 1757; he received a doctorate in music in 1762. His duties were not onerous since 'he was not expected to teach or examine, nor was he insulted with the customary salary of £100 a year; all that was expected of him was an occasional composition, such as that which he provided for the installation of the Duke of Bedford as Chancellor'.[16] Mornington was a talented musician, and his appointment, though honorary, did no dishonour to the subject, but the chair remained unfilled after his resignation in 1774, and was not revived until 1847.

The confident and dignified spirit of the age still breathes strongly through the Georgian buildings of the Front Square, an ensemble that has been described by Maurice Craig as 'the most ample piece of collegiate architecture' in the British Isles. The creation of the ensemble began six years before Andrews became Provost and was not completed until four years after Hely-Hutchinson's death, but the history of the development may be outlined at this point. In its assured and elegant expansiveness, the project was typical of these two great Provosts, and Andrews is thought to have played a part in its inception.

Richard Castle died in February 1751, and within a few months the College was petitioning Parliament for a grant to rebuild the West Front. Money was readily forthcoming because the Irish Exchequer was in surplus at the time, and preferred to spend the balance in Dublin rather than remit it to London. In all, £30,000 was voted between 1752 and 1759, and the older name of Parliament Square embodies a tribute to this generous allocation of public money. No attempt was made to adapt or extend existing structures. Beginning with the north range in 1752, the residences that had been put up in the latter part of the previous century to form a 'great court' to the west of the original quadrangle were demolished. The decent Jacobean West Front, completed less than sixty years earlier, also was pulled down. The Board appointed Hugh Darley, and not Castle's assistant and successor John Ensor, to supervise the work. It is known that Castle had drawn up plans for a new West Front a good many years before, so the decision to break with his firm marked a new but perhaps not surprising departure. Castle had scored a success with the Printing House, but his subsequent work on a new Dining Hall, which was being built in the mid-1740s, proved less than satisfactory. The vaults gave way in 1758, and the building had to be demolished and rebuilt. The work was completed about 1761. Many of the materials from Castle's structure were reused, including the chimney-piece now in the Common Room.[17]

Until 1976 the superb design of the present West Front was credited to Henry Keene and John Sanderson, and they were certainly associated with the work, for there is a record of a payment of £74 to them for 'Plans and

Elevations'. But evidence has been found indicating that they were executing a design which the Board had accepted from a distinguished amateur named Theodore Jacobsen. Jacobsen was the architect of the Foundling Hospital in London, and it now seems certain that he was the real author of the College's majestic Palladian façade, with the professionals Keene and Sanderson merely supplying the working drawings.[18] The West Front, together with the residential wings that run back from it, was completed by 1759. Jacobsen's original design included a central dome with two flanking cupolas. One cupola was erected on top of the north pavilion, but was removed in 1758.

The completion of Parliament Square by the erection of the Theatre and the Chapel, with their answering porticoes, was due to the initiative of Hely-Hutchinson. In 1775 he secured a building grant of £2,500 from the Erasmus Smith Trust and commissioned the distinguished British architect William Chambers to draw up plans for a new assembly hall. Early in 1777 work began on what is now the Public Theatre (commonly known as the Exam Hall), with on-the-spot supervision provided by a local architect, Christopher Myers. Chambers's plans were published in 1780, and show that his scheme envisaged the Chapel in its present position opposite the Theatre, and also a reconstruction of the west range of Library Square. But only the Chapel and Theatre were realised. Chambers, who was busy with Somerset House in London, resigned in July 1778, complaining of lack of information from Dublin. Both buildings were completed under the direction of Myers, the former in the mid-1790s, and the latter in about 1800. The new Chapel was solemnly consecrated on 8 July 1798. At the same time the last vestiges of the Elizabethan quadrangle, including the late seventeenth-century Hall and Chapel, were removed, opening up the view of Parliament Square as far as the western range of Library Square. Marsh's Chapel, which was about the same size as the new one, did not appeal to eighteenth-century taste. Not long before its demolition, it had been described as a mean and gloomy building, 'destitute of monumental decoration within and no better than a Welsh church without'. The present Chapel, with its fine pillared porch, dignified classical interior, and splendid plasterwork, made a fitting finale to the great Georgian building programme.

Antonio Maroni's portrait of Andrews (painted in Rome and now in the Provost's House) shows a portly figure with a double-chin. He enjoyed good food as well as good company, and the regime of a *bon viveur* eventually undermined his health. He died on 12 June 1774, at the age of fifty-six, in Shrewsbury, while he was on his way back from convalescence in Italy. He was buried in the College, which he remembered generously in his will, bequeathing £3,000 for the building of an Observatory, together with an annual charge on his estates for the salary of a Professor of Astronomy. The College supported the bequest with additional funds, leading to the first appointment of a Professor in 1783, and the completion of the Observatory at Dunsink, close to Dublin, in 1785.[19] The Observatory continues to provide viewing facilities, but the professorship was suspended in 1921. Under letters patent issued in 1792, the professor was granted the title of 'Royal Astronomer of Ireland on the foundation of Doctor Francis Andrews' This chair of astronomy was occupied by a succession of distinguished men, most notably by John Brinkley (1790–1827), William Rowan Hamilton (1827–65), and Sir Robert Ball (1874–92).

Like his predecessor, Provost Hely-Hutchinson had the energy and ability to combine parliamentary office with his College duties, but he was a much less amiable man, and the tedious quarrels that now began to rack the House were largely generated by his assertiveness and the high-handed and self-seeking way in which he chose to conduct College business. He was born at Gortroe, County Cork, in 1724, and entered the College under the name of John Hely. He assumed his double-barrelled name in 1757 when he inherited, through his wife, the estates of Richard Hutchinson of Knocklofty, County Tipperary. After graduation in 1744, his career took him away from College and into public life. He studied at the Temple in London, was called to the Irish Bar in 1748, and in his mid-thirties he entered Parliament, retaining a seat in the House as a member for Cork for the rest of life. Promotion to the post of Prime Serjeant soon followed in 1761, and he ended up in the imposing sinecure of Principal Secretary of State. A contemporary account of him as a parliamentarian refers to his natural fluency, enlivened by wit and satire, and says that he helped to improve the standard of speaking in the House by his 'classical idiom'. The same source adds that 'his acceptance of the Provostship of Trinity College was an unwise step, injurious to his peace, and almost clouding every prospect in his profession.'[20] How this came about will now be briefly related.

The provostship had become a lucrative post, worth more than £2000 a year, with a fine residence thrown in. It was effectively in the gift of the Viceroy and the Chief Secretary, and when it became vacant on Andrews's death they used it in a scheme of political jobbery outrageous even by the standards of the time. Hely-Hutchinson was induced to resign his post as

Prime Serjeant, which was needed to oblige another claimant, and was compensated by being installed as the head of a startled College, with which he had had no direct connection for thirty years.

Hely-Hutchinson was by nature an ambitious and acquisitive man, and Lord North's quip about him bears repetition: 'If you were to give him the whole of Great Britain and Ireland for an estate, he would then ask for the Isle of Man for a potato garden.' The Provost's House offered him a secure base at the heart of Ireland's social and political life, and he was happy to take it. If he could outface parliamentary opponents, he was not going to be deterred by the hostility of mere Fellows. His appointment traversed the statutes and previous practice in three respects: he was a layman, he was married, and he had not been a Fellow of any College. The first two obstacles could be, and were, overcome by royal dispensation; the third was a continued source of friction since the Fellows resented the imposition of a career politician with no pretensions to scholarship.

The first three years of his provostship were particularly chequered and turbulent. He managed to make a substantial improvement in the College's income by instituting a new survey of its estates, as a result of which low rents were raised to an economic level. But he also set the place at loggerheads by some shameless politicking in relation to the parliamentary elections of May 1776. Trinity had the right to return two members, and the Provost made it his aim to secure one of the seats for his son Richard. The electorate consisted of the Fellows and the Scholars who were not minors, and Hely-Hutchinson applied various pressures to this constituency. He secured the support of two Senior Fellows, Dr Leland and Dr Dabzac, each clandestinely married, by obtaining dispensations for them. He also installed his family tutor, the Reverend Wensley Bond, in rooms in College, using him as an agent to push his interests with the Scholars, and not hesitating to use intimidation and cajolery to secure their votes. At the election, he acted as returning officer, and declared his son elected, but the result was overturned after an enquiry, and at the subsequent by-election the seat went to John FitzGibbon, afterwards Earl of Clare. At a later election in 1790, which was also bitterly contested, Hely-Hutchinson did manage to secure a seat for his younger son, Francis.

His bitterest opponent among the Fellows was Patrick Duigenan, an uncouth man but an able lawyer, who had risen from humble origins with the aid of a sizarship, and was now Regius Professor of Laws. The two men quarrelled openly at a Board meeting on August 3 1775, where Duigenan is recorded in the Register as having 'used improper and disrespectful expressions to the Provost'. Hely-Hutchinson then employed a typical piece of diplomacy to side-line his adversary. He persuaded Duigenan to exchange his professorship for another chair, that of Feudal and English Law, at a considerably enhanced salary. This professorship had been established by letters patent in 1761 with the object of bringing university teaching in law into closer contact with legal practice in the courts. The post was open only to a barrister of at least two years' standing, but it was a further condition that any Fellow elected to it must vacate his fellowship. By accepting the position, which he held from 1776 to the end of his long life in 1816, Duigenan automatically lost his fellowship, but he did not lose his animosity against the Provost. The next year, 1777, saw the publication of his celebrated and much-quoted diatribe, *Lachrymae Academicae,* in which Hely-Hutchinson's character and conduct were vigorously and venomously lampooned. Duigenan censured the jobbery that had ensured his appointment as Provost, and his subsequent attempts to manipulate the University electorate. He accused him of setting a bad example to the students by indulging in duelling (which he had done), alleging that the College Park and even College rooms were being used for target practice, and that 'scarce a week passes without a duel between some of the students' in which 'some of them have been slain, others maimed'. He also pilloried Hely-Hutchinson for his fondness for horse-riding in the College grounds, and for the noise created by 'his infant children, their nurses and go-carts'.

Hely-Hutchinson undoubtedly brought a new style to the provostship. He promoted a riding-school in the College, and also engaged instructors to offer lessons in fencing and dancing. Such gentlemanly accomplishments, he argued, were not merely desirable in themselves, but would fit his charges for tutorial posts in great houses. Realising also that some knowledge of European languages would be useful to those of the students who might travel abroad, he secured government money to finance the establishment of two 'professorships' in modern languages. One instructor was appointed to give tuition in French and German, and a second in Italian and Spanish. These appointments have been acclaimed as the first 'chairs' in these subjects in the British Isles, but this is to make too much of them. The languages were not taught as part of the regular curriculum, and the 'professors' were hired tutors rather than top-ranking members of the academic staff. Nearly a century was to elapse before any modern European language formed part of the degree course.

These fashionable innovations were avidly seized upon by cartoonists and satirists, and a collection of lampoons came out in 1775 under the title *Pranceriana,* in which the Provost is harshly caricatured as:

A Harlequin genius, cognomine Prancer [swaggerer].
A Duellist, Scribbler, a Fop and a Dancer.

When reviewing the state of the College towards the end of his reign, Hely-Hutchinson claimed that standards had greatly improved in the scholarship and fellowship examinations. This may have been partly due to the fact that by 1790 numbers in College were more than twice what they had been twenty-five years before. But some credit should also be given to the Provost for his active management of the institution. In January 1786 he ordered the tutors to make a fortnightly return of the pupils attending their tutorials, indicating which were 'satisfactory' and which not. A typical quarrel at once flared up: the tutors resent the demand as unprecedented, non-statutary, and tending to violate the confidentiality of the tutor-pupil relationship. Towards the end of March, after receiving a letter from the Vice-Chancellor, Hely-Hutchinson decided to withdraw his order 'to prevent new contests between his Grace the Lord Primate and him, and to restore tranquillity and good humour to the Society'. These prudent sentiments are recorded in his manuscript history of the College, and he also pays a handsome tribute to his opponents when he notes that 'many of the gentlemen who opposed this order were as able and as diligent Tutors, as this, or probably any other College, had ever produced'.

One suspects that some of the tutors may have fallen short of this standard, and that their resentment was designed to protect their own position as much as that of their pupils. The Provost comes quite well out of the incident, and one feels some sympathy with him in this, as in some other of the vexed academic issues of his tenure. It is notable that in a major visitation in 1791 the newly elected Vice-Chancellor, Lord Clare, found in the Provost's favour in respect of his powers to assign pupils to tutors both at entrance and afterwards. The main point in which the visitation went against him was in respect of his claim to have a veto over Board decisions that he did not like. This old issue, known as 'the Provost's negative', turned on a disputed phrase in the statutes, which said that decisions of the Board were to be reached by ' a majority of the Senior Fellows together with the Provost' (*maior pars Sociorum seniorum una cum Praeposito*). Domineering Provosts like Hely-Hutchinson took this to mean that no decision was valid unless the Provost was an assenting party, but Lord Clare ruled against this interpretation. He held that the contested words simply meant that the Provost was a member of a body that was empowered to decide matters by a majority of the whole. This ruling was a constitutional landmark in the history of the College, and Provosts were never again able to rule in the autocratic manner of Hely-Hutchinson and some of his predecessors.

Hely-Hutchinson's health began to fail after the 1791 visitation, and he was often absent from Board meetings during the last three years of his provostship. Day-to-day administration passed into the hands of the Vice-Provost, Dr Richard Murray. It was perhaps a consequence of this state of affairs that the second centenary passed without any recorded notice or celebration. In the summer of 1774 John Hely-Hutchinson had gone to take the waters at Buxton, Derbyshire, and he died there on 4 September. His remains were brought back to Ireland and buried in Christ Church Cathedral.

It is difficult to write about Hely-Hutchinson without highlighting his more obvious defects of character and his many clashes with his academic colleagues. But there was a more estimable and constructive side to his public career which should not be forgotten. He was a patriot in the mould of Molyneux in his firm support of the Irish Parliament's right to legislative independence. Like Molyneux, too, he protested against the restraints that England placed on Irish trade. He also showed sympathy for Catholic Emancipation, and advocated the end of educational discrimination against Catholics. In one of his speeches he said: 'I would have them go into examinations, and make no distinction between them and the Protestants but such as merit might claim.....The present laws are disgraceful; they prohibit the Roman Catholics from having any education at all, and therefore should be abolished — the Roman Catholics should receive the best education in the established university.'[21]

In so far as he could, he put these principles into practice, as is shown by the case of Martin Toomey, the son of a Kerry farmer, who entered Trinity with a sizarship in 1786. Toomey testified before a parliamentary committee that he was a Roman Catholic, that he had been elected to a scholarship, and that no pressure had been put on him to conform to Church of Ireland practice in the College. Indeed, he added that some of the Fellows recommended him as a private tutor to their pupils and that he was able to earn a considerable income in this way.

The main problem for such a student was not so much election to scholarship as the acquisition of a degree. Students matriculating in Trinity had never been required (as they were at Oxford) to declare assent to the Thirty-nine Articles. The Scholar's oath had never contained any specifically Anglican clause, though in practice a student who did not attend College Chapel had little chance of election. But under the Penal Laws passed early in the eighteenth century, Catholics could not proceed to a degree unless they were prepared to take an anti-transubstantiation oath, which was repugnant to their conscience and beliefs. Times, however, were changing, and support for Catholic Emancipation was growing in the country as in the College. In 1792–93 the British government decided that the growing military threat from France made further conciliation of Irish Catholics imperative. The result was the Relief Act of 1793, which did away with the obnoxious test in regard to degrees. Under its Section II, there was also explicit exemption for non-Anglicans from the obligation to attend College Chapel. From then on, the education offered by the College from entrance to graduation was fully open to all Christian denominations, and also to Jews. Trinity's ethos, however, remained strongly Anglican, and the Statutes still required a candidate for fellowship (as distinct from scholarship) to abjure 'Pontifical religion' and the authority of the papacy.

The end of Hely-Hutchinson's provostship is a convenient point at which to outline some significant changes in the undergraduate course made under him and his predecessor. The most important change was the introduction, about 1760, of instruction in Euclidean geometry (books 1-3 and 5-6) in the Freshmen years. This was the first formal prescription of a branch of mathematics in the undergraduate course, and credit for the change appears to be due to Francis Andrews. The Freshmen still had to concentrate on logic, but their task was made more palatable by the dropping of Smiglecius and Burgersdicius in favour of a simpler textbook by a Trinity Fellow. A compendium of formal logic by Richard Murray, first published in Latin in 1759, and later in an expanded English version, was now prescribed. Murray succeeded Hely-Hutchinson in the provostship, and the 'Provost's Logic', as his book became known, held its place on the course for over a century until it was replaced by 'Abbott's Logic', which some older graduates still remember on the course for 'Little-go'. Besides their 'Murray', Senior Freshmen also had to study Locke's *Essay* for three terms. This work may have surprised, if not confused them, by its radical attack on Aristotelian method, but it is likely also to have enlivened and broadened their minds by its candidly empirical treatment of philosophical problems.

By 1794 the natural science course taken by Junior Sophisters had become noticeably more mathematical in its bias. The first term was devoted to astronomy, the second to mechanics, the third to hydrostatics, and the fourth to optics. Optics was studied with the aid of a textbook published in 1787, and written by a young Fellow, John Stack, who had been an unsuccessful candidate for the chair of astronomy in 1792. The appointment of the brilliant young Cambridge scientist, John Brinkley, must have helped to keep the teaching in astronomy fully up to date.

Ethics still remained the staple subject for Senior Sophisters, but their reading list now contained only one avowedly theological work, John Conybeare's *Defence of Revealed Religion* (1732), which was prescribed for the final term. In the earlier terms the students studied an ethical text of Cicero (*De Officiis*), Locke's *Essay on Government*, and a treatise on natural law by Burlamaqui, a professor at Geneva; this last was a widely read work, first published in 1747. The course reflects the spirit of the times. In the educational practice of the College the era of theological controversy can finally be seen to have given way to the age of reason and enlightenment.

The curriculum was dominated by Locke in epistemology and politics, and by Newton in science. They were included with ancient worthies like Homer, Plato, and Aristotle in the first set of fourteen portrait-busts placed in the Long Room of the Library. This was to be expected in an eighteenth-century academy that had long been predominantly Whig in outlook (though now beginning to incline to Toryism). The intellectual habits and principles that it sought to inculcate in its students have been well summarised as 'mathematical precision in demonstration, an appreciation of the ordered harmony of the universe, rational empiricism as a habit of thought, liberal oligarchy as the basis of government, the avoidance alike of deism, enthusiasm and superstition.'[22]

Notes

1. For this strange story, see further W.B.S. Taylor, *History of the University of Dublin* (1845), 248–51. See also Maxwell, *History*,108–09, who prints a letter from a descendant, J.R. Baldwin, dated 1892. This letter gives substantially the same account as Taylor, but locates the accident in Sedbergh School in Yorkshire and attributes it to the blow of a cricket ball. The archivist at Sedbergh has not been able to find any record relating to Baldwin, but it is of interest to note that a Trinity graduate, Dr Thomas Dwyer (Scholar, 1686) became an early headmaster of Sedbergh.
2. A poem dated 1731 and describing a College examination has the lines: 'Lo! Baldwin comes, how dreadfully serene / how grand his looks....' Quoted by Stubbs, *History*, 203. Lawson says that he continued to examine to the end of his life 'with great acuteness'.
3. From a contemporary pamphlet quoted by Maxwell, *History*, 113.
4. British Museum Add MSS 40851 contains a verbatim report of the trial. It is summarised and discussed by R.B. McDowell in *Trinity* 2 (1950) 20–22.
5. Quoted by Maxwell, *History*, 112.
6. For details of the complex relationship between Trinity College and the Royal College of Physicians in Ireland, the reader is referred to T.P.C. Kirkpatrick, *History of the Medical Teaching in Trinity College, Dublin, and of the School of Physic in Ireland* (Dublin 1912).
7. The details come from the Erasmus Smith Trust *Registry Book* 1674–1732, which is in the keeping of the Dublin High School. For the Hebrew lecturer's salary, see the *Book* p.106.

8. Lawson's work in facsimile, edited with an Introduction by E.N. Claussen and K.R. Wallace, was published by Southern Illinois University Press in 1972.
9. See W.B. Stanford, *Ireland and the Classical Tradition* (1976), 209–14. In reference to the educational influence of the Classics, de Valera in a letter to Stanford in 1960, stated: 'Young minds are affected far more than is is generally appreciated, I believe, when they come upon noble thoughts suitably expressed.' *The Irish Times,* 21 November 1991.
10. Madden published his scheme in pamphlet form in 1731. A similar scheme was soon applied also to the encouragement of industry and agriculture through the (Royal) Dublin Society, which Madden helped to found. 'Premium' Madden, as he became known, was the son of a Dublin doctor, John Madden who had married a sister of William Molyneux. All the Maddens were Trinity graduates, and a cousin, another John Madden, was a Fellow from 1710 to 1724. Samuel Madden was a close friend of George Berkeley, and both held similar views on how landlords could best contribute to rural prosperity. Berkeley's *Querist* came out in parts between 1735 and 1737, and Madden's *Reflections and Resolutions proper for the Gentlemen of Ireland* in 1738. The Madden Fund was instituted somewhat later, in 1798, from a substantial bequest by his son, Samuel Molyneux Madden. It was specifically devoted to consolation prizes for fellowship candidates.
11. Bishop Berkeley became an early and effective participant in the premium movement by his annual presentation, from about 1734, of a gold medal for the encouragement of Greek. The Berkeley medal was designed by the good Bishop himself, and its Homeric motto, which may be translated 'Always strive for excellence' encapsulates the emulatory spirit of the Madden scheme. The prize was endowed in perpetuity under his will in 1752.
12. The books are listed in sequence for the Freshmen and Sophister years on three pages at the beginning of the Register (TCD MSS:Mun V/27 (l), 1, 2, and 6). The lists are undated, but their position in relation to other dated material on nearby pages indicates the 1730s, and Stubbs's date of 1736, followed by McDowell and Webb, is probably not far off the mark.
13. McDowell and Webb (*History,* 45–49) provide fascinating detail on the contents and flavour of the various books listed for the science course. Their general conclusions are also significant for any assessment of the education provided by Trinity at this period. They stress how cosmopolitan the course was, with seven out of the ten books written by Dutch, French, or German scholars. The choice of Eustathius's *Ethics* for the first term of the Senior Sophister year seems pleasingly non-sectarian: the author, Father Eustache de St Paul, was a French Cistercian. In respect of 'science' in the modern sense of the word, the prescribed books were reasonably up to date, with Newtonian influence beginning to make itself felt. Otherwise, reliance was placed on rather venerable and unadventurous works, all published before 1700, a fact that gives the course a somewhat old-fashioned pre-Enlightenment look.
14. E.J. McParland in *Country Life* CLX (October 1976). See also M. Craig, *Dublin,* 182–83. The Provost's lodgings were previously in the south-west corner of the original quadrangle. In keeping with the rising grandeur of the provostship, the new house stood somewhat apart from the ordinary residence blocks. Building work started in 1759, and the structure was completed in 1761. Most of the internal work was finished by the mid-1760s. Supervision was by a local architect named John Smith (who received the rather paltry fee of £22 15s for his services). The design was adapted from that of a London mansion (now demolished), designed by Lord Burlington for General Wade. The exterior of the central block is practically identical with that of Wade's house, with the low wings as a successful addition. The interior arrangements however, are quite different. Edward McParland suggests that the perfection of the interior designing, seen to best advantage in the superb main staircase and saloon, is due to Henry Keene rather than John Smith. The total cost was almost £11,000. The building programme since 1751 had cost £55,000 in all.
15. F. Hardy, *Memoirs of the political and private life of James Caulfield, Earl of Charlemont* (1810), 76.
16. McDowell and Webb, *History,* 58.

17. The supervisor for the reconstruction of the Dining Hall was George Darley, another member of a family whose association with building work in College spanned more than a century. Their history, as given by McParland (*art. cit.* in n. 14), may be summarised as follows: The family haled from Yorkshire or Derbyshire, and settled in the North of Ireland in the late seventeenth century where they owned quarries in Newtonards. Henry Darley and his son Moses worked as stone-masons on Burgh's Library, and Moses went on to work on the Printing House. The granite and limestone for the West Front were largely supplied from Darley quarries at Golden Hill and Ardbruccan, where George employed a hundred men preparing stone for the College. A descendant, Frederick Darley, became official College architect in the next century, and was responsible for the design and erection of the north and east ranges of New Square between 1838 and 1844, and also the Magnetic Observatory in 1838.

    Richard Castle was responsible for two other buildings in College which have not survived: a tennis court, and an elaborate Bell Tower, begun in 1740 and completed in 1746 (according to Stubbs). The lower part of the Bell Tower formed a monumental entrance to the old Hall at the north-west corner of the Elizabethan quadrangle. The Bell Tower was therefore on the same line as its predecessor, the steeple of All Hallows, and its successor, the present Campanile, but considerably nearer the Front Gate. It was a tall and dominating feature of the eighteenth-century College, but was later found to be insecure. The upper portion was taken down in 1791, and the great bell removed to a meaner structure in Botany Bay. The rest of it, together with the old Hall, was demolished before 1800.
18. The question is fully discussed by McParland in *Country Life* CLIX (May 1976). The crucial document is TCD MS, Mun/P/2/98, a letter of 15 February 1755 from Hugh Darley to John Keene reporting progress on the building of the principal front and proposing emendations to Mr Jacobsen's plans. There is independent evidence for working links between Keene, Sanderson, and Jacobsen, apart from the West Front project.
19. The College transferred ownership of the property to the state in 1947, and its management then became the responsibility of the Dublin Institute for Advanced Studies. For a detailed history of the Observatory, see P.A. Wayman, *Dunsink Observatory, 1785–1985*, Dublin (1987).
20. From the pen picture by Hardy, *Memoirs*, 72–74
21. Quoted in Maxwell, *History*, 128. These liberal and tolerant sentiments had been anticipated by Bishop Berkeley in his *Querist*, section 191: 'Whether, in imitation of the Jesuits at Paris, who admit Protestants to study in their colleges, it may not be right for us also to admit Roman Catholics into our college, without obliging them to attend chapel duties, or catechisms, or divinity lectures?' W. Macneile Dixon, *Trinity*, 123f, notes as a 'striking fact' that 'when the proposal to establish a separate College for Catholics was discussed in Grattan's Parliament, a strongly worded petition against it was presented by the Roman Catholics of the kingdom'.
22. McDowell and Webb, *History*, 72.

CHAPTER 7

Provost Murray, 1798, and the Union

In the months before and after Hely-Hutchinson's death, the Fellows lobbied hard to avoid the imposition of another 'outsider' as his successor, and in the end were successful in persuading the Crown to give them their own choice from their own number. The Reverend Dr Richard Murray (1726–99) was duly sworn in as Provost on 29 January 1795. He was an elderly and respected figure who had devoted his life to the service of the College in which he had graduated more than fifty years before. His scholarship was respectable, if undistinguished (his textbook on logic has already been mentioned) and he was Professor of Mathematics from 1764 to his election as Provost. Innovation was not to be expected from him, but he was a safe man to head the House at a difficult time.

The political climate in Ireland became increasingly unstable as the violent momentum of the French Revolution intensified. England had been at war with France since early in 1793, and a French agent was arrested in Dublin in April 1794. The planning of reform was overtaken by the plotting of revolution. In May the government tried to suppress the United Irishmen. In September of the following year the clash between Peep o' Day Boys and Defenders at the Diamond in Armagh led to the founding of the Orange Order. Radicalism and republicanism were in the air, and the College was about to become an arena for conflict between 'Orange' and 'Green'.

The conflicting strands of nationalism and unionism were already beginning to stand out all too clearly in the tangled web of Irish politics. They can be seen in a particularly pure form in the careers of two Trinity graduates which may serve as paradigms of the increasingly polarised loyalties of the time.

Theobald Wolfe Tone (1763–98), son of a Dublin coach-maker, entered the College as a pensioner in February 1781. He was ambitious to do well, and was very disappointed not to win a premium in his first year examinations, but competition for these was extremely keen. In the following year he was involved as a 'second' in a duel which had a fatal outcome, and was sent down for twelve months. After his return to College, he worked more steadily, and secured election as a Scholar in 1785. As a Junior Sophister, he was now entitled to join the College Historical Society where he soon made his mark as a debater, winning twelve 'merits' and three medals.[1] He graduated in 1786, and after studying law for a time in London, he took his LLB and was called to the Irish Bar in 1789. In 1791 he helped to found the Society of United Irishmen, whose stated object was to unite Irishmen of all denominations in a movement for Catholic emancipation and parliamentary reform. A Junior Fellow of the College, Whitley Stokes, a kind-hearted man who was later to win a considerable reputation as a doctor and a scientist, was among the early members. As a 'moderate', Stokes soon found that he could not support the recourse to revolutionary violence espoused by Tone, but Tone continued to admire him and regard him as a friend.[2]

Tone's effective participation in the events leading up to the French invasion of 1798, and the courage he showed in his final hours after capture by British forces, can receive only the briefest of mentions here. His career is central and seminal in the rise of Irish republicanism, and it is to be remarked that even towards the end of his life he was able to write: 'I look back on my College days with regret, and I preserve, and ever shall, a most sincere affection for the University of Dublin'.[3]

William Blacker (1777–1855) came from a landed family that had been established in County Armagh since the sixteenth century. His father was Dean of Leighlin, but the Blackers also had strong military traditions, and an ancestor had fought on the Williamite side at the Boyne. William was educated at Armagh Royal School. As a member of the local militia he took part in the battle of the Diamond on 21 September 1795, and two weeks later he went to Dublin with his father to make arrangements for his entry to Trinity as a fellow commoner. He prepared for his first examination at home, and after passing it with tolerable credit he moved into a 'double' in Library Square. His room-mate was Hans Caulfield, son of a Tyrone clergyman. Blacker's journal records that his 'library' consisted of ' a dog-eared Lexicon, two-thirds of a Latin dictionary, a Murray's Logic, somewhat blackened from doing occasional duty as a kettle holder, and Elrington's Euclid, a greasy Virgil, and a Homer redolent of Anglesey Street....'[4]

Student feelings were running high enough to produce vicious outbreaks of violence in College, and there was even a duel fought between representatives of the contending parties. In the summer of 1796 trouble broke out in the North, and Blacker obtained a captain's commission in the yeomanry, but continued to come for term examinations, though 'Locke's logic had little success with Dundas and tactics'. In October 1797 he joined the third company of the College Corps formed in that year, and describes the drilling in the squares. He was reprimanded by the Board for his part in a brawl where student friends of his were attacked in Dame Street. He took part in the general visitation held by Lord Clare, the Vice-Chancellor, in the spring of 1798, and designed to purge the College of United Ireland sympathisers. In the course of the proceedings, Blacker clashed with Whitley Stokes, who had named him as a leading Orangeman. Although he was in obvious and outspoken sympathy with the aim of the authorities, he had reservations about the conduct of the affair, which he describes as 'a summary process, smacking, I must say, a little of the inquisitorial'. Blacker went on to become High Sheriff of County Armagh and Vice-Treasurer of Ireland, wrote some tolerable poetry, and had the pleasure of entertaining Sir Walter Scott to dinner when he visited Dublin in 1825.

Clare's notorious visitation followed soon after a disciplinary case in which a Scholar called Arthur Ardagh and his friend David Power were expelled by order of the Board upon reports of a meeting in College rooms at which seditious toasts were drunk. Both students were of good character and ability, and there was considerable sympathy for them in the College. Another student, Purcell O'Gorman, published a paper reflecting adversely on the Board's action, and he too was expelled for refusing to retract his comments. The Board's decision in the Ardagh-Power case was far from unanimous, and the Visitors in their judgment expressed strong criticism of one Board member, Arthur Browne, Jurist and MP for the University, for giving public vent to his dissatisfaction with the severity of the sentence. In general, the Visitors confirmed the existence of four Committees of United Irishmen in the College, and expelled eighteen students (including five Scholars) on various charges, including grave suspicion of seditious conspiracy, and contumacy in refusing to appear before the tribunal. Five were Catholics, the rest Protestants. The expelled included Robert Emmet, described by Clare as 'the most wicked and extreme' of the College radicals. Emmet had been in College since 1793, and had impressed his contemporaries by his intellectual prowess and oratorical powers. The sentence on Whitley Stokes was that he should be precluded from acting as a tutor, and disqualified for three years from co-option to senior fellowship.

They were harsh and stressful times, but College life went on even under the imminent threat of invasion and rebellion. In his Board notebooks for 3 May 1798, Thomas Elrington recorded: 'Board will not subscribe to water cart for College Green — Slates broke by balls — Wall of College Street — Composition Premiums stamped'.[5] However, the crisis became so severe after the initial successes of the uprising in Wexford that no candidate presented himself for the fellowship examination at the end of May, and the election had to be postponed to October.

After the 'year of the French', the country returned to relative tranquillity. The struggle in Parliament over proposals for legislative union with Britain was bitter and protracted, but the necessary bills were pushed through by August 1800, and the formal union of the two countries took place at the start of the new century on 1 January 1801. The rebellion had won no sympathy among the senior members of the College, but the Union was much more controversial. A majority of the Fellows, together with the new Provost, John Kearney, were opposed to it, and doubts were also voiced in Parliament by the Trinity members, George Knox and Arthur Browne, though in the end Browne voted for it. His only reward was to lose his seat, for University representation was cut from two to one, and the right of returning two members to Parliament was not restored to the College until the Irish Reform Act of 1833.

Notes

1. The College Historical Society (the 'Hist') can claim to be one of the oldest debating societies of its kind in the world. Its roots go back to April 1747 when Edmund Burke, then a Senior Sophister, founded a club for the discussion of historical and philosophical questions and for practice in public speaking. The club had seven members initially, meetings were held twice a week, and minutes in Burke's hand are extant. But it does not seem to have survived Burke's departure from College. We hear of a Historical Club formed in October 1753, but no records of its proceedings are extant. Such associations clearly met a need, and a new one was formed in 1770, 'mainly for the cultivation of historical knowledge and the practice of the members in oratory and composition'. This was the beginning of the College Historical Society, which still continues to flourish.

   The 'Hist' at first consisted of thirteen members, all Trinity students, and the Board granted them the use of the large upper room over the entrance to the Dining Hall (now the Staff Common Room). In the first session the membership increased to fifty, and 'historical examination' was soon neglected in favour of debate as the main business. In 1783 an alliance was formed with the Speculative Society of Edinburgh (established in 1764). In 1789 graduates of Oxford and Cambridge were permitted to become candidates for membership — their Unions had not yet been founded.

   Membership gradually increased to over six hundred, many being graduates of some standing. In April 1794 a dispute broke out with the College authorities over the attendance of a member who had been barred from frequenting the College. Political factions were active in College at this time, and the Board wished to ban outside influences as far as possible. The Society was ordered to exclude from its debates those not on the College books, and on its refusal to comply found itself locked out of its room. The 'Hist' then began to hold meetings outside the walls, but a split soon occurred, with some of the students agreeing to the Board's terms, including the exclusion from debate of 'any question of modern politics'. For a time there were two Societies, one internal, the other external.

   After the Union, the external Society declined, and in February 1806 dissolved itself, handing over its property to the group within the walls. This group had started with twelve members, including the future Provosts Kyle and Sadleir, and Thomas Lefroy, youthful 'sweetheart' of Jane Austen, and later MP and Lord Chief Justice of Ireland. Tom Moore and Robert Emmet joined later. The internal Society continued to meet in its old room until 1815 when further disputes with the Board and Provost Elrington led to a long period of exclusion. The Society was reconstructed; it functioned outside College until 1844 when it finally gained readmittance. It continued to restrict membership to men until 1968. Mary Harney was the first woman to be elected Auditor (President).
2. Stokes's dilemma was felt by many another intellectual at the time. Like all his College contemporaries, he had been brought up on Locke, and the views expressed in Paine's *The Rights of Man* (1791) could be seen as a natural development of Locke's liberalism. Paine's book was written in answer to Burke's *Reflections on the Revolution in France* (1790). The College came down officially on Burke's side when the Board in 1793 voted him an honorary degree. During the rest of the decade conservative reaction against the heady new wine of 'human rights' was progressively strengthened by the excesses of the Jacobins and by the anti-religious vein of many of the revolutionaries. Stokes wrote a reply to Paine's *The Age of Reason* (1795), and in 1798 Elrington, one of the younger Tory Fellows, brought out an edition of Locke's *Essay* for which he received the thanks of the Board. Elrington argued that when Locke spoke of the will of the 'people', he really meant the will of the 'men of property'. In 1799 the Board voted to take down Grattan's portrait from the walls of the Public Theatre and to replace it with one of the Earl of Clare. As McDowell and Webb well say: 'the break with the days of Andrews and Hely-Hutchinson was complete'. (*History*, 78)

3. This sketch of Tone is much indebted to Marianne Elliott's biography, *Wolfe Tone, Prophet of Irish Independence* (New Haven and London, 1989).
4. Blacker's Journal, though full of vivid touches like this, was in fact written many years later. Extensive extracts from it are printed as an Appendix by Maxwell, *History*, 257–74.
5. TCD MS 9721.

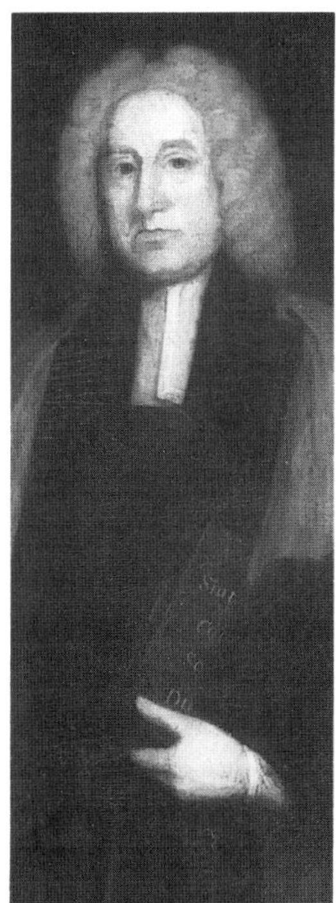

13 *Richard Baldwin (c.1668–1758), Fellow (1693–1717), Provost for forty-one years from 1717 to his death, the longest tenure of any incumbent of the office.*

14 *Francis Andrews (1718–84), Fellow (1740–58), Provost from 1758 to his death, builder of the Provost's House.*

15 *John Hely-Hutchinson (1724–94), Provost from 1774 to his death.*

16 *Edmund Burke (1729–97) graduated from the College in 1748. His denunciation of the French Revolution in 1790 gained him an honorary degree from the College in 1793. The statue by John Henry Foley was erected in 1868.*

17 *The College buildings in 1780, including Richard Castle's bell-tower (1746, demolished by 1800), taken from the perspective drawing by Samuel Byron.*

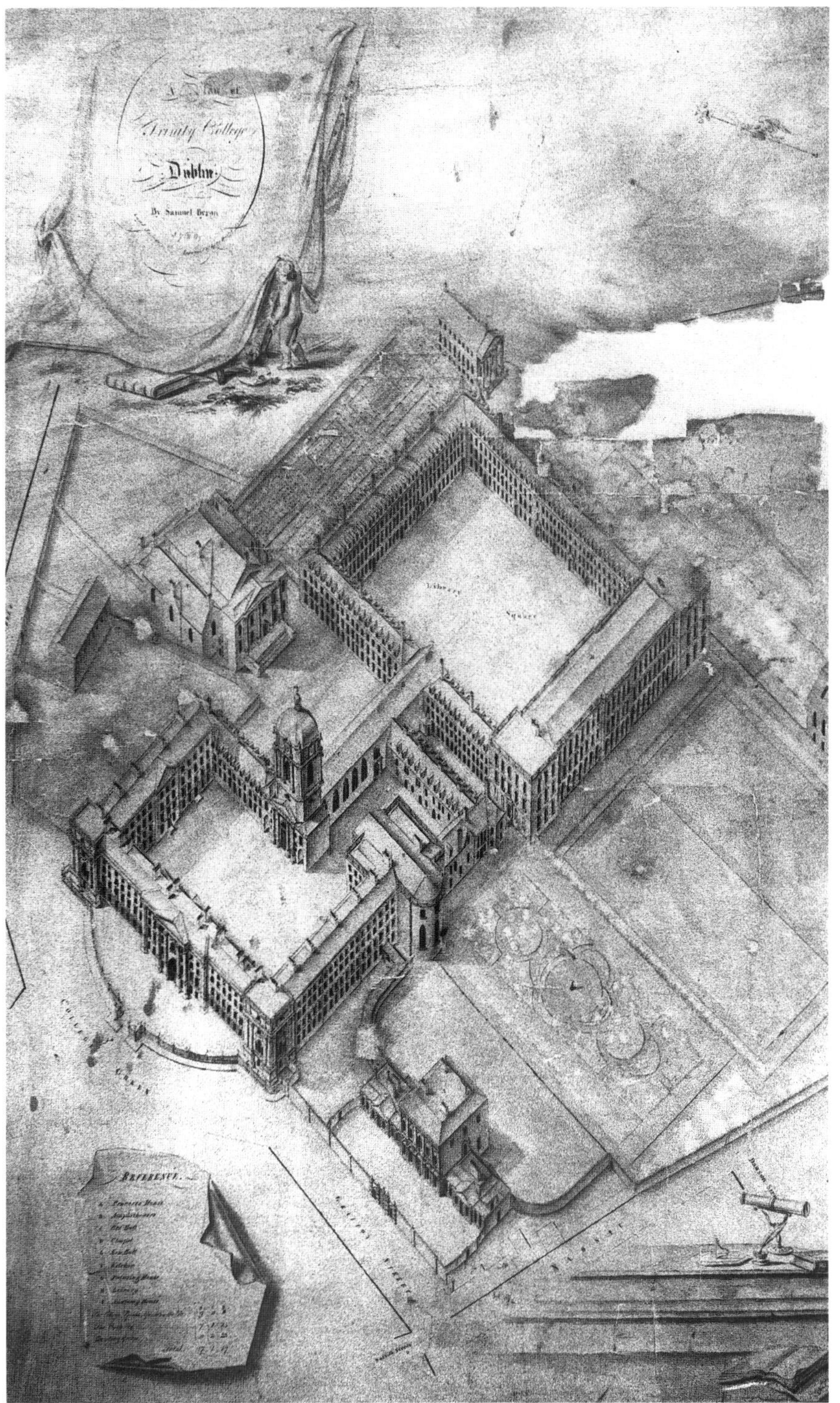

18 *The College grounds and buildings as drawn by Bernard Scalé (1761). The drawing shows the recently completed Provost's House and Dining Hall. The bowling green at the east end of the College Park is also clearly marked.*

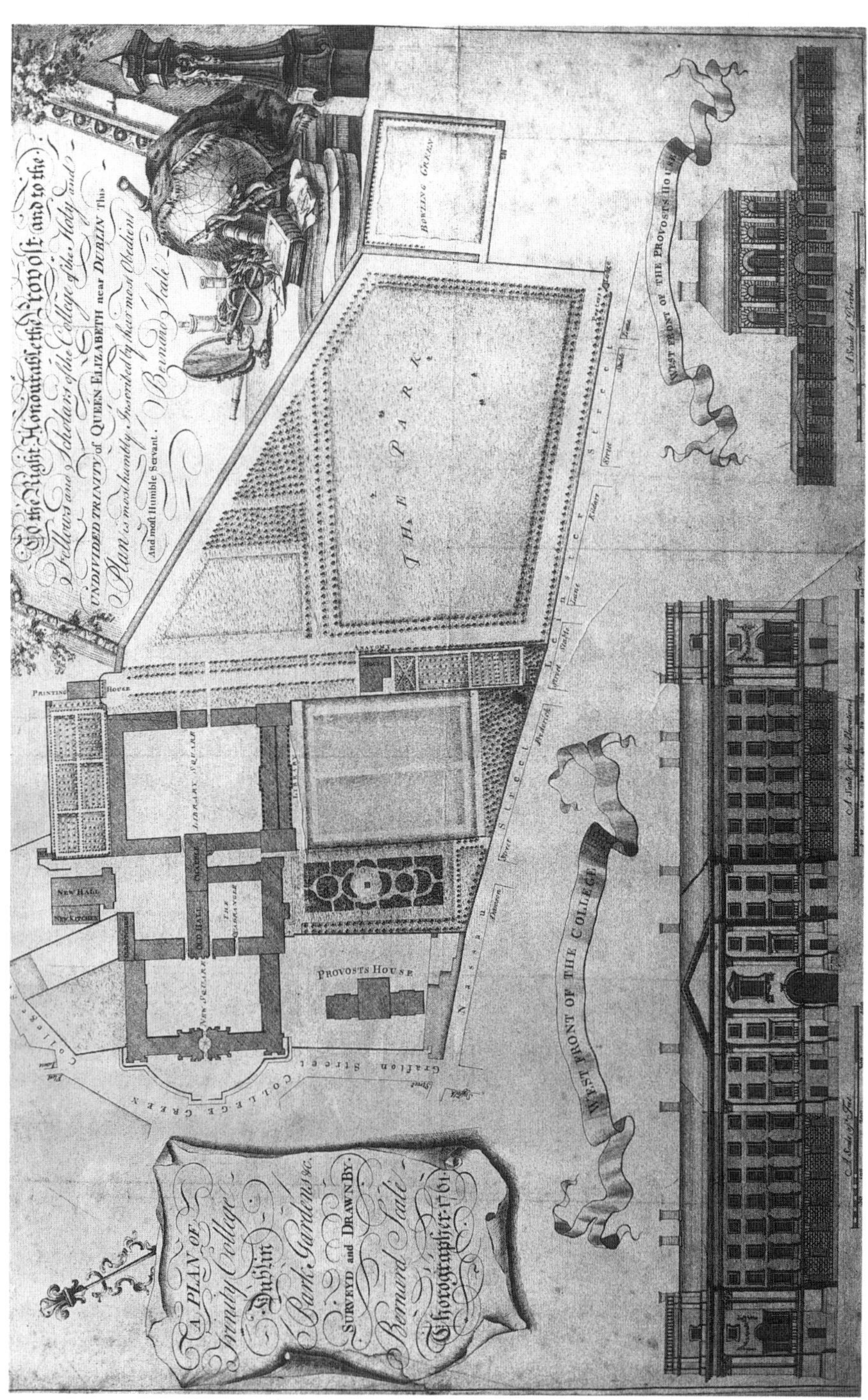

19 *The Provost's House, No. 1 Grafton Street. In background (left) the 1937 Reading Room, the Old Library, the Museum Building; (right) the Arts Building.*

20/21 (over)
Two photographs of the saloon in the Provost's House, showing it used as a drawing room in about 1900, and today, when it is used mainly for receptions and concerts. Gainsborough's portrait of the Duke of Bedford is visible on the end wall in the modern view.

22 (Previous page) *The interior of the College Chapel.*

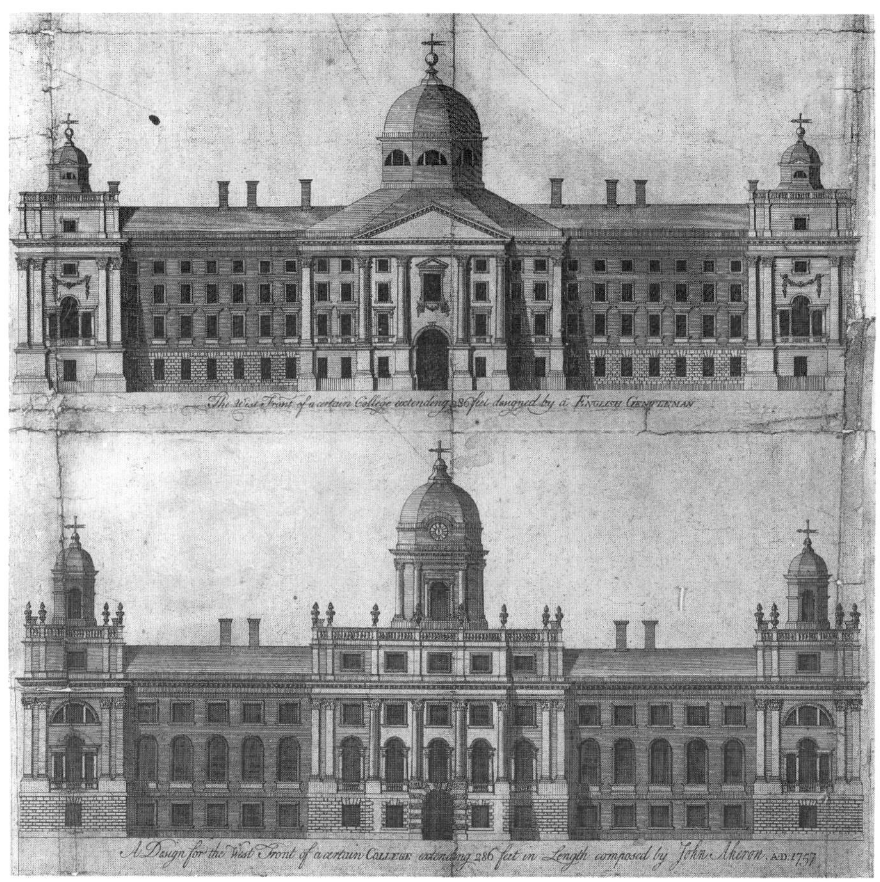

23 *Elevations of Theodore Jacobsen's original design for the West Front (above) with (below) John Aheron's proposed revisions. The cupola on the left was erected, but soon removed.*

CHAPTER 8

From the Union to 1831

While allowing that the Act of Union was a watershed in Irish history, McDowell and Webb argue that it did not mark a significant divide in Trinity's academic life. Here, they think, if one is looking for the true end of the eighteenth century, one should go back to the death of Hely-Hutchinson. On the other hand, a typically nineteenth-century attitude to higher education did not emerge until the provostship of Bartholomew Lloyd, which began in 1831. Their analysis reveals a period of some thirty years in which the College performed quietly but adequately in a fairly set pattern, living, as they well say, in a kind of 'limbo' between the Georgian and Victorian eras.

Murray died in office on 20 June 1799, and between him and Lloyd came four Provosts with much in common. They were all in holy orders, all graduates of the College, all solid Tories, each had held senior fellowship, and each left the office to become a bishop of the Church of Ireland. They form a worthy but unadventurous quartet, and under them the College, like Dublin, lost much of the élan of former years, and became a somewhat duller though by no means a torpid place.[1]

Mahaffy called the period between the provostships of Hely-Hutchinson and Lloyd a 'disgraceful forty years', and 'probably the least creditable in all the three centuries'.[2] He noted that no fine buildings were erected, that the custom of presenting silver plate was allowed to lapse, and that when the new Chapel was consecrated in 1798 the alabaster-topped monument of Luke Challoner (which had been housed in the former Chapel) was put out into the open where the effigy soon weathered into a shapeless mass. The sad result of this piece of thoughtlessness could be seen up to 1968 in the little cemetery that occupies a corner between the present Chapel and Dining Hall, and the authorities of the day are much to blame for it.[3] But Mahaffy paints too black a picture, and when he goes on to complain that 'no public display brought the College into notice except the lavish feast to George IV in 1821', his prejudice against the somewhat parsimonious successors of the great Georgian Provosts becomes only too clear. Mahaffy was also wrong in stating that these years earned Trinity the title of 'Silent Sister', a reproach that went back to Baldwin's time when there was a very fallow period between 1722 and 1753. In fact the senior members of the College now formed a more distinguished group than were to be found in any Oxford or Cambridge College, and their record of research and publication was good and varied.[4]

College numbers fell during the 1790s, but soon picked up after the Union, and by 1811 the intake was back to what it had been twenty years before, with about 200 students entering each year. But over the next thirteen years a steep rise took the annual intake to 300 by 1817, to over 400 by 1820, and to a maximum of 466 in 1824. This last figure was not improved upon until after World War II.[5] These statistics mean that in a decade-and-a-half the undergraduate population went up from about 800 to close on 2000. No comparable increase had occurred before in the College's history, and to match it again one has to come down to the 1960s and 1970s. The peak of 1824 was not sustained, and during the rest of the century the annual matriculation figures declined by stages until in 1900 the intake was back to about 220.

No full explanation has been found for these fluctuations. Population growth and the rise of the middle class must be factors in the increase, and it is interesting to find that in the first quarter of the nineteenth century Cambridge experienced a growth very similar to Dublin. But the subsequent downturn in Dublin was not matched in Cambridge. Nor can we correlate the scholarly reputation and achievements of the university with student numbers, for Trinity's reputation stood high in the Victorian age, at a time when its numbers were declining.

The creation of three new fellowships between 1808 and 1811 was probably a response to the increase, but the staff-student ratio obviously worsened in the period we are considering, while the workload of the Fellows must have gone up very considerably. They seem to have borne this with commendable absence of complaint, but it should be remembered that the per capita basis of payments ensured a corresponding rise in their emoluments. An increase in the proportion of students who attended only for examinations was another mitigating factor.

By 1814 it had become clear that there was a pressing need to provide more residential accommodation, and this was met by the completion of the Square which has been known to successive generations of students as Botany Bay.[6] Planning had begun back in the early weeks of Hely-Hutchinson's provostship when he got the Board to agree that the area of the kitchen garden behind the north range of Library Square should be designated for residential expansion. In 1786 the College repossessed the lease of the area along its northern perimeter, known as Marsh Park, and demolished a number of small houses which had been built there. This was done to make space for the new Chapel, as well as the projected residences. Houses 11 and 12 were nearly complete in 1787, but development was suspended in the 1790s when numbers went into a temporary decline, and was not resumed until Elrington's provostship. The remainder of the Square dates from 1814–1817, and was financed with the aid of a government loan of £20,000.[7] In design, materials, and finish, the ranges show a marked falling-off from the high standards of the Front Square. The best that can be said for them is that they are practical if plain. Before World War II the interior of the Square was a rather squalid expanse of muddy gravel dotted with stunted hawthorn bushes, but in 1955 its appearance was much improved by the construction of three hard tennis courts donated by the Endowment Fund 'out of monies subscribed by graduates of the University', and by the addition of well-planted surrounds.

The most important academic development of the period occurred in the Medical School. By the turn of the century the long-standing jealousy and distrust between the members of this School and the authorities of the College of Physicians had generated a complex set of regulations for obtaining a medical degree. Students had to go backwards and forwards between the two institutions with various documents and fees, and the tediousness of the procedures combined with the attractions of Edinburgh to reduce the number of candidates to a very low level. A further complication arose from a quarrel about the administration of the monies deriving from Sir Patrick Dun's estate. This dispute inhibited the establishment of the clinical lectures desired by Sir Patrick. The difficulties could be sorted out only by legislation, which came in the form of a new School of Physic Act in 1800, one of the last measures to go through the Irish Parliament. The Act provided for a payment of £100 each to the King's professors, and further stipulated that a hospital suitable for clinical teaching should be built with the surplus of Dun's estate. This was the genesis of the famous teaching hospital bearing Sir Patrick Dun's name, which remained closely associated with Trinity's Medical School until its closure in 1986. After the passing of the Act, the problem of the clinical lectures was solved by their temporary accommodation in the Meath hospital and Steevens's hospital, and they were then moved to Dun's when it was finished about 1815.

The stage was now set for a revival and expansion of the Medical School, and this happened from 1812 on, largely because of the appointment of James Macartney as Professor of Anatomy. Macartney was a Presbyterian from the North who had trained in London and had been a lecturer in comparative anatomy at St Bartholomew's hospital. He soon attracted such large numbers to his classes that the Board had to agree to an expansion of the facilities, and this led to plans for new medical premises at the east end of College Park. The new School building was completed between 1823 and 1825, and portions of it still survive where the building that presently houses the Health Sciences Office adjoins the departments of anatomy and chemistry.

One immediate consequence of the Union was the passing of a new Copyright Act in 1801 which extended to Ireland the operation of existing English legislation. Trinity College Library now became a legal deposit library and was entitled to claim free copies of all items (books, pamphlets, maps and periodicals) published by British publishers registered with the Stationers' Company. Unfortunately the university presses of Oxford and Cambridge were not so registered, and it was sometimes difficult to get publishers to obey the law. But, despite these difficulties, the privilege was a valuable one, its working was improved and extended by the Copyright Act of 1836 and it lies at the root of the Library's present day eminence.[8]

Before 1801 the collection was built up in part by purchase, but the main source of accessions lay in the generosity of benefactors. Archbishop Ussher's library of some 10,000 books and manuscripts was acquired in this way, and the tradition was worthily continued in the eighteenth century. William Palliser had been a Fellow from 1668 to 1682, before his elevation to a bishopric. He was Archbishop of Cashel from 1694 for over thirty years, and after his death in 1727 the College received by bequest from his collection every book that was not already in the Library. The Palliser donation, with other similar benefactions, is commemorated in gold lettering on the frieze above the bookcases in the Long Room.

The bookcases were not completed at the time, but the Long Room had come into use as a reading room when the next major accession was received. This was in 1735 by gift from Claudius Gilbert, who resigned his fellowship in that year to go out on a College living. Gilbert had been Vice-Provost during the first eighteen years of Baldwin's term of office. His entire library of some 13,000 volumes came to the College during his lifetime, and is still shelved in the Long Room in its original order. Gilbert also remembered the Library in his will, and at his death the College received the sum of £500 'for the purchase of busts of men eminent for learning to adorn the library'. The Board used the money to commission a set of fourteen busts as the start of the splendid collection now in the Long Room, and these were in position by 1749.[9]

The next really major accession came by purchase in 1802. It consisted of the 20,000 volumes of the personal library of Hendrik Fagel, Greffier (Chief Minister) of Holland, which he had put up for sale in London some years before. His asking price of £8000 (the equivalent of about £1 million today) was far beyond the means of the Board, but the Erasmus Smith Trustees agreed to finance the purchase and, after some rather protracted negotiations, the prize was secured. The total holding of the Library at the time was about 50,000 volumes, so the Fagel collection increased this by 40 per cent at a stroke. It was estimated that the new books would require over a mile of shelving, and the necessary cases were made to order in a very handsome style in the first-floor room of the East Pavilion where Fagel's volumes are still housed. The collection was a broadly humanistic one with its main strength in European history, and substantial sections also in geography, politics and law, so it admirably complemented the Library's existing strengths in theology and biblical exegesis. It is a great antiquarian treasure, and also provides valuable teaching resources for the departments of French, history, philosophy, and the history of art.[10]

The enterprise shown in the Fagel acquisition belies Mahaffy's claim that the period we are describing was 'stagnant', but it was generally stable, and no fundamental changes were made in the curriculum. The undergraduates still toiled away at their Latin, Greek, logic, Locke, physical and mathematical science, and ethics. They derived no benefit from the Fagel books, for admission to the main Library was confined to graduates. For their basic textbooks they relied on a lending library established for their use in the earlier part of the previous century.

Algebra was added to the Senior Freshman course in 1808, but otherwise the subjects remained as before. The course may be criticised for being unadventurous and somewhat arid, but it was better balanced than contemporary courses at Oxford or Cambridge, and more rigorous than those of the Scottish universities. Being compulsory for all students, it had to be tempered to the pace of the dullest. The aspirations of the brighter students could be satisfied by success in the scholarship examination, which they would normally take in their third year. There was also the system of premium awards at term examinations, first instituted in the 1730s, and significantly extended in the period now under review.

In 1793 the award of a gold medal was instituted for students who had performed consistently well throughout their course. This was not won easily, for the student had to answer at the level of *valde bene* at every one of his sixteen term examinations. In 1815 the Board established a new basis for the gold medal award, and this was a significant innovation foreshadowing the later separation of pass and honor courses. It was now arranged that, when they reached the stage of their last examination, students who had won a premium at any of their previous examinations should be treated differently from their peers. They were placed in a separate group and given a stiffer examination on a more advanced and extensive course. On the result sheets they headed the list, arranged in an order of merit, under the title 'outstanding in their class' (*primarii in sua classe*). Two gold medals were awarded, one to the best student in classics, and one to the best student in science (philosophy and mathematics). Here can be seen the germ of an honor system with merit classes and separate moderatorships in more specialised subjects.[11]

The first quarter of the nineteenth century was a time when the College became noted — and some might say notorious — for its examination system. The statutes of Oxford and Cambridge had long laid much more stress on lecture attendance than examinations, but since 1637 the emphasis at Trinity had been different. The Laudian Statutes had expressly required the termly testing of the knowledge of the Scholars in Hall, and this system had grown into a rigorous and remorseless cycle of quarterly examinations.[12]

Trinity, it has been remarked, 'possesses the questionable distinction of being the cradle of the public examination system.' The authors of this generalisation go on to paint a graphic picture of the scene at examination time:

> . . .the week that preceded each term was full of indescribable ferment and bustle, with two or three hundred students from the country or from England who were never seen in College at other times helping to crowd the squares, with Masters of Arts (who assisted the Fellows as examiners when needed) emerging from their burrows in obscure corners of Botany Bay, and with undergraduates running to and fro between the examination hall and their books or their grinder for a last-minute tip, or shuffling together their hastily composed or dearly

> bought themes, while the great bell of the College from its ramshackle penthouse in Botany Bay tolled out its solemn, almost funereal note.[13]

The examination of each class took two days with a morning and an afternoon session each day (8 to 10 and 2 to 4). The 'theme' was a Latin essay set on the first day and due for submission on the second. It was the only written part of the examination. All the rest of the testing was done *viva voce*, with the class split into divisions of between thirty and forty students, and two examiners, one in Classics and one in Science, assigned to each division. In the 1820s Trinity could not be regarded as old-fashioned in this respect because the printed examination paper had not yet been invented — it was first used at Cambridge in 1827. A pamphlet written in 1828 by Richard MacDonnell, then a Junior Fellow, criticised the chanciness and time-wasting nature of the system, particularly for the average pass-man who might only face his examiners for ten minutes out of the eight hours, and might then fluff a formula or be asked to construe an author he had not had time to prepare. But there were pros as well as cons. The oral system set a premium on mastery of detail and quick recall, which are not to be despised, and it spared the examiner a mountain of turgid scripts. The dons at least liked their 'vivas', which long continued to play an important and even dominant part in Trinity's examinations, particularly those for fellowship.[14]

Notes

1. John Kearney (1742–1813) was a Dubliner distinguished more for wit and literary taste than for scholarly attainment. He was appointed in July 1799 within a month of Murray's demise, and presided over the College for six-and-a-half years before resigning to take up appointment as Bishop of Ossory on 23 January 1806. Perhaps his main claim to fame lies in his recognition and encouragement of the talent of Thomas Moore, who had been an undergraduate during the stormy 1790s.
   His successor, George Hall (1753–1811), was the only non-Irishman of the group, having been born in Northumberland and educated in England. He died in the College on 23 November 1811, five days after his consecration as Bishop of Dromore.
   Thomas Elrington (1760–1835) was born in County Dublin, and held the professorships of Mathematics (1795–99) and Natural and Experimental Philosophy (1799–1806) before succeeding Hall at the end of 1811. He ruled with vigour and decisiveness for nine years before becoming successively Bishop of Limerick (1820–22) and Bishop of Ferns (1822–35). He is commemorated by a handsome prize, founded by subscription on his death. The prize (now worth £500) was for long offered in the Divinity School, but is now awarded annually for an essay by a Senior Freshman in the School of Hebrew, Biblical and Theological Studies.
   His successor, Samuel Kyle (1771–1848), came from County Derry and was not in favour of Catholic Emancipation, a fact that gained him his appointment in October 1820 at a time when the issue was a particularly sensitive one for the British cabinet. He headed

the College with competence but no special distinction for eleven years until his appointment as Bishop of Cork in 1831.

2. In *The Book of Trinity College, Dublin, 1591–1891* (1892), 83.
3. In May 1968 the Board approved the recommendation of its Challoner memorial committee for the removal of part of the original monument to the Chapel crypt, and the provision of a new slab over the monument in the cemetery.
4. One may instance as substantial works of scholarship Arthur Browne's two treatises on civil law and ecclesiastical law (1798, 1799), Matthew Young's *An Analysis of the Principles of Natural Philosophy* (1800), William Magee's two-volume treatise on the Atonement (1801) and John Brinkley's *Elements of Astronomy* (1808), both of which went through seven editions, Bartholomew Lloyd's *A Treatise on Analytic Geometry* (1819), John Walker's eight-volume edition of Livy (1797-1822), and Whitley Stokes's *Observations on the Population and Resources of Ireland* (1821). One should not forget the eccentric John ('Jacky') Barrett, Librarian from 1791 to 1808, who wrote on Swift and the zodiac and edited an important early palimpsest of St Matthew's Gospel (Codex Z) which he identified among the College manuscripts.
5. The figures here and elsewhere down to 1952 are taken from McDowell and Webb's *History*. They were the first to highlight the early nineteenth-century expansion, and their Appendix 2 (Statistics relating to students), with its graphs and analysis, will remain fundamental for all future study of the phenomenon.
6. The origin of the name is uncertain: it may derive from the previous location there of the College's kitchen garden, in which botanical specimens may also have been grown. Others consider it a nickname given by the original student residents, with a joking reference to themselves as 'convicts' banished to a location as remote as the original Sydney colony. See Maxwell, *History*, 167. Trinity's contacts with Australia in fact began with the 'first fleet', in which a Scholar of the House, Thomas Jameson (1766) sailed as surgeon's mate on the *Sirius*. For this and other instances of Trinity men who contributed to Australian development, see J.J. Auchmuty, 'The Anglo-Irish influence in the foundation of Australian institutions', *Melbourne University Gazette*, May 1969. Henry Grattan Douglass, whom he regards as the main instigator of the University of Sydney, held a medical degree from the College, and there were two Trinity men (both Catholics) on its original Senate: John Hubert Plunkett, the Attorney General of New South Wales, and Sir Roger Therry, a judge; the first Chancellor of Melbourne University (Sir Redmond Barry) and the first Registrar (Edward Graves Mayne) were also Trinity graduates, as was the first Premier of Southern Australia (Sir Robert Torrens). Auchmuty states that 'the majority of the professional men . . .who came to Australia [*sc.* in the first colonial century] were educated within the walls of Trinity College'.
7. See TCD MSS Mun/P/2/219, 220. The loan was repaid in instalments of £1200 from 1818 on. Proposals were taken in 1813 and the main work was undertaken between 1814 and 1817. Houses 15 and 16 were measured in September 1814.
8. The present (1991) position is that Trinity's library is a 'copyright library', receiving Irish and British publications in the same way as the British Library, the Bodleian, Cambridge University Library, and the national libraries of Scotland and Wales are sent, gratis, British and Irish publications. Since Ireland's independence, Irish legislation as well as British has been necessary to maintain the legal deposit status of these libraries on a reciprocal basis. Separate Irish legislation gives legal deposit status *for Republic of Ireland items only* to the National Library of Ireland, the University Colleges in Dublin, Cork and Galway, and St Patrick's College, Maynooth.
9. The busts were sculpted by Peter Scheemakers, a fashionable sculptor of Flemish parentage working in London. The idea was copied, like the Library itself, from Trinity College, Cambridge. Their subjects were Homer, Demosthenes, Socrates, Plato, Cicero, Shakespeare, Milton, Locke (as in Cambridge), Aristotle, Bacon, Robert Boyle, James Ussher, Thomas, Earl of Pembroke. See further Anne Crookshank in *Treasures of the Library* (1986), 21–25.

10. For a detailed account of the Fagel Collection, see Vincent Kinnane in *Treasures of the Library* (1986), 158–69.
11. Medal candidates in classics had to read some additional texts, and were advised to be well-versed in ancient history, to understand the nature and history of Greek drama, and to be 'well acquainted with the prosody and other niceties of the Greek language'. For the science medal, fairly advanced work in algebra, trigonometry, astronomy and optics was required, and the course in mathematics included calculus, analytical geometry, and conic sections.
12. The first College Calendar came out in 1833. After the historical introduction, its first sentence reads: 'Terms in the University are kept, during the Undergraduate course, not by residence, as at Oxford and Cambridge, but by answering at the Examinations held for this purpose at the beginning of each term.' One should add that undergraduates *in residence* were also required to attend their tutors' classes and the 'Morning' (science) and Greek lectures on pain of fines and loss of standing.
13. Quoted from McDowell and Webb, *History*, 123. The great bell, cast in Gloucester in 1742, was originally hung in Castle's domed bell-tower over the west end of the Old Hall, but this structure was removed as unsafe in 1791. The bell was then placed in a makeshift penthouse in Botany Bay before being hung in the present Campanile in 1854. The Campanile also houses a smaller bell, the Provost's bell, which was cast in the fourteenth or fifteenth century, and, according to E.H. Alton (*TCD*, 9 June 1943) 'in all probability' came from the steeple of All Hallows.
14. In the quarterly examinations, the examiners in effect awarded grades on an eight-point scale in each subject. In the upper part of the range a candidate could be adjudged to have performed *optime* (a rare distinction), *valde bene*, *bene*, or *satis bene*; in the lower, *mediocriter*, *vix mediocriter*, *male*,or *pessime*. A 'judgment' below *mediocriter* led to a 'caution', which meant failure in the examination; two failed examinations meant the loss of a year.

    There were sixteen examinations in the four-year course leading to a BA, and the student was required to pass at least eleven of these, including five in the Freshman years. He was said to be 'answering for his degree' at the Michaelmas examination of his Senior Sophister year, but for pass men, as distinct from candidates for medals and the honors list, this examination did not differ in kind from those that preceded it. Before the degree was conferred, the traditional exercises of a Latin declamation and a syllogistic disputation had to be performed.

CHAPTER 9

Reform and development 1831–1851

Change was in the air when Provost Kyle resigned in the spring of 1831. Catholic Emancipation had been achieved in 1829, a new Whig government was in power, and the great Reform Bill was about to come before Parliament. The installation of Bartholomew Lloyd as the new Provost on 9 April 1831 was in keeping with the spirit of the times, for it was the prelude to two decades of major reform and development in the College.

Bartholomew Lloyd (1772–1837) was a native of New Ross, County Wexford, and had been a Fellow since 1796. He had a good record as a scholar and administrator, having been Professor of Mathematics (1813–22), Professor of Natural and Experimental Philosophy (1822–31), and Bursar (1816–19). Author of two first-class mathematical textbooks, he had shown a versatility typical of his generation in adding the Regius Chair of Greek to his responsibilities for most of the years between 1821 and 1829. Lloyd was in every way the outstanding candidate among the Senior Fellows, and his eminence was further recognised during his provostship by his election as President of the British Association in 1835 and President of the Royal Irish Academy from 1835 to 1837.

Lloyd's main previous achievement had been to modernise the courses in mathematics and mathematical physics by introducing a knowledge of the analytical methods developed some years earlier in France by Lacroix, Poisson and Laplace. By so doing, he laid the foundations for the eminence of Dublin mathematics later in the century. Thanks to him, the quality of teaching and research in the school soon rivalled Cambridge and far outstripped Oxford. The subsequent achievements of Rowan Hamilton, McCullagh and Salmon would not have been possible without his foresight and initiative. The British Association held its annual meeting in Dublin in 1835, and at the concluding banquet in Trinity the Viceroy conferred a knighthood on Hamilton, an unusual but fitting tribute to him and his

College.[1]

When Lloyd became Provost he had to contend with a Board where there was always the possibility that the conservative vote would be strong enough to block change, but by a combination of tact and tenacity he managed to put through a series of major reforms in the academic structure and practice of the College. These reforms included changes in terms and vacations, always a difficult matter on which to secure the agreement of academics, a reorganisation of the tutorial system, the revision of the Divinity course, the institution of new professorships and the substitution of new conditions for existing ones, and, most important of all, the introduction of radical changes in courses and examinations which effectively distinguished pass-men from honors-men in all four years of the undergraduate course.

The term structure was defined by the Laudian Statutes, and had not been altered since 1637.[2] It was an arrangement that produced terms and vacations of very unequal length. The main feature of Lloyd's reform was to introduce three terms instead of four. Hilary term began on 10 January, Trinity term on 15 April, and Michaelmas term on 10 October. Under this system, which was close to the Cambridge pattern, the length of the terms was much more constant, varying only between ten and eleven weeks, the summer vacation became even longer (over three months), and there were three-week breaks at Christmas and Easter. The change took effect in 1834, a year after the appearance of the first official Calendar. A Junior Fellow, James Henthorn Todd, who had been elected in 1831, took the initiative in compiling the material for it, and contributed a long and important introduction on the history of the College.

The change to a three-term structure called for a redistribution in the work prescribed for each class, but Lloyd took the opportunity to introduce a much more radical reform. In effect he devised two courses, a basic one to be read by all students, and a more varied and extended one available for students aspiring to honors. The pass-men still had to study much the same subjects as before, but they now took their basic mathematics in their first year and their Locke and formal logic in their second year. Their third-year course comprised mechanics, astronomy, and optics, and ethics filled up the last year. The reduction in the number of terms allowed for a reduction in the number of prescribed books, and the cutback in classical texts was extensive. These changes produced a shorter and easier course which the average student could hope to master. The honors-men did more advanced work in the same subjects.

The pass examinations took two days, as before, and were followed by an honor examination on the more advanced course. Only students who performed very well at pass level were allowed to proceed to this stage, and they had to be individually recommended by the examiners. They could be recommended for further examination in either classics or science, or in both. Candidates successful at honors level in their BA degree examination were now designated as 'Moderators', a term peculiar to Trinity. It derived from an earlier custom by which the best performers in the degree exercises were drafted in to 'moderate', i.e. chair, the disputations of the less brilliant. This system very soon led to further specialisation at degree level. Candidates could opt to be examined in one or more of three disciplines: classics, mathematics (including theoretical physics), and 'Ethics and Logics' (i.e. philosophy). Separate 'moderatorships' were awarded in these subjects, and the successful candidates were divided into two grades, senior and junior. There was a regulation that the number of Senior Moderators (who were awarded a gold medal) should not exceed 2 per cent of the total of the graduating class, with Junior Moderators (who received a silver medal) similarly limited to 5 per cent.[3]

Senior moderatorship now became a 'glittering prize', lifting standards in its subjects, and encouraging more specialised lecturing by Fellows and Professors. Pass-men still depended on their tutors, and here the quality of teaching was considerably improved by a fundamental change in the tutorial system. Previously, tutors received a fee from every pupil in their chambers and were in turn responsible for most of their instruction. In 1834 Lloyd persuaded them to specialise in a more limited range of subjects and to admit the pupils of other tutors to their lectures. The standard of instruction was improved by this eminently sensible division of labour, and at the same time the financial inducement to compete for pupils was almost eliminated by a rationalisation of the method of payment. All the tutorial fees were pooled in a common fund, the tutors were ranked in three grades according to seniority, and each grade received an allocation from the fund in the ratio of 4: 3: 2. The new arrangements proved popular, and the system so established lasted with only minor changes for more than a century.

The principle of specialisation was also applied to the conditions of tenure of some professorships. Before Lloyd's provostship most chairs carried only a fairly small salary (£200 or less). As noted earlier, certain 'professors' were really only part-time lecturers, and would have had to supplement their small stipends by taking on other work. The Fellows did most of their teaching as tutors and derived most of their income from tutorial fees. For them a professorship meant some extra lecturing and some additional money, but did not imply success in, or commitment to, research in the subject. They moved readily enough from one professorship to another, and sometimes even held two at the same time, as Lloyd himself did in the 1820s. His own experience may have convinced him that change was academically desirable, particularly at a time when the very large increase in numbers had overloaded the Fellows with tutorial work. At all events, as soon as he became Provost, Lloyd decided to turn the now vacant chair of Natural and Experimental Philosophy into a post more akin to current notions of a chair. His proposal was that the new professor (who would be appointed from the ranks of Fellows) should be exempt from tutorial duties, and should receive a salary of £700 a year. In return, he would be expected to engage in advanced teaching and research. The proposal might have gone through without much opposition but for the fact that his preferred candidate for the new post was his own son, Humphrey, who had been elected to fellowship in 1824. Not surprisingly, a storm of controversy was stirred up, but the Provost eventually got his way, and Humphrey, who was an excellent physicist (and a future Provost), soon justified his appointment by some original and successful experimental work.

A similar principle was applied in a reorganisation of the Divinity School, initiated by the Provost in 1833. The reform centred on the post of Archbishop King's Lecturer in Divinity, which had become something of a sinecure, usually given on a yearly basis to a Senior Fellow. The Board now decreed that in future this lectureship should be held by a Junior Fellow on the same basis as the 'new' professorship in physics. Since he was relieved from tutorial duties, the new lecturer was able to devote much more of his time to teaching, and this made it possible to extend the postgraduate instruction in divinity from a one-year into a two-year course. The Regius Professor was given responsibility for lecturing the senior year as a whole, and Archbishop King's Lecturer was given responsibility for the junior year. A regular system of term and annual examinations leading to the testimonium (a 'professional' qualification for ordination) was soon instituted. The King's lectureship was raised to a professorship in 1906, and the structure of the School was progressively strengthened by the foundation of additional chairs: Irish in 1840, Ecclesiastical History in 1850, and Pastoral Theology in 1888. Mention should also be made of the chair of Biblical Greek, founded in 1843 but not formally attached to the School until 1909. All these changes were made within the pattern established under Lloyd, and the divinity testimonium continued to be organised as a two-year course until its discontinuance in 1978.

The Lloydian reorganisation came at a timely moment, for separate theological colleges were becoming popular in Britain, and Richard Whately, who had been appointed Archbishop of Dublin at the same time as Lloyd was admitted Provost, spent much time and energy promoting just such a scheme for the Church of Ireland. A new seminary for the training of ordinands in Dublin would have cut across one of Trinity's traditional functions, and College opinion was in no way prepared to acquiesce in Whately's scheme, whatever merits it may have had in the abstract. The Board was fortified in its opposition by the thought that by 1839 (when the government finally turned down the scheme) the new courses in the Divinity School were working very well.

Whately did succeed in contributing to College development in a different field, that of the new and fashionable science of political economy, in which he himself had considerable interest and expertise. He had held the professorship in the subject for two years at Oxford, and soon after his arrival in Dublin he offered to endow a similar post at Trinity, an offer the Board accepted with no great enthusiasm. In fact, the new chair (which nowadays would probably be called a post-doctoral fellowship) was a success, and Whately continued to provide the stipend of £100 a year from 1832 until his death in 1863.

The first incumbent was a Junior Fellow, Mountiford Longfield, who published his lectures in book form in 1834. The work contained some fresh and seminal theorising that was well ahead of its time. Longfield had a keen mind, and went on to make a distinguished career for himself as a judge and privy councillor. Whately had stipulated a maximum tenure of five years, and Longfield was succeeded in 1836 by another rising Trinity lawyer, Isaac Butt, who was destined to achieve fame as the leader of the Home Rule party in the 1870s. The connexion thus established between the chair and the Irish Bar was fruitfully maintained for many years.[4] The first six professors were Trinity graduates, many of them published good original work, and one, John Elliot Cairnes, who occupied the chair from 1856 to 1861, went on to hold similar chairs in Galway and London, and became one of the leading economists of the British Isles.[5]

On 24 November 1837 Provost Lloyd died suddenly in his sixty-sixth year, and the Whig government moved quickly to appoint Franc Sadleir (1775–1851) as his successor. In political terms, Sadleir stood out as an able Whig among an undistinguished and mainly Tory group of Senior Fellows. Though already into his sixties when admitted Provost in late December, he proved to be a capable if cautious head of the College. He brought considerable administrative experience to the post, having previously been Librarian (1821–37) and Bursar (1824–33). While in no way outstanding as a scholar, he had also been Professor of Hebrew (1822–24), Professor of Mathematics (1825–35), and Regius Professor of Greek (1833–38). One would not be far wrong in concluding that he was a pluralist with a shrewd eye for a lucrative post. The bursarship was still remunerated by poundage on fees and rents when Sadleir held it during the peak period of numbers in the mid-1820s, and it will be observed that for the nine years of his tenure he was also Librarian and a Professor.

Sadleir remained Provost for fourteen years, and under him the College continued to develop and diversify its activities, though the pace of reform was not as intense as during Lloyd's six-year rule. The most significant constitutional change came early in his term of office, and received his strong support. This was the abolition of the celibacy rule for Fellows.

The rule was designed to ensure that Fellows would reside in the College and devote themselves wholeheartedly to their studies and teaching duties. It does not seem to have been questioned in earlier times when fellowship was normally only an interim stage in a clerical or professional career, and tenure was short. Fellows who stayed on to devote their life to academic work were either content to remain bachelors, or could seek a personal dispensation. From about 1750, a third solution — the semi-clandestine marriage — came more into favour. Provosts Marsh and Peter Browne had acted to deprive married Fellows of their fellowship, but College opinion gradually turned against the strict enforcement of the Statute (which was also held to offer a loophole by a supposed ambiguity in its wording), and by 1811 sixteen out of the twenty-five Fellows were married. In that year the situation was radically altered by Provost Hall, who, on his own initiative, obtained letters patent reimposing the celibacy obligation in unambiguous terms. Existing married fellows were given full indemnity and the 'right' of existing unmarried Fellows to marry was recognised, but all Fellows elected from 1812 were strictly bound to celibacy on pain of forfeiting their fellowship.

The celibacy issue now became to some extent linked with the problem of College livings. Previously a Fellow who wanted to get married could always resign and take up less arduous and better paid duties in a country rectory, when, of course, he would no longer be bound by the rule. The College had twenty-one livings in its gift, at least six of which were worth over £1500 a year, and a further seven or eight over £1000. An income of £1000 was more than double what even a Senior Fellow could hope for in the eighteenth century. So when a living was offered down the list of

cont. p87

Pl 1 The Long Room of the Old Library.

Pl 2 A view of Library Square (in foreground), the Campanile, and the Front Square. The Canadian maple on the left is said to be the largest specimen in Western Europe.

Pl 3 Folio 200v of the Book of Kells: part of the genealogy of Jesus Christ (St Luke 3, 23ff).

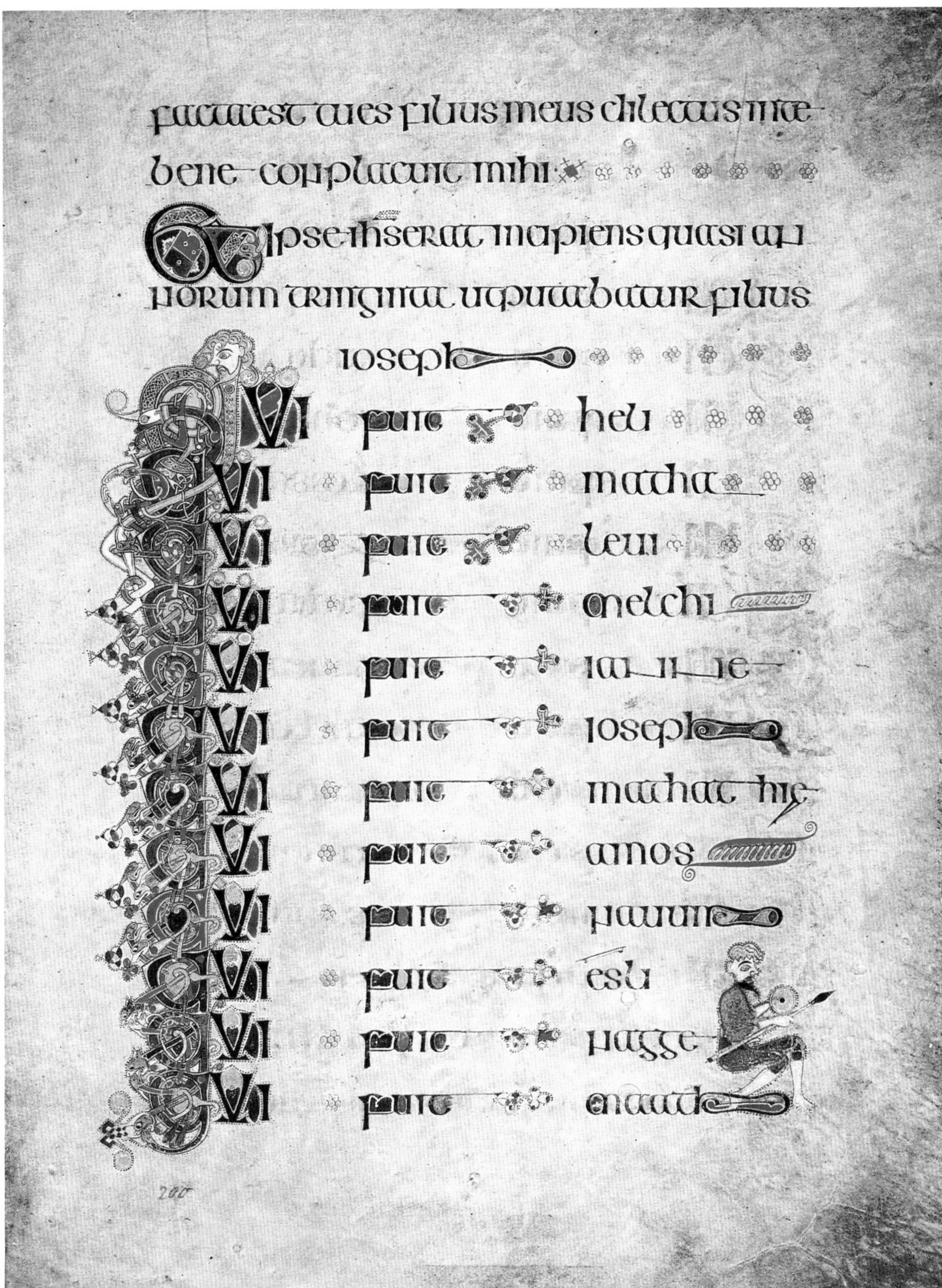

Pl 4 The Public Theatre (Examination Hall) set up for an examination.

Pl 5 The east range of Library Square, known as the Rubrics, a residence block completed soon after 1700, and the oldest surviving building on the campus.

Pl 6 The Museum Building, east side, looking towards College Park.

Pl 7 (Opp.) *Entrance hall of the Museum Building by Thomas Deane and Benjamin Woodward (1857).*

Pl 8 *A view of the northern façade of the Arts and Social Sciences Building from Fellows' Square. In the background, the Berkeley Library.*

Pl 9 *The Berkeley Library from the New Square, by Paul Koralek (1967).*

FIRE EXIT

Pl 10 Archbishop Adam Loftus (c.1533–1605), the first Provost of the College. Loftus was also Lord Chancellor of Ireland, and is shown holding the pouch of the Great Seal.

Pl 11 A prospect of the Library from the south-west, drawn by Joseph Tudor in 1753. An arcade runs south to the Anatomy House beyond the Fellows' Garden. A portion of the south range of the Elizabethan quadrangle is visible at the west end of the Library.

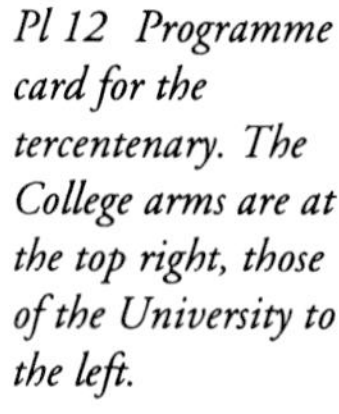

Pl 12 Programme card for the tercentenary. The College arms are at the top right, those of the University to the left.

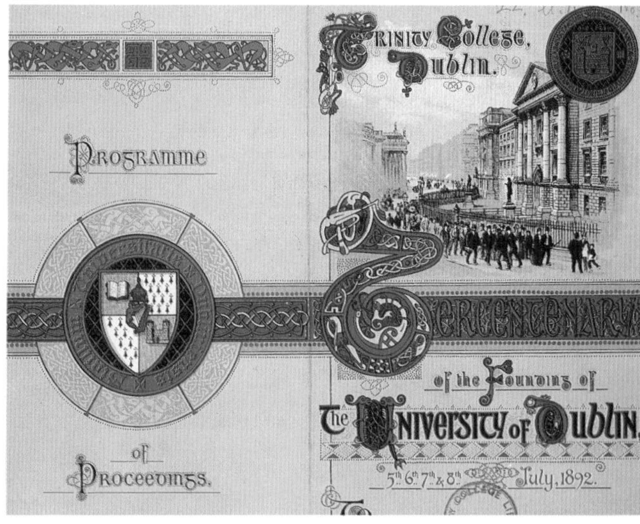

cont. from p86

Fellows, it would always find a taker, and this ensured a steady turnover among Senior and Junior Fellows alike. But soon after 1800 the livings began to become financially less attractive as increasing numbers of students brought the remuneration of Fellows, and particularly Senior Fellows, to hitherto unprecedented levels. It could now seem a more desirable option to wait on in College, hoping for co-option to senior fellowship, and once this dignity was achieved, resignation became even more unthinkable. James Wilson, who accepted Clonfeacle in 1824, was the last Senior Fellow in the history of the College to resign on a living.

The refusal of Senior Fellows to move out to livings soon pushed up the average age of the Board, and it was easy to see that if the tendency was to spread downwards to the Junior Fellows, circulation within the whole body corporate would be dangerously impaired. Board members therefore appreciated the advantage of maintaining the celibacy rule, if only because it put additional pressure to resign on connubially inclined Junior Fellows. But by 1840 the weight of liberal opinion against the rule became too strong to resist, and, at the request of the Board, letters patent were issued for its repeal. In making its request to the Crown, the Board had suggested that the rule might still remain for the nine most junior of the Fellows — a typical conservative compromise. But the Crown rejected this in favour of an expansion of the fellowship body by creating ten additional fellowships, which were to be filled at the rate of one a year over the next decade. Only four of these new Fellows were to be allowed to hold tutorship. This solution suited the Scholars since it maintained a steady flow of vacancies, but it soon produced a new problem in the shape of an aggrieved class of very poorly paid non-tutor Fellows.

In 1841 the city terminus of Dublin's first railway line lay just outside the eastern boundary of the College, making even the most sheltered academic aware that the Industrial Revolution had begun to impinge on Ireland. Trinity's response to the problem of providing well-qualified professional men for such developments was commendably prompt. The initial stimulus came from three Junior Fellows: Humphrey Lloyd, the distinguished Professor of Natural and Experimental Philosophy; James McCullagh, the brilliant young Professor of Mathematics; and a mathematical colleague, Thomas Luby. In April 1841 they sent a memorandum to the Board proposing the foundation of a professorship of civil engineering, and outlining a curriculum for the school. The Board agreed before the end of Trinity term, creating the proposed new chair, and also one in 'Chemistry and Geology applied to the arts of construction'. (A separate chair of geology and mineralogy was created in 1844.) In thus recognising engineering as an academic discipline, Trinity followed hard on the heels of Durham, Glasgow and London, and is the proud possessor of one of the oldest Engineering Schools in the world.

In the first two decades of its existence, students of the School read for a diploma and not a degree, degrees in Engineering being as yet unheard of. But, from the start, the Board was keen to integrate them as much as possible into academic life, and stipulated that they must matriculate and pass the Junior Freshman year in Arts, with its strong emphasis on mathematics. Being members of the College, most of them decided to continue with Arts along with their professional studies, emerging in due course with a BA, as well as their engineering diploma.

The diploma course was originally designed to last for two years, but was soon lengthened to three. The first year consisted of mathematics, theoretical mechanics, and chemistry.Work in drawing, surveying and levelling began in the second year, and was continued in the third, together with appropriate fieldwork. By 1860 the School was deemed successful enough for its students to appear at Commencements to receive a licence rather than a diploma. The degree of Master in Engineering also was instituted for licentiates holding a BA, provided they had spent at least three years in engineering practice. Finally, from 1872 on, a degree of Bachelor of Engineering was awarded instead of a licence to successful students, provided they had also taken their BA. This was a notable pioneering development, for Dublin's BAI and MAI appear to have been the first degrees in the British Isles to be awarded outside the traditional faculties of divinity, law, medicine, and music.

The first Professor of Engineering was an Irishman, John McNeill (later Sir John), who had worked under the famous Scottish engineer and bridge-builder, Thomas Telford. After Telford's death in 1834, McNeill had gone on to complete a research project into the water resistance of canal barges which they had begun together. He proved a distinguished first head of the School. From 1843 to 1847 the School was housed in the East Chapel Building. Demands for increased space then led to the construction of a temporary building for it, located between the Examination Hall and the Library, and subsequently removed when the School was allocated permanent accommodation in 1855 in the newly completed Museum Building.

The School was popular and successful from the start. One of the first two students to complete its course was James Barton, who designed and built the Boyne viaduct. Well over a hundred students had qualified by

1861, and more than half of these went to find work abroad, notably in India. McDowell and Webb comment as follows on the significance of this development: 'they were the advance-guard, soon to be joined by graduates from other faculties, of the army of T.C.D. men who were to provide the British Empire for nearly a century, in numbers far exceeding their proportion of the total roll of graduates of the British Isles, with administrators, jurists, doctors, missionaries and engineers'.[6]

In 1849, after some protracted discussion with the Royal College of Physicians, the Board was able to introduce a revised medical curriculum, including a new course in surgery. The other 'units', each of six months' duration, were: chemistry, anatomy, practical anatomy, materia medica, institutes of medicine, practice of medicine, and midwifery. A further 'unit' consisted of two half-courses: botany, and either medical jurisprudence or practical chemistry. Students could take the 'units' in any order they chose, and were not liable for any examinations except the final one. Otherwise, the course was reasonably up-to-date and comprehensive. They also had to gain credit for eighteen months' hospital attendance, which included clinical lectures. The obligation to graduate BA before an MB could be obtained still held good, apart from a brief break with tradition between 1839 and 1846 when the requirement was temporarily reduced to completion of the first two years of the Arts course.

A professorship in surgery was instituted for the development of the new course, and less than two years later a number of medical students petitioned the Board to found a diploma in the subject. At that time surgeons still qualified by a different route from doctors, though there was naturally a considerable overlap in their fields of study. After finding out that the Army, the Navy, and the East India Company would recognise such a diploma, the Board approved it in principle, and drew up a four-year curriculum. The course was further strengthened in 1852 by the institution of a second chair, the university professorship of surgery, specifically to oversee the examinations for the diploma. Its first occupant, J.W. Cusack, was the first Catholic to be appointed to a professorship completely under the control of the College. Letters patent of 1868 dignified this chair with the title of 'Regius'.[7]

These developments ensured formal recognition for surgery as an important branch of the School's work. In medicine, the Regius professorship was held with great distinction by William Stokes. William had been assisting his father Whitley in the post from 1840, and succeeded as professor on the latter's death in 1845. His tenure lasted until 1878. He developed to a fine art the use of the stethoscope in clinical diagnosis, and won a European reputation for his two books on diseases of the lungs and heart. The high repute enjoyed by the School in the latter half of the nineteenth century was due more than anything else to his work and writings.

Pride in the Irish nation and a strong desire to encourage self-reliance in her people have been conspicuous qualities in many of the choicer spirits educated in Trinity College. The case for legislative independence was ably argued by Molyneux and supported by Swift. Berkeley displayed a shrewd and practical patriotism in his economic prescriptions. Grattan's Parliament may have been stronger on rhetoric than achievement, but its period of office was far from inglorious, and Wolfe Tone gave his life for the ideal of total independence from England. It is not then surprising to find a Trinity graduate at the heart of the mid-nineteenth-century resurgence of Irish nationalism that became known as the Young Ireland movement.

Thomas Davis was born at Mallow on 14 October 1814. His father had come from England as a surgeon in the Royal Artillery, and had married a Mary Atkins from County Cork. Davis was brought up as a unionist, but all this changed after his entry to Trinity in 1831. He there came strongly under the influence of a slightly older student, Thomas Wallis, a Dubliner, who converted him to nationalist views. Davis did not win any great distinction in College, obtaining only a junior moderatorship in ethics and logics, but he remembered his student days with pleasure and affection. After spending some time in London and on the Continent, he was called to the Irish Bar in 1838, and was also elected Auditor of the College Historical Society for the 1838/39 session. As president of the Society in the following year, he delivered an address that was profoundly impressive in its quietly eloquent plea to his hearers to devote themselves to the cause of Ireland.

Still only in his mid-twenties, Thomas Davis now emerged as the leading political thinker among his contemporaries. He became a member of O'Connell's Repeal Association in April 1841, and in 1842 joined forces with a brilliant young journalist, Charles Gavan Duffy, and John Blake Dillon (who had been educated at Maynooth and Trinity) to found *The Nation*. This immensely successful weekly newspaper became an influential channel for the dissemination of a broad and tolerant nationalism. Among its contributors was John Mitchel, also a Trinity graduate, who was transported to Van Diemen's Land (Tasmania) for his part in the 1848 uprising. Davis remained the moving spirit and chief contributor until his sudden and premature death from scarlet fever at the age of thirty on 16 September 1845. His enthusiasm, his liberalism, and his belief in the value of education never faltered.[8]

The spirited journalism of *The Nation* inspired another Trinity student to contribute perhaps the best known ballad that it ever printed, 'The Memory of the Dead', with its rousing opening line, 'Who fears to speak of Ninety-Eight?'. Although the ballad was published anonymously in April 1843, its author was John Kells Ingram, elected Scholar in 1840 and Fellow in 1846. Ingram lived to become one of the most prolific, versatile and respected of Trinity's late Victorian scholars. He was a pillar of the College, holding office successively as Librarian, Senior Lecturer, Registrar, and Vice-Provost, and to the end of his long life — he died in 1907 — he retained a liberal and tolerant outlook.

Notes

1. Sir William Rowan Hamilton, one of the greatest mathematicians that Ireland or the world has seen, was born in Dublin in 1805 of Scottish parents, and graduated from Trinity in 1827. Such was his youthful brilliance that the Board appointed him Professor of Astronomy shortly before he took his BA. He did very important work in optics and dynamics, but is probably best known for his discovery of quaternions. The basic formula flashed into his mind when he was walking in from Dunsink to a Royal Irish Academy meeting in Dublin. He was passing the Royal Canal, and on impulse took out his pocketknife and carved the formula on a stone of Brougham Bridge, as well as entering it in his pocketbook. The centenary of the date, 13 November 1843, was marked by the issue of a special commemorative Irish stamp.
2. Prior to 1637, there had been a sensible enough arrangement of four terms, independent of the 'movable feasts', of nearly equal length (eight to nine weeks). Christmas term ran from 15 January to 10 March, Easter term from 16 April to 8 June, John the Baptist term from 9 July to 8 September, and Michaelmas term from 15 October to 8 December. This allowed for four vacations of thirty to thirty-seven days each. Laud imposed the Oxford pattern, governed by the Church year, under which Hilary term (called after the feast of St Hilary on 13 January) began on the Monday after Epiphany and ended on the day before Palm Sunday. Depending on the date of Easter, this term could be as short as sixty-nine days, or as long as ninety-seven days. Easter term began on the eighth day after Easter Sunday and ended on Whitsun eve, and was therefore of fixed length (forty-one days). Easter term began on Trinity Monday and ended on 8 July; it could vary in length from twenty-two to fifty days. Michaelmas term began on 1 October and ended on 16 December (seventy-seven days).
3. The records show that 'in the first ten years of the system there were thirty-seven Senior Moderators in Mathematics, twenty in Classics and thirty-eight in Ethics and Logics, while the corresponding figures for Junior Moderatorships were fifteen, fifteen and fifty-nine' (McDowell and Webb, *History*, 174).

4. The pattern of an effective Law School was established in 1850 by agreement between the Board and the Benchers of the King's Inns. The Benchers undertook to establish two new professorships at the Inns, one in constitutional and criminal law, and the other in the law of personal property, pleading, practice and evidence. The Board restored the credibility of the Regius Professorship of Civil Law (which had become a sinecure for Senior Fellows) by new regulations, under which the holder had to be a doctor of laws with at least six years' experience as a practising barrister. These professors, together with the Professor of Feudal and English Law, were to provide courses in all the main branches of law, and the courses were to be open to students of the Inns and Trinity alike.
5. The Board endowed the chair from College funds in 1866, and in 1887 abolished any restriction on tenure. This enabled C.F. Bastable, who acquired considerable fame for his work in economics, to hold it for fifty years from 1882 to his retirement in 1932. One should mention that the salary was never increased, and Bastable, who was interested in law as well as economics, also held the chair of Jurisprudence at Queen's College, Galway from 1883 to 1903. He then returned to Trinity to teach in the Law School, becoming Regius Professor of Law in 1908. The professorship of Political Economy was reconstituted as a full-time post in 1934, and in 1979 Whately's name was restored to the title of the chair in due recognition of the part which he played in its foundation.
6. McDowell and Webb, *History*, 185.
7. In England and Scotland the Crown normally claims a right in a 'Regius' appointment, but this has never been the case in Ireland. In addition to Surgery, three other Trinity professorships are currently denominated 'Regius': Physic (effectively founded in 1662, but not called Regius before the nineteenth century), Laws (founded by Charles II in 1667; first appointment 1668; date of title Regius uncertain), and Greek (founded as a Regius chair in 1761). The Regius Professorship of Divinity (dating from the early 1600s, but not so called until 1761) is suspended, and the Regius Professorship of Feudal and English Law (1761) was discontinued in 1934.
8. See 'Thomas Davis 1814–1845 : A Commemorative Address', by Bolton C. Waller, Dublin 1930; also the short biography by T.W. Moody in *Of One Company*, Icarus, *T.C.D.* 1951.

CHAPTER 10

Victorian heyday 1851–1892

In April 1850 Royal Commissions were announced for Oxford and Cambridge, and a similar body was soon appointed to enquire into the University of Dublin. The Commissioners were Richard Whately, Archbishop of Dublin and one of the Visitors; Mazière Brady, Lord Chancellor of Ireland; James Wilson, Bishop of Cork; William Parsons, the third Earl of Rosse; Mountiford Longfield, a former Fellow and now Professor of Feudal and English Law; and Edward Cooper, a country gentleman from County Sligo. Wilson, Brady and Longfield were Trinity graduates; the other three were Oxford graduates. The Commission began work in September 1851 and reported early in 1853, finding the general state of the university to be 'satisfactory'. The modernisation programme of the previous twenty years had put Trinity in a position where it was better able to stand scrutiny than Oxford or Cambridge. Their Commissions came up with far-reaching proposals for radical reform, but in Trinity's case the thirty-four recommendations were directed towards improving rather than remodelling the institution.

The Board itself had power to initiate some of the recommended changes; for others a Queen's Letter, or Act of Parliament, was required. In the former category was the Commission's proposal for the creation of scholarship awards that would be open to dissenters. Between 1788 and 1810 a small number of Catholics and nonconformists succeeded in gaining a foundation scholarship, but as a general rule the Board did not elect candidates unless they were practising members of the Church of Ireland. This criterion was more rigidly enforced from about 1810, but it was a restriction that stemmed from custom rather than from any particular College statute. If it had any legal basis in the general tenor of the Statutes, this had obviously been undermined by the Act of 1793, and the practice was challenged in a celebrated case in 1843. In that year Denis

Caulfield Heron, a Catholic student, came fifth in the scholarship examination — there were sixteen vacancies — but was passed over because of his religion. He appealed to the Visitors, who at first refused to hear his appeal, but were later directed to do so by the High Court. The Visitors were the two Archbishops of the Church of Ireland, and their eventual dismissal of the appeal was hardly surprising, though the soundness in law of their verdict was open to question.

The Commissioners naturally debated the issue, but were unable to reach agreement on the only satisfactory solution, namely, to open foundation scholarships to all students, irrespective of their religious affiliation. They suggested as a compromise that Exhibitions open to students of any denomination should be 'given in the same manner as College Scholarships but without making the holders members of the Corporation'. The College was divided on the merits of this proposal, but it went through with majority support, and the first four 'non-foundation scholars' were elected in 1855. The group was appropriately headed by Thomas Maguire, later to become the first Catholic Fellow. The denominational distinction between 'foundation' and 'non-foundation' scholars operated for eighteen years until it was rendered null and void by Fawcett's Act in 1873. In this period a total of thirty-eight non-foundation scholars was elected, as against 249 foundation scholars, figures that closely reflect the proportion of dissenters on the books. The distinction was reinstated in 1906 to facilitate the election of women to scholarship. It still survives (but without any status implication) as a convenient device for increasing the number of scholarships awarded (when merit requires) above the statutory maximum of seventy.

Much of the Board's time in the immediate aftermath of the report was devoted to the contentious business of preparing and agreeing a draft Queen's Letter on the recommendations that required statutory change. This task took nearly two years to complete, and the Letter was issued on 31 January 1855. Many of the changes embodied in it were not of any great moment since the Board took the opportunity to seek the repeal or updating of many obsolete clauses in the existing statutes. The Scholars, for example, were no longer required to read a chapter of the Bible during Commons, and in the case of admission to the Library a 'declaration' was substituted for an 'oath'. More importantly, the Board, subject to the consent of the Visitors, was given discretion to vary the form and content of the fellowship and scholarship examinations, and the number of lay Fellows was increased from three to five. The Commissioners had recommended that the obligation on Fellows to take orders should be abolished, but College opinion was not ready for such a decisive break with tradition. The College had been founded with the twin objects of fostering learning and piety, and most educated people still held to the view that the clergy should play a leading role in higher education. Nevertheless, the concept of lay Fellows was beginning to gain wider acceptability, the extra lay places were rapidly taken up, further dispensations were sought and granted, and by 1867 the number of lay Fellows in the College had risen to ten.

Other important recommendations that called for a response related to the University Senate and College finance. The Commissioners had unexpectedly proposed the abolition of the Senate on the grounds that its functions had become purely ceremonial. The Board instead wished to reform it, making some small increase in its powers. To everyone's surprise, a further Queen's Letter of 24 July 1857 decreed that the Senate (defined as the Chancellor or Vice-Chancellor, Doctors in the several faculties, and Masters of Arts of the University) should be established as a corporate body distinct from the College, with its own common seal, and the right to own property and to sue and be sued. If this measure was intended to bring a new access of power and independence to the Senate, it proved singularly unsuccessful. The Senate has never acquired any property, has never sued anyone, and has remained firmly under the College's control. It has the power of rejecting proposals, but it cannot initiate them, for it is limited to the discussion of business that the Board brings before it. The Registrar of the College is *ex officio* its Registrar, and when it votes to elect the Chancellor, it votes on a nominee put before it by the Board.[1]

On College finances the most far-reaching recommendation related to the remuneration attaching to College offices held by Senior Fellows. Hitherto, they had received a portion of their income from poundage on rents and fees, and the rapid increase in student numbers earlier in the century, even though not fully sustained, had pushed up their emoluments to a level that was the occasion of some scandal.[2] In a bumper year for graduations, a Senior Proctor might receive as much as £900 on top of his basic salary of about £1500, and at the time of the Commission the Bursar was found to be in receipt of annual emoluments of £3400 — considerably more than full professors were receiving in the early 1960s. The Commission therefore proposed that, in future, College officers should be remunerated with a fixed salary. Not unnaturally, this proposal met with strong opposition at Board level, and it was not until 1858 that, under pressure from the government, the Chancellor, and the Dublin newspapers, it was agreed that degree fees were to go into the central fund of the College, that the Proctors were to receive a salary commensurate with their duties, and that the Bursar and Senior Lecturer were to be paid by salary instead of by poundage. The Board, however, refused to publish the College accounts as requested. The only concession on this front was an agreement that they should be open to inspection by the Junior Fellows, and that a second Auditor, not a Fellow, should be appointed by the Board, subject to approval by the Visitors.

In the first half of the nineteenth century there was no suggestion of a Catholic 'ban' on Trinity College. Many eminent Catholic laymen received their higher education there, and remained loyal alumni. Sir Thomas Wyse, for example, who graduated in 1812, spoke most appreciatively of his time as an undergraduate and put it on record that there had been no attempt to interfere with his religious beliefs. Daniel O'Connell himself sent his sons to Trinity, and there was a future Catholic Archbishop (Michael Slattery) on the roll of graduates. Nevertheless, after Catholic Emancipation, the need for an enlargement of the Irish university system was clear; the problem was how to achieve it.

The first step was taken by Sir Robert Peel in 1845. Through Parliament, he provided generously enough for the foundation of three new colleges situated in Belfast, Cork and Galway, and in 1850 they were federated to form the Queen's University. England had London University to give nonconformists an acceptable alternative to the older Anglican strongholds of Oxford and Cambridge. Peel's aim was to establish something on the same lines for Irish dissenters. The new colleges were strictly secular and nondenominational in concept and constitution, but this did not please everyone. The High Church wing of Peel's own party attacked them as providing 'a scheme of godless education', a cry soon taken up by the Catholic hierarchy in Ireland. The Belfast College prospered in the more nonconformist atmosphere of the North, but Cork and Galway were not at first very successful.

The issue of the new colleges was debated at the first national synod of the Irish Catholic Church in modern times, held in Thurles, County Tipperary, in 1850. By no means all the bishops were averse to members of their flock attending them, but the upshot of the proceedings was not in their favour. With the encouragement of the Pope, the Synod decided to set about founding a Catholic University, and an institution bearing this name, with a charter from Rome but none from the Crown, came into being in Dublin four years later. It was located at 86 St Stephen's Green, was under the control of the bishops (though not all of them supported the idea), and had John Henry Newman as its first Rector .

The members of the Thurles Synod were obsessed by the moral and spiritual dangers inherent, as they saw it, in the increasing trend towards secularisation in education. This tendency was exhibited in the Queen's Colleges, and so they concluded their proceedings with a 'synodical address' to the faithful, exhorting them to attend only 'Catholic' colleges. The message fell some way short of an outright 'ban' on either the Queen's Colleges or Trinity, but it marked the end of any tacit acceptance by the hierarchy of the latter's suitability for Catholics. Clerical opposition was further sharpened when Archbishop Cullen succeeded Murray in the see of Dublin in 1852. From 1854 on, Cullen's desire to foster the embryo Catholic university in his diocese went hand in hand with increased hostility to Trinity.

The post-Famine period from 1850 to 1875 was a decisive time in the evolution of modern Irish Catholicism. Ultramontanist views were in the ascendant, and a 'devotional revolution' set a pattern of rites and practices that has persisted ever since. The Church developed its character of whole-hearted and conspicuous loyalty to Rome, and, while strongly opposed to Fenianism,[3] moved into ever closer association with the rising tide of Irish nationalism that was soon soon to be manifested in the Home Rule movement and the formation of the Gaelic Athletic Association. The Young Irelanders' attempt to define Irishness in more comprehensive terms was superseded by a narrower and more exclusive concept of patriotism. Against such a background, the rift between Trinity and the Catholic hierarchy unfortunately was bound to widen.

The Irish university question again became a House of Commons matter during Gladstone's 1868–74 administration. Since 1867 a radical member of his party, Henry Fawcett, had been using the device of a private member's bill to try to have all remaining religious tests in Trinity abolished.[4] By 1871 he had convinced the College authorities that such a reform would be timely, and they had even accepted the need for some constitutional changes. But at this point Gladstone decided that Fawcett's scheme should be merged in a much more comprehensive measure of reform. Accordingly he himself introduced a far-reaching Irish University Bill in 1873. Declaring that the Queen's Colleges had been 'a comparative failure', he proposed to dissolve their existing federal structure, and to conjoin two of them (Galway was to be closed on financial grounds) in a new National University. Essentially this new university was to be an enlargement of the University of Dublin, with constituent colleges, including Belfast, Cork, Magee College in Derry (a Presbyterian training college) and the by now sadly depleted Catholic institution in St Stephen's Green.

The desperate radicalism of Gladstone's attempt to satisfy both Liberal and Catholic opinion is only too apparent when one considers the disparate nature of the elements he wished to unite, not to mention the restrictive arrangements laid down for the teaching and examining of the 'sensitive' subjects of theology, philosophy, and modern history. Trinity felt gravely threatened. It would certainly lose its autonomy and its Divinity School; it would probably lose a portion of its endowments; and, worst of all, its freedom to offer its students a broad and liberal education would be severely curtailed by the proposed treatment of the disciplines just mentioned. The Irish hierarchy, with Archbishop Cullen in the van, were also vehemently opposed to the measure since it did not meet their core demand for a chartered and endowed Catholic university.

Despite Gladstone's masterly advocacy, the Bill came under increasingly severe criticism in the House. It was a 'close-run thing', but in the end a major split in the Liberal vote ensured its defeat by a mere three votes. The vested interests in Ireland breathed again, and the Irish university question remained unsolved.

If Trinity was to be rendered more acceptable to Catholics, a revival of Fawcett's measure seemed the only practicable way forward. He was accordingly given leave to bring forward his Bill in its original simpler form without any proposals for reform of College government, and it passed into law in May 1873.

The most significant provision of Fawcett's Act was the abolition of religious tests for all posts except those in the Divinity School. This opened fellowship (and also foundation scholarship) to candidates of any faith or none, and two Catholics Scholars were in fact elected on to the Foundation in that year. The Act also did away with the obligation for Fellows to be in holy orders, and between 1873 and 1915 only five of the thirty-nine elected were, or became, clerics.[5] Ironically, one consequence of the Act was to make Trinity less, rather than more, acceptable to the Catholic hierarchy. Taking note of what they regarded as its secularisation, the Maynooth Synod of 1775 extended Catholic condemnation of the 'godless' Queen's Colleges to include Trinity as well. The formal 'ban' on Catholic attendance at Trinity may be regarded as dating from this decision. So much for the good intentions of Fawcett and his supporters!

Between 1873 and 1915 (when fellowship elections were temporarily suspended) the working of the Act brought laymen more into the heart of the College but did not materially alter its Anglican character, two-thirds of the new Fellows being also members of the Church of Ireland. Other denominations were slower to avail of their opportunities, with only six Presbyterians, three Catholics, and one Moravian gaining fellowship during the period. In the student body, the proportion of Presbyterians remained constant over the next two decades, and that of Catholics declined as episcopal opposition sharpened and became more articulate. Nevertheless the Act stands out as a significant milestone in Trinity's evolution. In the long run it helped to mould 'an atmosphere that was religious but not clerical, tolerant but not indifferent, neither formally secular nor exclusively denominational. All posts were open to men of any creed or none, and this was true in fact, as well as in theory'.[6] Fawcett's legislation was admirably liberal and non-discriminatory in intention; it gave equal status to all members of the College, and in the 1960s it was still being quoted as relevant, in spirit at least, to the debate on the admission of women to fellowship.

Four Provosts presided in the forty years from the Royal Commission to the tercentenary. Richard McDonnell (*c.*1787–1867) was a Cork man who had gained fellowship in 1808 but had published nothing afterwards except a pamphlet on the defects of the Trinity examination system. He had gained experience at the Bar, and showed a good practical grasp of affairs when he served as Bursar between 1836 and 1844, and also in the evidence he gave to the 1851 Commission. A colleague described him as 'clever but very lazy'.[7] Of a generally liberal and reformist cast of mind, MacDonnell made an adequate if unexciting choice for Provost. Already in his mid-sixties when he was admitted to the office on 24 January 1852, he served competently enough for exactly fifteen years, dying on the same date in 1867.

The early years of his provostship saw the erection of two buildings that greatly enhanced the College's distinguished architectural heritage: the Campanile and the Museum Building. The Campanile was the princely gift of Archbishop Beresford to commemorate his election as Chancellor, on 12 November 1851. Sadleir is said to have implanted the idea of a bell tower in his mind by taking him to Botany Bay to see the makeshift housing of the great College bell there.[8] But Sadleir died a few weeks later, and McDonnell was in charge when the work was completed towards the end of 1854.

The commanding site between Parliament and Library Squares had been lying vacant since 1837 when its eighteenth-century residence block was demolished. Frederick Darley, who built the north and east ranges of New

Square between 1838 and 1844,[9] produced drawings for a handsome new building that would meet the need for a museum and additional lecture rooms. But an eminent English architect, Decimus Burton, whom the Board consulted on the matter, advised against the insertion of a large building into the vista from Front Gate. Burton, however, thought that 'a small but highly architectural object' might with advantage be located there. This prescient suggestion bore splendid fruit in Lanyon's Campanile, whose noble and shapely silhouette has become the architectural symbol of the College. The Campanile raises its dome and cross very close to where the steeple of All Hallows once pierced the skyline, and as its smaller bell probably came from the monastery, it is a fitting embodiment of the continuity of study and worship on the site.

Burton recommended the south side of New Square for the new lecture block, but Deane and Woodward's splendidly ornate building is a far cry from the 'simple and grave architecture' that he thought appropriate. The Museum Building, 'arguably the loveliest in College' (in Edward McParland's opinion), was designed to house geological specimens, and also to provide permanent accommodation for the Engineering School. Completed in 1857, it was a daring and successful experiment, framed on romantic Ruskinian principles, and executed with a wealth of native Irish materials and craftsmanship. The Venetian quality of its exterior, and the Moorish elements in its grand hall and staircase are particularly notable features of the design. McDonnell and his Board of 1853 deserve much credit for accepting the plans and finding the money (well in excess of £24,000) to implement them.

McDonnell's successor, Humphrey Lloyd (1800–81), was a Dubliner, a son of the reforming Provost of the 1830s, and probably the most distinguished scholar to hold the office since Narcissus Marsh. An eminent mathematical physicist with a long list of publications, he was a Fellow of the Royal Society, held an honorary doctorate from Oxford, and had been President of the British Association as well as the Royal Irish Academy. Lloyd was in advance of his time in the importance he attached to research as a function of the University. His own research centred on the earth's magnetic field, and was organised from the Magnetic Observatory in the Fellows' Garden, with the aid of a team of observers stretching as far as India.[10]

Classics also blossomed during his provostship, a development that stemmed from changes in the fellowship examination introduced under McDonnell in 1855. In the first half of the century, mathematical candidates had held an advantage, and this led to a preponderance of mathematicians and mathematical scientists in the fellowship body. The examination was now widened in scope to enable moderators in classics and philosophy to compete with the mathematicians on more equal terms. The changes led to the election of John Pentland Mahaffy (in 1864), Arthur Palmer (in 1867) and Robert Yelverton Tyrrell (in 1868). Louis Claude Purser's election came somewhat later, in 1881, and John Bagnell Bury's in 1885. Together they formed a team of indigenous classicists of unsurpassed brilliance. There had been a Regius chair of Greek since 1761, but Latin had always been so central and fundamental a part of the Trinity curriculum that it had not been thought necessary to distinguish it by a separate professorship. But now, in an era of advancing specialisation, the School of Classics received sharper definition by the creation of a chair of Latin in 1870 and a chair of Ancient History in 1871. The former was held by Tyrrell from 1871 to 1880, and then by Palmer, while Mahaffy was the first occupant of the latter.[11]

A significant change in the fellowship election system made by the letters patent of 1880 also call for notice. Up to 1879, elections were not necessarily held every year, but only when there were vacancies in the fellowship body, which was fixed at a maximum of thirty-five. But from then on there was a statutory stipulation that one Fellow, and one only, should be elected every year, irrespective of the total number in the body. This system was followed down to 1915.

Lloyd died in his eighty-first year in 1881, and was succeeded by John Hewitt Jellett (1817–88). A native of Cashel, County Tipperary, he gained fellowship in 1840. In 1847 he became the first holder of the university professorship in natural philosophy, and held that post until 1870, giving it a marked bias towards applied mathematics. In 1857 he was proposed as the first Registrar of the newly incorporated Senate, but the Board insisted that the post should go *ex officio* to the College's Registrar (then J.L. Moore). Jellett was a scholar of considerable eminence; he was elected President of the Royal Irish Academy in 1869, received the Royal Society' s Medal in 1881, and the cachet of an honorary degree from Oxford in the year before his death. His most notable work was a treatise on friction published in 1872. A student of the day remembered him as 'a very handsome man, with a fine presence and keen glance'.[12] Though no reformer, he was the only member of the Board to support the admission of women when this was first mooted in the early 1870s. His politics were also sufficiently liberal to make him an acceptable candidate to Gladstone, who appointed him Provost in April 1881. In his comparatively short reign — he died in office on 19 February 1888 — no new chairs were created and no new moderatorships established. The number of the latter, like the Senior Fellows, remained fixed at seven: mathematics, classics, philosophy, experimental science, natural science, history and political science, modern languages.

The Conservatives had opportunely returned to power in the month that Jellett died, and the cabinet did not take long to name George Salmon (1819–1904) as his successor. Salmon was conservative by temperament, sound in judgment, and a witty and sardonic conversationalist. His distinction as a scholar was outstanding even among the galaxy of eminent men then gathered in Trinity. An English mathematician, Thomas Hirst, who visited him in 1862, described him in his *Journal* as a 'simple-minded modest man', but 'endowed with an intellectual power and a capability of work such as we rarely meet.'[13] Born in Cork, Salmon entered Trinity at fourteen, and had gained fellowship before turning twenty-two. He held the Donegall lectureship in mathematics from 1848 to 1866, but also lectured in the Divinity School, with theology as a competing strand of interest in his mind. When the Regius chair of Divinity became vacant in 1866, the Board nominated him for the post, but his acceptance meant that he had to resign his fellowship.

Up to this time, Salmon's published work had been in mathematics, where four notable books on analytic and algebraic geometry gained him a European reputation. Now his talents became concentrated in the fields of theology and biblical criticism. The fruits of decades of study and reflection were garnered in a very solid treatise, *An Introduction to the Study of the New Testament*, published in 1885, which soon went through seven editions. The work pursued a magisterial *via media* between simplistic fundamentalism and the destructive rationalism of German higher criticism. A rather lighter but very trenchant refutation of extreme Romanist claims, *The Infallibility of the Church*, appeared three years later. Oxford, Cambridge and Edinburgh honoured him with doctorates, and he was also a medallist of the Royal Society. He was active as a churchman, publishing five volumes of sermons, and holding the chancellorship of St Patrick's Cathedral from 1871 to his death. Perhaps his most significant contribution to church affairs was made in the years immediately after Disestablishment, when his incisive and well-balanced mind dominated the deliberations of the General Synod, and he was successful in restraining its members (two-thirds of whom were laity) from a too radical revision of the 1662 Book of Common Prayer.

The period after 1851 can show no reforms as far-reaching as those of the

1830s, but significant if somewhat piecemeal changes continued to be made in the undergraduate course. The innovations in part came as a response to recommendations of the Royal Commission, but more generally they reflect the broadening intellectual horizons of the times and the progress of science.

Up to 1855 foundation scholarships were awarded only in classics, but from then on students also could compete in 'science', defined as philosophy, mathematics and physics. In 1858, the scope of the moderatorship in experimental physics (instituted in 1849) was widened to include some geology, palaeontology, botany, and zoology. The name of the moderatorship was altered to experimental and natural sciences, and, by a natural progression, separate moderatorships in each branch were instituted in 1871.

From 1855, English literature emerged as a recognised subject in the degree course, and courses in Sanskrit and Arabic were also introduced. The former development stemmed from the enterprise of John Kells Ingram, the latter from a change in British imperial administration. From 1866, more prominence was also given to modern European languages, particularly French and German.

When MacDonnell became Provost in 1852, Ingram succeeded him in the Erasmus Smith Chair of Oratory. No lectures in the subject had been given for nearly twenty years, and Ingram threw himself into his new duties with vigour and enthusiasm. In 1855 he persuaded the Board to allow him to widen the scope of his teaching to include English literature as well as oratory, the change being recognised by an alteration in the title of the chair. This led almost at once to the institution of a new moderatorship course in which English literature could be studied along with history, jurisprudence, and economics. This somewhat odd conjunction of subjects lasted until 1873 before being broken down into different specialisms. Modern languages then received fuller recognition with the institution of a moderatorship in modern literature, in which English could be combined with any one of French, German, Italian or Spanish. The last two were soon dropped because no one opted for them, but French and German proved popular choices. Douglas Hyde took this moderatorship in 1884, and gained a 'first' with a large gold medal. A separate chair of German had been established in 1866, and a chair of Romance Languages in 1869. The talented philologist Robert Atkinson was the first Professor, and he seems to have looked after the teaching of French.[14]

The recognition of English literature was taken a stage further in 1867 when the subject was finally detached from oratory and honoured with a separate chair. The first Professor was Edward Dowden, one of the brightest stars in late Victorian Trinity. By all accounts his lecturing was spellbinding, and his writings gained him a European reputation, particularly as an editor and critic of Shakespeare and biographer of Shelley. He remained Professor for forty-six years until his death in 1913. His successor, Wilbraham Trench, came to Trinity after a fourteen-year tenure of the chair of English at Galway. Trench was not lacking in distinction in his own rather idiosyncratic way. The writer has a distinct recollection of him as a tall gangling figure with a flowing beard, rather reminiscent of the Ancient Mariner, as he lectured enthusiastically in the Graduates' Memorial Building on Aristotle's doctrine of the tragic *katharsis*, an occasion which must have been within a few months of his death in 1939.

The creation of a chair of Arabic in 1855 (with Hindustani added to the title in 1866 and Persian in 1873) and of a lecturership in Sanskrit and Comparative Philology in 1858 (raised to a professorship in 1862), had a distinctly utilitarian aim in view. The new chairs were intended to provide appropriate teaching for candidates for the Indian Civil Service. Lord Macaulay had immersed himself in Indian affairs in the 1830s, and by the 1850s his reforming zeal had led to the abolition of selection through family connections, and the substitution of an open competitive examination. The future administrators of the subcontinent obviously needed some introduction to its linguistic complexities, and Sanskrit and Arabic were recommended as suitable for this purpose. Trinity students, well-grounded in classics and mathematics, and well-schooled in stiff examinations, seized avidly on this new career outlet, and between 1855 and 1912 no less than 180 of them were recruited.[15]

An important constitutional change occurred midway through Lloyd's provostship when a University Council was constituted by letters patent in November 1874. The reform went ahead with the assent of the Board and Senate. It was a natural consequence of the broadening of courses and the growth of new professorships just described. The non-Fellow Professors now numbered over twenty, and they were beginning to complain of their lack of influence. The Junior Fellows had also been pressing for more say in the governance of the College. Their expectations had been roused by Fawcett's 1871 proposal to include more of them on the Board, and Fawcett had also outlined a scheme for a mainly elective Council, to which Catholics and nonconformists could at once be elected.

From the Board's point of view, the new legislation had the merit of devolving some academic power to other interest groups while preserving intact the Board's own composition and ultimate control of College affairs. The new Council was empowered to nominate to all professorships with the exception of those in the Divinity School, and those, like the Erasmus Smith chairs, where the mode of election was independently specified. The Board was bound to accept the Council's nominee unless it was prepared to justify its refusal to the Chancellor. The duties and tenure of future professorships became a matter for agreement between the two bodies. The Council was also given an equal say with the Board in the regulation of courses, lectures and examinations, the consent of both bodies being needed for any change. It remained, however, a fundamentally subsidiary body, with no control over finance, and no power to create new chairs (though the Board could not proceed to do so without its consent).

The membership of the new Council consisted of the Provost as *ex officio* chairman and sixteen other persons, all of whom had to be members of the Senate of the University. Four of them were elected by the Senior Fellows, four by the Junior Fellows, four by the non-Fellow Professors, and four by the remaining Senate members. There was provision for rotation of membership after a normal term of four years, but sitting members were eligible for re-election. In the spirit of Fawcett, both the Fellow constituencies initially went outside their own ranks to elect a Catholic into one of their seats. After some initial sparring, which served to clarify the limitations on its powers, the Council settled down amicably enough to co-operate with the Board in running the academic side of the College.

Trinity was a major influence in the spread of organised sport in Victorian Ireland, so it will be appropriate at this point to trace the early development of sports facilities and clubs in the College. The original statutes expressly prohibited the students from playing games in the College squares or grounds, but in the more relaxed atmosphere of the Restoration the authorities permitted the laying-out of a bowling-green in 1684. A plan of 1761 shows it occupying an area about two hundred feet square, to the east of College Park, on ground where the Medical School Building now stands. The next sporting facility to be provided was a fives-court, commissioned by the Board in 1694, and built at the east end of the Fellows' Garden.[16]

Nothing more was officially done for student recreation until 1740 when Richard Castle submitted a plan and estimate for the construction of a 'real' tennis court. The court was finished the following year.[17] It was housed in a building about eighty feet long, situated right on the northern perimeter, somewhat to the east of the Printing House. A survey of 1804 shows it still standing, but it subsequently disappeared, perhaps as a result of the construction of Brunswick Street (now Pearse Street). In 1784 the Board purchased some ground near the northern boundary for re-laying the bowling-green, and in 1813/14 Provost Elrington made some provision for handball by latticing the east windows of the Dining Hall. Some years later householders in nearby Brunswick Street were complaining that their windows were being broken by balls coming from the College ball-court opposite.[18]

At the start of his provostship, Hely-Hutchinson secured the agreement of the Board that 'a field for the exercise of the scholars ought to be provided when it can be done with convenience', but action was long delayed. It was not until the next century that the gradual conversion of the College Park into a sports arena began. The low marshy area now occupied by the cricket field was first drained in 1813, and provided a convenient space where balls could be knocked around or races run. With the rise of organised games in the early Victorian period, a demand arose for regular cricket and football pitches. Cricket was being played in College in the 1830s, but a formal Board decision to lay out a cricket pitch was not taken until 1842. From the 1850s, football was played on a muddy strip of ground between the cricket square and Nassau Street. The area of the present Rugby field, previously used as a rubbish dump, remained a 'wilderness' of scanty grass, meagre hawthorn bushes, and stunted poplars. Repeated requests were made for its clearance and use as a playing pitch, but the Board's consent was not obtained until November 1900, and then only after a violent storm the previous November had blown down most of the trees.[19]

The authorities were equally reluctant to make any new provision for indoor games. In 1849 the students petitioned for ball-courts, but there was no positive response until 1862 when the Board gave a grant of £100 towards the construction of a rackets court 'in the north-east angle of the College Park'. Ten years later the first gymnasium was completed alongside the court with the aid of a Board loan of £1000. The complex, with some modifications, served the needs of indoor sport for more than a century.[20]

The beginnings of formally organised clubs can be traced well back into the nineteenth century. The Boat Club vies with the Cricket Club for the honour of being the senior College club, and one hesitates to adjudicate between their claims. A good but later secondary source (Lawrence's *Handbook of Cricket in Ireland*, 1866) assigns a foundation date of 1835 to the Cricket Club, which would make it the second oldest in Ireland —

Phoenix Cricket Club was founded in 1830. The Boat Club can counter with the actual record of a meeting held in a hotel in College Green on 3 September 1836.[21] This was the inaugural meeting of the Pembroke Club (called after the Earl of Pembroke's estate at Ringsend where the rowing took place), whose initial membership consisted mainly of Trinity undergraduates. The first major Irish regatta was held at Ringsend in 1840. Three years later the students broke away from the Pembroke Club to form their own club under the name of the University Rowing Club. They again amalgamated with Pembroke in 1847 under the name of Dublin University Rowing Club, making some provision for non-university members. However, tension between the two elements continued, leading to a second split in 1867, when mass student resignations led to the emergence of Dublin University Boat Club, with an exclusively university membership.

There is a mention of football as an evening amusement in College Park in the 1780s, but this was played on an informal basis without any club organisation. The game involved hacking and tripping, and is described as 'vulgar, fatiguing and rough'.[22] The Football Club, formed in 1854, was the first of its kind in Ireland, and has a strong claim to be the oldest continuously existing rugby club in the world. (Guy's Hospital in London had a football club from 1843, but it lapsed for a time later in the century.) Most of the earliest members of the Trinity club had been to school at Cheltenham or Rugby, and it was they who introduced the Rugby code into Ireland. The distinctive practice of running with the ball as well as kicking it was introduced in a school match at Rugby by William Webb Ellis in 1823. Ellis's father served in the British army in Ireland, and young Ellis could have been conditioned to make his innovation after seeing ball-handling in local village contests played in the old Gaelic style. If so, the subsequent GAA ban on 'rugby' as a 'foreign' game takes on a somewhat ironic tinge. Rugby School had produced a written code as early as 1846, but Trinity seems to have operated without one until 1868 when Wall, the secretary of the Club, and a Rugbeian, Charles Burton Barrington, drafted a set of rules in Wall's rooms in Botany Bay. Barrington captained the club from 1867 to 1870, and his uncle, another Trinity man named Charles Burton West, is the 'East' of Thomas Hughes's *Tom Brown's Schooldays.*

The College Park must long have been the scene of informal contests in running and jumping. Students used to challenge each other to leap the drainage channel known as the ha-ha, a broad ditch up to twenty feet in width, which earlier marked the north-east boundary of the Park. It ran from the Printing House diagonally across to the neighbourhood of the present Pavilion. The ha-ha was in existence in Charles Lever's time in College (1823–28), but subsequently was filled in.

The first organised athletic meeting to be held in Ireland took place in College Park on Saturday 28 February 1857. It was run by the Football Club, and proved so popular that a second meeting was held within a month. In the hands of an athletic committee, the event then developed into the annual College Races, and led in due course to the formation of the Dublin University Athletic Club in 1885. The attendance of the Lord Lieutenant at the first meeting added social cachet to the occasion, and the Races soon became highly fashionable, as well as very successful financially. The occasion came to be regarded as the premier out-of-doors social event of the Dublin year. A Trinity man later recorded his memory of cycling and long distance walking (races of four and seven miles) as leading features of the Races, mentioning the 'exceptionally tall' undergraduate Bram Stoker, the future author of *Dracula*, as an outstanding champion in the walking events.[23] Some of the accumulated profits were applied to equipping the gymnasium in 1869, and most of the money for Thomas Drew's Pavilion (begun in 1884 and opened on 13 June 1885) came from this source.

In the late 1870s the Races suffered disturbance from unruly crowds up to twenty thousand strong, and there were accusations of money-grubbing and unfair handicapping. The evening of the second day of the 1878 meeting was marred by a student riot in Botany Bay, in which three porters were injured and a carpenter's store destroyed by fire. Some of the offenders were sent down, more were suspended or fined, and the Board refused to allow the Races to be held the following year. The incident was the prelude to a turbulent period in College, with more student disturbances in April 1880, leading to the banning of the Races in that year too. They were not resumed until 1881, and then on a one-day basis, with much tighter control of ticket sales, and under the supervision of the Junior Dean. In 1886 a Harriers Club was formed to promote cross-country running, and athletes combined with harriers to found the Dublin University Harriers and Athletic Club in 1921.

Trinity students were playing hurley by 1810, but the first reference to an organised club comes sixty years later with the publication of the Laws of Hurley as played by the Dublin University Hurling Club. These Laws appeared in Lawrence's *Handbook*, and the editor stated that he had received enquiries about them from clubs in England. The rules, together with team photographs of the time, make it clear that the club favoured the northern variant of the game, which was played with a narrow-bossed stick and in winter rather than summer. The southern variety, which became the basis of the modern game, was played in summer with a much broader stick. It was the variant espoused by Michael Cusack when founding the Dublin Hurling Club in 1882/83. Trinity hurling was already beginning to evolve towards what is now called hockey — both terms were then in use for the game — with hitting allowed with one side of the stick only, and a prohibition on winding the hurl round the head 'when in close quarters'. The last rule stipulated that 'the ball shall always be the object of play'. Some other Dublin clubs emerged in association with existing cricket clubs like Phoenix, Leinster, and Merrion, and the game was taken up by schools such as High School and King's Hospital. But despite the formation of an Irish Hurley Union, which took place at a meeting in Trinity in 1879, the Trinity type of hurling did not spread beyond the Dublin area. The Trinity Club lapsed in the 1880s, but its traditions, together with its colours of green and black, were inherited by the Dublin University Hockey Club, founded in 1893.

In February 1882 an Athletic Union was formally constituted to organise the Races, and to disburse surplus funds in grants to the sports clubs. In this latter respect it was a forerunner of the Dublin University Central Athletic Committee (DUCAC), and it was managed by a committee that included staff and student members. All the existing clubs were represented. They numbered eight, of whom four — Boat, Rowing, Cricket and Football — were allowed to nominate two representatives each. The rest had to be content with one representative apiece. These were the Bicycle Club, the Gymnastic and Lawn Tennis Club, the Racket Club, and the Hurley Club.[24]

Eighteen eighty-four was a sad year in the development of sport in Ireland since it saw the beginnings of a split in athletics along political lines. The rift between Catholic nationalism and Protestant unionism was now so deep and embittered that such a development was probably inevitable. Michael Cusack launched the Gaelic Athletic Association (the GAA) at a meeting in Thurles on 1 November — a meeting attended by a Trinity rugby international, St George McCarthy — and in the following January it was resolved that any athlete who competed at meetings held under other laws would be ineligible to compete at GAA meetings. This resolution at once led to the formation of a rival body, the Irish Amateur Athletic Association, and introduced a division into Irish athletics that was not resolved until the 1960s. The partitioning of athletics was soon followed by a general 'ban' on 'foreign' games. Trinity's good work in keeping a form of hurling alive in the dark days after the Famine was forgotten, and her continued support for the other games she had done so much to popularise came to be viewed as yet another instance of disloyalty to the national cause.

Five future Provosts were prominent in the sporting life of the College in the later Victorian period. A. Traill captained the College in football and cricket, being perhaps the first, and certainly one of the very few, to achieve this distinction. He was also fourteen times rackets champion, gaining his last success at the age of fifty-two. J.P. Mahaffy was a first-class cricketer, who particularly excelled as a bowler. In the development of the facilities and organisation of College sport, they received enthusiastic support from another distinguished sportsman and Fellow, the physicist G.F. Fitzgerald, who died too young to be considered for the office. Mahaffy's successor, J.H. Bernard, was a good hurley player, W.E. Thrift was a champion cyclist when the sport was at a peak of popularity in the 1890s, and E.H. Alton played as a forward on the cup-winning rugby football team in 1897/98.

In 1892 the College commemorated the tercentenary of its foundation with impressive pageantry and panache. The ceremonies were concentrated into four days towards the end of Trinity term, and achieved dignity, and indeed splendour, without becoming over-ostentatious. Trinity's scholarly achievement was then at its zenith, and its worldwide reputation is reflected in the distinguished list of those who accepted invitations to be present at the celebration. Delegates brought greetings and good wishes from seventy-five universities and learned bodies spread over Europe from Holland to Russia, and further afield from India, Australia, Canada and the United States of America. Eminent visitors from Britain included Lord Acton, Lord Kelvin, the physicist J.J. Thompson, the classicists A.W. Verrall and J.P. Postgate, the composers Sir Charles Parry and Sir John Stainer, the artists Frederick Leighton and Sir Lawrence Alma-Tadema. There were also present in an *ex officio* capacity the Vice-Chancellors of Oxford and Cambridge, the Directors of the British Museum and the National Gallery, and the President of the Royal Academy. It is probably true to say that 'Dublin had never seen before and has not seen since so many men of real eminence gathered together'.[25]

The programme of events was devised by a committee chaired by Mahaffy, who predictably complained of the parsimony of the Board in pruning back his more extravagant plans. The celebrations began on the morning of Tuesday, 5 July with the Provost welcoming the delegates and guests at a reception in the Public Theatre. It may be noted in passing that Salmon's personality made a deep impression on the visitors, and many of them recalled the easy assurance and open friendliness with which he presided over the various occasions. The opening reception was followed by one of the most colourful and flamboyant parts of the ceremonial when over one thousand persons in gowns, robes, and uniforms proceeded through the Front Gate of College, and went on foot up Dame Street to St Patrick's Cathedral for a service of thanksgiving and commemoration. The afternoon was enlivened by a cricket match in College Park and a garden party in the Fellows' Garden. The evening featured a concert by the University Choral Society at which a specially composed Tercentenary Ode was sung. The day's festivities concluded with a reception and ball in the Mansion House, hosted by the Lord Mayor, Joseph Michael Meade (who had received an honorary LLD from the University at the Summer Commencements shortly before).

Wednesday's events were equally notable. The Senate convened at noon in the Public Theatre for the conferring of honorary degrees, with Tyrrell deputising as Public Orator for Palmer, who was ill. The graduands were so numerous that they had to be presented in groups (mathematicians, astronomers, and so on) rather than individually . When presenting the 'physicians and surgeons', Tyrrell ended his five-line citation with an apt quotation of the Hippocratic maxim: 'Life is short, the art long'. The only recipients to be personally named were Leighton and Alma-Tadema, then at the height of their fame, and Sir Henry Irving, whose reputation has held firmer than theirs. Irving was the first actor to be honoured in this way, and he was lionised by the students, who chaired him across to the Dining Hall steps after the ceremony, and insisted on his making an impromptu speech.

In the afternoon the Lord Lieutenant and his Countess gave a garden party at the Viceregal Lodge, and the evening was marked by a grand banquet in Leinster Hall attended by six hundred guests. At the high table the Provost was flanked by the Archbishops of Armagh and Dublin, the Bishops of Oxford and Derry, the Lord Chancellor and the Lord Lieutenant, the Marquess of Londonderry, Lord Kelvin , the Earl of Rosse (the Chancellor), the Master of Trinity College, Cambridge, and W.E.H. Lecky.

Lecky was the main speaker at the dinner, and gave a typically balanced and judicious appraisal of Trinity's contribution to Irish life:

> It may be said of Trinity College that for three hundred years it has steadily mingled with most of the best things in Irish life. It has not been merely a University of great mathematicians, of classical scholars,

> of great divines, or metaphysicians; it has also been the University of Swift and Goldsmith, and Congreve and Burke, of Henry Brooke, of Moore, of Lever, and of Davis. Whatever its enemies may say of it, it has been the University of the nation, and not merely of a party or sect. . . . It can count among its pupils men of every variety, and every extreme of political opinion — Clare and Grattan, Flood and Sheil, Duigenan and Wolfe Tone, Whiteside and Butt — and men connected with it have borne a leading part in elucidating the most distinctively Irish history.

Lecky went on to refer to the Celtic researches of scholars like Todd, Ferguson, Stokes and Reeves, and, in a quietly eloquent peroration, expressed the hope that 'whatever new powers may arise' Trinity would remain 'the home of sober thought, of serious study, of impartial judgment, of an earnest desire for truth, building up slowly, steadily, and laboriously the nobler and more enduring elements of national life.'

Thursday's programme was equally full, but slightly more low-keyed. The delegates presented their congratulatory addresses in the morning. In the afternoon there was a garden party, hosted by the Forces Commander Lord Wolseley at the Royal Hospital, Kilmainham. The evening saw the University mount an entertainment at the Gaiety Theatre with a double bill featuring Sheridan's *The Rivals* and a farce about College life entitled *Botany Bay,* written by Robert H. Woods and Charles W. Wilson. The College Races were run with their traditional pomp and glitter on the Friday afternoon, and that evening the guests, some doubtless rather weary, repaired yet again to the Leinster Hall for the concluding Ball.

Such was the course of the festivities by which Dublin's University celebrated its tercentenary. Dublin Corporation reciprocated the honour done to its Lord Mayor by conferring the freedom of the city on the Provost. At the ceremony the Lord Mayor rose to the occasion when he recalled the Corporation's gift of the site 'near Dublin' three hundred years before, and went on to say with commendable pride and not too much exaggeration that 'the City has flung around you her hospitable arms, and converted your outlying acres into a site, which, for extent and convenience, is not equalled by any university site in the populous cities of Europe'.

A record of the occasion was provided by the publication of *The Book of Trinity College*, and a commemorative medal was struck, bearing the heads of Queen Elizabeth I and Queen Victoria. An initiative by the graduates also resulted, after the lapse of a decade, in the completion of a major new

College building. This was the Graduates' Memorial Building, which stemmed from their desire to mark the tercentenary by a permanent addition to College amenities. The original idea was to provide a Union building like those at Oxford and Cambridge, in which student societies could be well and centrally housed. An appeal to graduates for this purpose realised £7500. But where was the new building to go? After considerable hesitation and prolonged discussion with the subscribers' representatives, the Board decided to add College money to a larger project which would provide more student rooms as well as the desired Union premises. The former redbrick range known as 'Rotten Row', was demolished to make way for the new building, designed by Sir Thomas Drew and completed in 1902 at an cost of over £15,000. When compared with the severity and restraint of Burgh's Library opposite, the 'GMB' may appear an over-ornate and rather pretentious structure, but it adds a touch of late Victorian style and interest to the grand ensemble of the Front and Library Squares. Forty new sets of rooms were provided in the houses at each end of it, and a spacious 'debating hall' was a useful feature of the central block. After lengthy argument, the Historical and Philosophical Societies convinced the Board that they already fulfilled the function of a Union, and they were allocated the accommodation they still retain.

The main staircase of the GMB is adorned with a fine stained-glass window commemorating Andrew Marshall Porter, who was killed in action at Lindley in the Boer War. Porter had a brilliant career as a student, gaining a scholarship and a first-class moderatorship in classics, and excelling also at hockey and cricket. He was one of more than twenty graduates who volunteered for service, and his beautiful memorial is a poignant reminder that the twentieth century was destined to be far less peaceful than its predecessor.

Notes

1. Down to 1976 the Senate seemed to have some discretion in the selection of the Chancellor. It voted on a panel of three names drawn up and submitted by the Board, but as McDowell and Webb (*History*, 223) explain, this was little more than a façade of democratic procedure.
2. Total College revenue nearly doubled between 1800 and 1850, due to a 30 per cent rise in the yield from the rents of the College estates (which amounted to about 170,000 acres), and the increase in student numbers. Despite assertions to the contrary, a Trinity education was not excessively expensive. In 1820 the fees for the four-year course totalled £70, and by 1900 the same charges had increased only to £83.
3. Fenian leaders educated at Trinity included John O'Mahony, Thomas Clarke Luby and John O'Leary.

4. Henry Fawcett (1833–84) was a courageous and single-minded reformer who had no particular connection with Ireland apart from his general desire to improve all the institutions of the British Isles. Though blinded in a shooting accident as a young man, he succeeded in becoming Cambridge's first professor of political economy in 1863, was elected MP for Brighton in 1865, and was appointed Post-Master General by Gladstone in 1880. He introduced parcel post in 1882. He was a close friend and follower of J.S. Mill, and remained very much on the left wing of the Liberals.
5. W.R.W. Roberts, J.H. Bernard, G. Wilkins, R.M. Gwynn and A.A. Luce. Since Luce's election in 1912, only one non-professorial candidate, J.R. Bartlett, elected in 1975, has been in holy orders. The Reverend H.F. Woodhouse and the Reverend F.E. Vokes, professors in the Divinity School, were elected as professorial Fellows in 1974.
6. McDowell and Webb, *History*, 256.
7. William FitzGerald, quoted by McDowell and Webb, *History*, 206–07.
8. See R.B. McDowell in *Trinity* 4 (1952), 21–23.
9. Under the provisions of the Reform Bill of 1832, masters in arts were granted parliamentary franchise. Over the next few years, so many Trinity BAs proceeded to take out their MA that the College received a substantial windfall in fees, which it applied to this building programme.
10. The Observatory, with its elegant Doric façade, was designed by Frederick Darley and was built as a laboratory for Lloyd in 1838.
11. For details of their work, see W.B. Stanford, 'Classical Studies in Trinity College, Dublin, since the Foundation', *Hermathena*, Vol. 57, 1941. See also J. Dillon in *Trinity College, Dublin: The Idea of a University* (edited by C.H. Holland, Dublin, 1991), 239–54.
12. The Reverend Newport J.D. White, *Some Recollections of Trinity College, Dublin*, quoted by McDowell and Webb, *History*, 286. White was admitted a Scholar of the House by Lloyd in 1880. He records (p.16) that this was the last occasion when Scholars knelt before the Provost when taking their oath. One of those elected, William Colgan by name, refused to do so, and the practice was immediately discontinued.
13. From Thomas Hirst's *Journal*, now in the Royal Institution in London. I owe this reference to my colleague Professor David Spearman, who included this and other interesting extracts from the *Journal* in his memorial discourse on Salmon on Trinity Monday 1991. Spearman outlines the history of mathematics in *Trinity College, Dublin: The Idea of a University* (Dublin, 1991), 280–93.
14. Between 1786 and 1797 there were separate 'professorships' of French and German, but the two were then reunited, as they had been in the original foundation of 1776. In 1866 the Board took power to appoint to a separate chair of French, but this was not in fact done until 1937 when Thomas Rudmose-Brown, who had been Professor of Romance Languages since 1909, was appointed.
15. For the sake of completeness, two further developments that strictly belong to the Edwardian period may be briefly noted. Modern history for long remained a sophister course only, and there was no separate moderatorship in the subject, but its status began to improve when an energetic young graduate, J.H. Wardell, was appointed to the chair in 1903. He soon persuaded Board and Council to extend the honor course back into the Freshman years. He also secured the appointment of an assistant, H.L.Murphy, whose well-researched monograph on the early years of the College remained unpublished until 1951, when it was deservedly rescued from oblivion by T.S.C. Dagg. The History School was further strengthened when an endowment for a new chair, received under the will of W.E.H. Lecky's widow, led to the appointment of Walter Alison Phillips as Lecky Professor in 1914.

    The religious overtones of instruction in Irish have previously been mentioned. In 1906 the Fry Commission commented adversely on the College's lack of interest in the language for its own sake. This criticism, when combined with E.J. Gwynn's enthusiasm for the subject, stimulated the Board into instituting a moderatorship in Celtic Languages (covering Welsh as well as Old, Middle, and Modern Irish), which was done in 1907.

16. The information in this section is largely derived from T.T. West's researches into the origins of sport in Trinity. I am greatly indebted to him for letting me see a draft of his *The Bold Collegians* (Dublin, 1991) in advance of publication. West's work supersedes the pioneering account of the sports clubs in K.C. Bailey's *History*, chapter VII. The plan of the College Park and Gardens (TCD MS Mun/MC 7) was drawn by Bernard Scalé. For the fives-court, see *Register*, Vol. 1, 316.
17. TCD MS Mun P/2/28 1, 2. The dimensions proposed are 80 feet 'in the clear' and 25 feet wide. The accounts show that the original estimate of £110 was exceeded by 28 per cent. Castle's plan is lost, but for later plans, see Mun MC/78.106. No account off this court has been given in any previous College history, but McParland listed it as one of Castle's projects in his *Country Life* articles.
18. TCD MS Mun/P2, item 257. Under the date 27 March 1819, Elrington's *Board Note Books* (TCD MS 9721) record that the Bursar is to get the ball court built if it can be done for less than £150.
19. An eyewitness account of this 'providential' event was published by R.M. Gwynn in *T.C.D.*, 2 December 1899.
20. A conversion of the rackets court into three squash courts was effected on the eve of World War II, and in 1961/62 an upper floor was inserted into this part of the building with the aid of a grant of £3500 from the Endowment Fund. Previously, the boxing ring had tended to monopolise the available space, but now better provision could be made for basketball, table tennis, and fencing. The old gym passed out of sporting use after the opening of the Luce Hall in 1981/82 (for which see Trevor West, *The Bold Collegians*, 96–97), and became a store for Library material.
21. TCD MS Mun/Club/Boat/1. For the history of the Club, see R. Blake, *In Black & White* (Dublin, 1991).
22. The reference comes from *Poems by the late Edward Lysaght Esq.* (Dublin, 1811). The information relates to Lysaght's student days in the 1780s.
23. N.J.D. White, *Recollections*, 8.
24. The Bicycle Club had been founded in the 1870s, and the Lawn Tennis Club in 1877, the same year as the All England and Fitzwilliam Clubs. Tennis was played first in the New Square, and from 1879 on asphalt courts near the gymnasium. The Hurley Club lost their representation when their numbers fell below thirty, and were replaced by the newly formed Association Football Club in 1884. The Dublin University Golf Club was founded in 1894.
25. McDowell and Webb, *History*, 337.

CHAPTER 11

Changing times 1892–1919

In 1904 Dublin University followed the route pioneered by London University in 1878 and admitted women to its degree courses on the same footing as men. The move put Trinity ahead of Oxford and Cambridge in one respect, though in other ways it had been lagging behind them for some time. It was behind in the sense that Cambridge since 1881 and Oxford since 1884 had permitted women to avail of much of the teaching and to take many of the examinations provided for men. It outstripped them because, from the start, Dublin allowed its matriculated women students to proceed to a degree without any reservations, whereas in Oxford this was not possible until 1920, and in Cambridge not until 1947.

The explanation of this paradox lies in the differing structures of the institutions. In multi-collegiate Oxbridge it was not difficult to establish separate colleges where women could reside and receive instruction in comparative seclusion. So Cambridge had Girton and Newnham, and Oxford Somerville and three other women's colleges, all founded before 1880, and most of them at a discreet remove from the centre. At single-college Trinity no such lines could be drawn, and the late Victorian conservatives remained doggedly opposed to women crossing the threshold of their all-male 'club'. But when the walls were breached, and women were admitted to lectures and practicals, there seemed to be no reason why they should not also have their degrees, since even male graduates had little or no say in running the university. But it was different at Oxbridge, where graduate votes counted in the business of Convocation or Senate, and that is why the final cachet was there withheld for so long.

The first move in the long campaign came in 1869 when Alexandra College (founded in that year) requested Trinity to provide examinations for its students. The Board responded readily enough by instituting two 'examinations for women', a junior one at matriculation level, and a senior one at second-year level. Certificates of proficiency were awarded to successful candidates, and the scheme was popular for some years, but from 1879 women seeking an academic qualification preferred to work for the arts degrees of the Royal University (founded in place of the Queen's University in that year) which could be taken by extern examination. In the early 1880s, reformers in Trinity who wanted the Board to follow the example of the Royal University used the forum of the new Council to raise the matter; but they failed to swing majority opinion to their side, and nothing was done.

By the time of the tercentenary, the women's cause had gained ground in Trinity, with influential Junior Fellows like Traill and Bernard (who later became Registrar for the Examinations for Women) giving it their support. In 1893 the Council, by a narrow majority, accepted a committee recommendation that women should be allowed to attend lectures and take examinations. Meanwhile the Association of Irish Schoolmistresses (ably led by Miss Isabella Mulvany, the Principal of Alexandra College, together with Miss Alice Oldham and Miss Henrietta White) was bombarding the Board with letters pressing its case and seeking a hearing. The Board refused to talk directly with the women, but in October 1894 agreed to meet a male deputation on their behalf. The case for admission was strongly presented by Mr Justice Madden (soon to become Trinity's Vice-Chancellor), W.G. Brooke, and D.J. Cunningham, the Professor of Anatomy. The Board felt constrained to take some action, and decided to seek legal opinion on the matter. The opinion delivered by two elderly counsel to a Board whose eight members could reckon six hundred years between them was that the proposed innovation was so radical that it could be effected only by an Act of Parliament.

The Board sat back with relief, declaring that it would not seek such legislation, and indeed would oppose it unless it applied also to Oxford and Cambridge. Only one small concession was made to feminine aspiration: those who had passed the junior examination for women might attempt a senior freshman honor examination, and those who had passed the latter examination a moderatorship. A successful candidate would receive a certificate, but not a degree.

The Board's general objections to mixed education in Trinity have been summarised in a passage that deserves quotation *in extenso*:

> Once a woman was in College it would be impossible to know where she went and how long she stayed, or, indeed, whether she ever came out at all. As to chaperonage, it would be impossible for the porters to

> decide whether, when two women entered together, one was old enough to act as guardian of the other. It was not to a college of this kind that parents sent their sons. Granted that most undergraduates of both sexes would behave well, an occasional scandal was bound to occur, and in any case many a susceptible boy would become entangled in an imprudent marriage. From such *liaisons dangereuses* and fortune-hunters the Board had a duty to protect its students.[1]

It will be seen that the objections were made on social rather than educational grounds. But in fairness to the authorities, it must be remembered that a strict code of morality was accepted by all parties at the time, that the current proprieties were rigidly observed, and that the conventions governing association between the sexes created difficulties that would not seem so daunting today. And if the staff were inordinately apprehensive about untoward consequences, it is also true to say that the undergraduates in residence did not pine unduly for female company.

The late 1890s saw Trinity isolated in the darkest hour before the dawn. In 1889 the Scottish universities were empowered to effect the full admission of women. Durham capitulated to the trend in 1895. Towards the end of the century a number of deaths among the Senior Fellows altered the Board's anti-feminist bias. Mahaffy, a strong protagonist of reform, had taken his seat in 1899, and when Tarleton took Conner's place at the end of 1901, the pro-women party found itself in a majority. Mahaffy, as Senior Lecturer, proposed 'that it was now expedient for the Board to make arrangements for admitting women to degrees in Arts' and this motion was carried by five votes to three, with the Provost voting against.

The educational equality that Plato had recommended more than two thousand years before was now won, but it took two more years before the necessary arrangements were in place. The Crown's law officers agreed that counsel's opinion had been too negative, and that the change could be effected by letters patent, provided that the Provost as well as the Board assented. Salmon bowed to the will of the majority, making it clear that, while his hand might sign, his heart remained opposed. Almost his last act as Provost — he died on 22 January 1904 — was to preside over the Board meeting that received the 'Royal Letters Patent permitting women to receive Degrees in the University of Dublin'.

The succession lay between John Pentland Mahaffy and Anthony Traill. Both were vigorous and assertive characters; the former was the better scholar, the latter the better administrator. Mahaffy's claim was weakened in College eyes by his previously expressed support for a federal solution to the university question, and there was also a general feeling that it was time to have a lay Provost (though Mahaffy was the least clerical of clerics). Mahaffy had the strong support of George Wyndham, the Chief Secretary, and was equally vigorously opposed by Arthur Dudley, the Lord Lieutenant. The choice lay with Arthur Balfour, the Prime Minister. He received a well-balanced assessment of the two leading contenders, and of J.B. Bury and J.H. Bernard, other suggested candidates, from D.H. Madden, the Vice-Chancellor, and finally decided that Traill would be the least unacceptable politically.

So the brusque, businesslike, and not unprogressive Ulsterman Anthony Traill (1838–1914) was sworn in during the same term that saw the admission of women. Isabel Johnston was the first to matriculate, in January 1904, followed by forty-five others before the year's end. In her case, by a nice irony, the *liaisons* so gloomily foreseen by some took the form of marriage to Stephen Kelleher, a Fellow of the College. The women's attendance was governed by some strict but readily accepted rules: they had to wear cap and gown at all times, they could not visit any set of rooms unchaperoned, and they were required to leave the premises not later than 6 p.m. In Hilary term 1905, a Lady Registrar was appointed to guide and supervise the women undergraduates, the first holder of the post being Lucy Gwynn, daughter of the Regius Professor of Divinity. Later in the same year the Elizabethan Society was formed to provide for women students the same facilities as the 'Hist' and 'Phil' made available for men. By 1914 women were constituting about 15 per cent of the annual student intake. Their application was intense, their intellectual standard high, and they were soon beating the men to gold medals at moderatorship. Olive Purser was the first woman to win a (non-foundation) scholarship, and in June 1918 she succeeded to the lady registrarship.

There was one immediate and unexpected consequence of this quiet revolution. Reciprocal *ad eundem* arrangements had long been in force whereby male graduates of Oxford, Cambridge or Dublin could take out a BA at either of the other universities without the need to pass any further examination. There were many women, including some from Ireland, who had performed all the required exercises at 'another place', but were debarred from putting the desired letters after their name. The Board agreed that the *ad eundem* privilege might apply to such women for a four-year period from December 1904. At first only a few availed of the concession, but the idea soon caught on, and by the end of the period more than seven hundred women, mostly from Cambridge, had crossed to

Dublin to pay their fee and receive their degree. The concession was not renewed despite much pressure, and the fees were largely turned over as a substantial addition to a subscription fund that had been started for the provision of a women's hostel. This was the origin of Trinity Hall in Dartry Road, about three miles south of the College, where the main house was purchased in 1908. Appropriately enough, the first warden, Miss E.M. Cunningham, was one of the Irish women who graduated via Cambridge in 1906. The property was greatly extended in 1910 when Mr (later Sir) John Purser Griffith and his wife purchased the neighbouring Palmerston House and most generously donated it to the College. At their request it was renamed Purser House in memory of their relative, Frederick Purser, a Fellow of considerable distinction in mathematics, who had died earlier in the year.

Despite the passing of Fawcett's Act, Catholic aspirations, as articulated by the hierarchy, remained firmly set on a Catholic university under Catholic control. The Queen's Colleges were still viewed as incurably 'godless', and the Act was discounted as mere window-dressing that did little or nothing to alter the unacceptably Protestant character of Trinity College. But the full Catholic demand had little chance of making political headway at Westminster. The Liberals were opposed on principle to endowing denominational education, and the Conservatives, who tended to regard Catholic Ireland as inherently disloyal, saw no reason to make concessions to its religious leaders. It seemed to both parties that the obvious (and cheapest) solution was for the Catholics to accept the existing colleges as suitable for the education of Catholic youth, given appropriate provisions and guarantees for the protection of their faith.

So for more than two decades nothing was done, but as the nineteenth century drew to a close, the situation again became more fluid. A conciliatory statement by the hierarchy in 1897 opened the way for another Royal Commission, which was set up in 1901 under the chairmanship of Lord Robertson. The Commission was to enquire into how higher education in Ireland might be reformed and rendered 'adequate to the needs of the Irish People', that is to say, made more acceptable to Catholic opinion. But its terms of reference (set by a Conservative administration) precluded it from considering Trinity College. In view of this exclusion, and also because of a the unimaginative and half-hearted character of its solution — in effect, a revamped version of the Jesuit-run University College in association with a remodelled Royal University — it is hardly surprising that its recommendations, issued in 1903, proved abortives.[2]

There the matter rested until the overwhelming Liberal victory of 1906 brought a new Chief Secretary to Ireland in the person of the formidably able and energetic James Bryce. Bryce at once recommended the appointment of another Royal Commission, which would devote its entire attention to Trinity College and its future role in the Irish university system. The chairman was an eminent judge, Sir Edward Fry, and the members included Douglas Hyde, then President of the Gaelic League. Hyde not unnaturally deplored Trinity's attitude to the Irish language, but was in general not unsympathetic to his *alma mater*.[3] There were two other Trinity graduates among the Commissioners, both, unlike Hyde, Catholics. The senior was the distinguished lawyer, Christopher Palles, whose views carried much weight, and whose loyalty to the College was never in doubt. The other was the relatively young and inexperienced Stephen Barnabas Kelleher, elected to fellowship in 1904, and the nominee of the Board. There were four academics from England, and the panel was completed by Denis Coffey, Professor of Physiology in the Cecilia Street medical school and soon to be the first President of the new University College, Dublin.

Trinity could expect sympathetic and fair-minded consideration from the Commissioners, and this it duly received. But some of the evidence submitted, notably from representatives of the Gaelic League and the Catholic Graduates and Undergraduates Association, revealed an intense and bitter hostility to the College. Like older antipathies, this was partly fuelled by sectarianism, but Trinity was also (and probably with justice) perceived as increasingly out of tune and touch with Irish cultural and national aspirations. Ironically enough, Trinity's popularity had sunk to new depths at the very moment when its scholarly reputation stood very high. But unpopularity was a political rather than an educational consideration, and did not weigh much with the Commission.

The Commissioners recommended (Kelleher alone dissenting) that a Catholic College acceptable to the hierarchy should be established in Dublin. Where they differed, and differed seriously, was on the question of how such a College was to be fitted into the existing pattern. Three recommended its affiliation to the Royal University, but five took the view that all the colleges in Ireland should be conjoined in a 'great national university'. Among the five was Henry Jackson, the Regius Professor of Greek at Cambridge. With appropriately Platonic detachment, he believed this to be the ideal solution, but felt that the time was not yet ripe to implement it. So the Commissioners, who reached unanimity on all their other recommendations, were split down the middle on the crucial issue of the future structure of Irish third-level education.

This disagreement, however, hardly mattered, for Bryce had already decided that the single-university option was the best, and had secured cabinet approval for it even before the Commission's report was published. The report appeared on 21 January 1907, and Bryce announced his scheme four days later. The hierarchy had already conceded that the main principle of Fawcett's Act, the absence of religious tests for offices or award, could be applied in a new Catholic college or university. On this basis, Bryce proposed the establishment of just such a college. It was to be situated in Dublin, would be given an adequate endowment, and would be joined in a reconstituted University of Dublin, together with Trinity College and the Queen's Colleges of Belfast and Cork. Galway was to be affiliated on a more dependent basis. The intractable problem of denominationally 'sensitive' subjects such as philosophy and history was to be overcome by a system of alternative examinations and dual professorships.

Such a scheme might appeal to a pragmatic politician, but it was bound to be anathema to liberal-minded academics, and Trinity reacted strongly against it. A Trinity College Defence Committee was established, with the Provost as chairman and E.J. Gwynn as an energetic secretary. 'Hands off Trinity' became the rallying cry, protest meetings were organised, and intensive lobbying maintained. Opposition was much helped by the fact that Bryce left Ireland almost immediately to take up a new appointment as Britain's ambassador to the United States of America. In any case his scheme had not been greeted with much enthusiasm. He was succeeded as Chief Secretary by Augustine Birrell, a cautious and scholarly man, sympathetic to Trinity, and naturally inclined to postponement and reconsideration.

The College was also fortunate in having another well-informed admirer in the cabinet in the person of R.B. Haldane. Haldane possessed a good grasp of the Irish university problem, and had in fact put forward his own solution to it some years before. The Haldane plan proved acceptable to Traill, and Birrell was soon induced to espouse it. By the end of the year, the Provost was able to reassure his colleagues that Trinity's interests and endowments would not be impaired by the forthcoming Irish Universities Bill.

The Bill was introduced in March 1908 and had passed all stages by August. Under it was instituted the university framework that (new universities apart) has persisted more or less unaltered down to the time of writing. Trinity College remained intact as the University of Dublin. The Queen's College in Belfast was given the status of a separate university. The Royal University was dissolved. In its place was established the National University of Ireland, incorporating as university colleges the existing Queen's Colleges in Cork and Galway. Its third member college was University College, Dublin, *de jure* a separate foundation, but *de facto* the lineal successor to the University College that had its roots in Newman's University.[4]

The Haldane plan was generally welcomed as a sensible and even-handed solution to the Irish university question. In its secular constitution, the new National University was less than ideal from the Catholic viewpoint, but in practice it provided an educational situation that the bishops could live with, and that nationalist sentiment could embrace with pride. A hopeful omen for the future could be seen in the appointment of Protestants to the chairs of Old Irish, Modern Irish, Welsh, and Irish archaeology.

The evidence given to the Fry Commission at least served to put the university question into sharp focus, and the reasonably satisfactory solution that followed in its wake has now been outlined. It remains to consider some of the specific recommendations made in relation to Trinity College, and the important constitutional reforms that flowed from them.

Constitutional reform in the College had more and more come to mean change in the composition of the Board. So far as the Fellows were concerned, the recruitment of its members (apart from the Provost) by seniority alone had become the central issue, but the reforming party was motivated by the practical consideration that promotion to senior fellowship had become excruciatingly slow, rather than by the argument that the mechanism was wrong in principle. The body of non-Fellow professors, now equal in size to that of the Fellows, had a different ground for complaint, in that they could not even aspire to a seat on the governing body. But neither Fellows nor Professors formed a united group in their pressure for change, and the Board was not forced into action until the Fry Commission took evidence and made its recommendations.

The evidence, as might have been expected, was disparate enough, ranging in tone from radically reformist to ultra-conservative, and in the light of what they heard, the Commissioners might have been excused for making no proposals. But in fact they called firmly and unanimously for a completely elective Board and for due representation for the Professors. This was a clear-cut proposal with much to commend it. When the

College came to consider it after the demise of the Bryce scheme, there was wide endorsement of the principles of representative government and the inclusion of the Professors. It was agreed that a joint committee of four Junior Fellows and four Professors should draw up a detailed scheme to embody these principles, and this was duly done. The scheme, which involved the creation of a unified constituency of Junior Fellows and principal (i.e. full-time) Professors, was approval by the Junior Fellows with only one dissentient. But when the Professors as a body came to discuss it, they split over the problem of defining 'principal' and 'secondary' chairs, declined to give their support to the committee's proposals, and made some new proposals of a somewhat divisive nature. The Junior Fellows were annoyed, and began to regret their conciliatory overtures, and the temporary coalition of non-Board interests fell apart.

The Board then produced a scheme of is own of a much less radical nature. The hard core of the governing body was to continue to consist of the Provost and the seven Senior Fellows (as it had done since 1627), but the membership was to be enlarged by the addition of two elected representatives of the Junior Fellows, and two elected representatives of the Professors, the latter to become members of the body corporate for the period of their Board service. In addition, there was an important provision that the offices of Bursar, Senior Lecturer, and Registrar should be open to Junior as well as Senior Fellows, and that any Junior appointed should also sit *ex officio* on the Board.[5]

By the end of Trinity term 1909, the Board had secured a somewhat reluctant assent to these proposals from both Fellows and Professors, and had instructed counsel to draft them in form for a King's Letter. Two Senior Fellows, the Reverend T.T. Gray (who had been a Fellow since 1862 and a successful Junior Dean) and G.L. Cathcart (a Fellow since 1870), had been vehement opponents of the scheme at Board level. They now continued the fight, first by seeking a restraining injunction in the High Court, and finally by a direct appeal to the Crown. But all to no avail. The Provost demonstrated that they were an unrepresentative minority by putting the proposed reform to the whole body corporate, Fellows and Scholars alike, and securing an overwhelming mandate for its implementation. The letters patent of 1911 duly altered the composition of the Board in the way desired, and up to the time of writing no further constitutional changes have been sought from, or imposed by, government. All subsequent modifications in the structure of the Board, or the Council, have been made by statutory change initiated and agreed within the confines of the College.

Trinity's pervasive ability to regulate its own affairs by ordinance was undoubtedly the most important legacy of the 1911 King's Letter. The College had been granted a large measure of autonomy under its original charter, but its independence had been greatly curtailed by the Caroline revision of 1637. At a time when Home Rule for Ireland seemed close, the Fry Commission recommended that the Board again be given authority to initiate statutory change, and this very significant legislative power, subject to certain conditions and safeguards, was confirmed to the reconstituted Board by the letters patent. The Board was prevented from making arbitrary or unwanted changes in the statutes by the provision that, if it desired to make a new law, statute or ordinance, or to alter or amend an existing one, it had first to obtain the assent in writing of a majority of the Fellows, and also the approval of the Visitors. The Board was also precluded by an 'entrenched clause' (alterable only by the Crown) from making any change in the constitution or powers of the new Divinity School Council established by the same King's Letter.[6] Finally, the Letter contained the blanket proviso that statutory changes 'shall not alter or affect the Constitution of the Body Corporate of our said College'.

This chapter covers the period when the 'east end' of College first began to take on much of its present appearance. The Schools of Medicine and Engineering were the first to enjoy some physical extension. In 1895 the Board recognised the growing importance of pathology when it agreed to provide new accommodation for the subject. A substantial building was erected on the mound by Lincoln Place at the south-west corner of College Park. Costing £9,000, it housed the departments of pathology and bacteriology, and was opened in 1898.[7]

At the start of the new century, money was also found for a plain but functional extension to engineering facilities in the shape of the low brick structure that lies just across the roadway from the rugby pitch. This first 'Engineering Lab' was designed and equipped to give students instruction in mechanical and electrical engineering. The building resulted from recommendations by a Board committee set up in 1899 to consider whether and how the course might be extended to include these subjects. The first stimulus probably came from Traill, who had good reason to be aware of the development possibilities in this field. Traill had been closely involved with his brother in a project that produced the first hydro-electric passenger tramway in the British Isles, a line running from Bushmills (near the Traill family home) to Portrush in County Antrim. The tramway provided a useful local service without subsidy for more than sixty years. So the first significant extension of the Engineering School, like its inception, was not unrelated to developments in public transport.

Traill was also instrumental in having the Board committee enlarged to comprise all the heads of the scientific departments, and its deliberations then took a wider sweep. It now included the very eminent physicist, George Francis Fitzgerald, and the equally distinguished geologist, John Joly.[8] These men were fully aware of the importance of current advances in science and the great expansion in resources taking place in British universities. Fitzgerald had recently presented a report to the Senate highlighting Trinity's sadly deficient provision of facilities for scientific research. Finance, as always, was at the root of the problem, and Fitzgerald's remark that the College 'must continue all the functions that it has fulfilled in the past, and in addition it is expected to provide for all the new developments that arise almost yearly' will strike an answering chord in the hearts of latter-day administrators. He referred to the building of the Clarendon and Cavendish laboratories at Oxford and Cambridge, largely financed by private benefactions, and to the local pride and money that had built up the resources of the newer universities from Liverpool to Bristol. These developments stemmed partly from the wealth generated by the Industrial Revolution (which had barely touched Ireland, apart from Belfast) and partly from the greatly enhanced prestige of the natural sciences in the post-Darwin generation. Physics, too, was just starting to get to grips with the phenomenon of radioactivity, and Fitzgerald was well aware of the significance of the discoveries currently being made by Röntgen, Rutherford and Madame Curie. What, he asked in effect, was Trinity going to do to keep up with its peers in the scientific field?

The Science Committee, chaired by Mahaffy, presented its first report in June 1899. It surveyed the needs of all the scientific departments, and recommended a development scheme which it estimated would require 'a capital outlay of about £70,000, and an annual expenditure of £5,000.' Since the total annual income of the College at the time was about £80,000, it is hardly surprising that the Board asked the committee to think again. In a second report, presented in 1902, the committee revised its estimate downwards by about 50 per cent, and urged priority treatment for physics and botany.

Even the revised figures seemed beyond the College's capacity to meet, and it was decided to launch an appeal to graduates and the general public. Early in the following year the Chancellor, Lord Rosse, took a happy initiative in writing to enlist the interest of Edward Cecil Guinness, the wealthy and philanthropic chairman of the brewery. Apart from being a graduate, Lord Iveagh as he then was, had no official connection with Trinity — he did not succeed Lord Rosse as Chancellor until 1908 — but he responded in a splendidly generous way. He undertook to provide a capital sum of £34,000 as soon as the committee's appeal produced enough to fund its recommended annual outlay of £2730. This would have needed nearly £80,000, and the appeal in the end realised only £19,000. However, it was calculated that this sum would produce enough to cover the increased annual expenditure on physics and botany, and this part of the scheme (together with the Engineering extension described above) went ahead, with Lord Iveagh paying the total cost — £24,450 — of new buildings for physics and botany.

The buildings, designed by W.C. Marshall, stand side by side beyond the east end of the rugby field. With solid cut-stone exteriors and well-designed interiors, they were good specimens of the Edwardian laboratory, and proved adequate for the teaching needs of their departments until the big expansion in numbers began in the late 1950s. The Physics building received a major extension in the 1960s, but the School of Botany, in its exterior form at least, remains as first built. There was no money left for geology at the time, but some years later Lord Iveagh agreed to give the balance of his original guarantee (nearly £10,000) to fund equipment and assistants for Professor Joly's researches.

Coming events were beginning to cast their shadows in the opening years of the reign of George V. From April 1912 members of the College followed the protracted debate on Asquith's Home Rule Bill with close interest and considerable apprehension. Their representatives at Westminster were Sir Edward Carson,[9] who was implacably opposed to the measure, and James Campbell (later Lord Glenavy) who proposed that Trinity be excluded from the jurisdiction of a future Irish parliament. To their credit, the Board and the College staff formally repudiated this suggestion, emphasising Trinity's roots in Ireland, and asking only for a guarantee that no change in the College's status would be imposed against its will. The Bill passed the Commons early in 1913, and was duly rejected by the Lords, but the Upper House had lost its power of indefinite veto, and by August 1914 the measure was within a few weeks of becoming law, when the outbreak of World War I led to an agreed postponement of its implementation until peace should return. By the end of the war, events had overtaken it, but fortunately any fears that Trinity may have had proved groundless, for the Free State government that emerged after the Treaty in 1921, though not overtly supportive of the College, showed no desire to intrude into its affairs.

The students and staff were only marginally involved in the labour troubles of pre-war Dublin, but the 1913 strike and lock-out touched the conscience of at least one of the Fellows, the Reverend R.M. Gwynn. Gwynn, whose whole life was a model of unselfish scholarship and charitable endeavour, supported the cause of the workers, though not in any doctrinaire spirit. According to some accounts, the evolution of the 'peace committee' (of which he was a leading member) into Connolly's Citizen Army began in his College rooms, though clearly he did not endorse its role in the 1916 Rising.[10]

In Trinity term 1913 Traill nominated Mahaffy as Vice-Provost, and the following year, as Traill's health began to fail, Mahaffy found himself in virtual charge. Traill did not long survive the start of the war with Germany on 4 August, and was dead by mid-October. The Gaelic Society, which had previously been in trouble with the authorities, chose this moment to invite Patrick Pearse to speak at its opening meeting. Given that Pearse was making anti-recruitment speeches at the time, one can understand why Mahaffy moved to prevent him appearing on a Trinity platform. The meeting went ahead outside the walls without incident, but Mahaffy's letter of refusal to the Society contained the notorious phrase 'a man called Pearse', and this gratuitous insult was to be long remembered against the College.

Mahaffy was already in his seventy-sixth year, but was far from senile, and his scholarly fame and all-round talents made him the obvious choice for the succession. To the general approval of his colleagues, he was duly admitted Provost on 20 November 1913. This final promotion came very late but very deservedly. Mahaffy was in many ways a great man, but it was ironic that one so given to social ostentation should have been called to preside over a College so cramped by war-time stringencies. Gone were the days of lavish entertaining, student numbers had halved, and sheep cropped the long grass in the College Park. Mahaffy worked hard to keep up the morale of his diminished establishment, and occupied his time with research into College history and the production of a catalogue of the College silver.

Although conscription was never in force in Ireland, more than three thousand graduates and undergraduates joined the armed forces, and casualties were high. The roll of honour includes the names of 454 who lost their lives. One VC,[11] over 100 DSOs, and nearly 300 MCs were won by this gallant group. Three of the Fellows fought on the western front: F. La T.Godfrey and A.A. Luce survived the ordeal, but a promising young mathematician, Samuel George Stewart, was killed in action only two weeks before the armistice. Another sadly late staff casualty was the distinguished physiologist Sir William Henry Thompson, a frequent traveller to London for consultations with the Ministry of Food, who perished when the mail-boat *Leinster* was sunk by torpedo in October 1918.

The Trinity response was in line with Redmond's wholehearted support for the British war effort, though most Trinity men fought as unionists, not home rulers. But constitutional nationalists and unionists alike were united in their condemnation of the 1916 insurrection, and this should be remembered in any consideration of Trinity's involvement in the fateful events of Easter week.

The seizing of the General Post Office and other strategic points in the inner city came on the morning of Monday, 24 April. Luce was the first of the Fellows to be confronted with the situation. He happened to be back on leave from France, and in the course of a walk to Nelson's Pillar was amazed to see armed men at the windows of the GPO. He returned at once to the College where word of the Rising had already been received and the porters had closed the gates in the face, it was rumoured, of an advancing column of Sinn Féiners. A three-man detail was on routine guard duty at the headquarters of the Officers Training Corps in the Parade Ground, and immediate responsibility for the defence of the College rested with them.

They acted at once to notify other members of the corps, but many cadets and the commanding officer, Major (later Sir) Robert Tate, were away from College for the Easter break. By mid-afternoon some two dozen had assembled under the command of the senior officer present, Captain E.H. Alton, one of the Fellows. Rifles were issued from the armoury, the windows of the headquarters were sandbagged, and sentries posted. By evening the garrison had increased to forty-four, including a number of Anzacs and other 'regulars' on leave in the city, who came in to take refuge in the College.

Given the strategic situation of the College at the heart of Dublin, and the fact that several hundred rifles and thousands of rounds of ammunition were in store, the defenders had every reason to fear that an attempt would be made to overrun their position. Detachments of the insurgents had occupied St Stephen's Green and the railway stations, including nearby Westland Row, armed patrols could be seen on the elevated loop line overlooking the Parade Ground, and sniper fire was coming from Nassau Street.[12] In the course of a tense and anxious night, the decision was taken to concentrate the defence in the older buildings to the west of College Park, so the OTC building was evacuated and arms and equipment were moved to the Front and New Squares.[13] Fire was then directed from the roof and pavilions of the West Front to impede insurgent communications and prevent further occupation of key points like the Bank of Ireland. By Tuesday evening the danger of incursion was receding as government forces arriving in the city began to engage the insurgents, and the garrison was reinforced by a detachment of the Leinster Regiment. On the night of Wednesday, 26 April the immediate safety of the College was assured, when, with the consent of the Provost, the first party of troops to come from Britain entered the premises and established their headquarters there. Over the next few days, large numbers of exhausted soldiers could be seen sleeping in the squares or on the steps of the buildings with their horses tied to the railings or grazing in College Park. Casualties were treated in an emergency hospital fitted up in No. 15, and manned by the medical unit of the OTC.

By the weekend, the tragedy that had overtaken the city was all too apparent in the rubble-strewn streets, the shattered and burning buildings, and the many hundreds of dead and wounded, three of whom found a last resting place in the College grounds. But equally tragic for the academic community was the conflict of loyalties so feelingly expressed some weeks later in an editorial in a student magazine. The writer was Cadet T.C. Kingsmill Moore, who later became an eminent judge and long-serving Visitor to the College. He had been a member of the garrison, and had witnessed the destruction and carnage caused by British artillery, including an 18-pounder mounted outside the Brunswick Street Gate. He wrote as follows: 'To be called upon to defend our University against the attack of Irishmen, to be forced in self-defence to shoot down our countrymen — these are things which even the knowledge of duty well fulfilled cannot render anything but sad and distasteful.'

In May 1917 Britain's Prime Minister, David Lloyd George, initiated a new move for an Irish settlement. He decided to summon the various parties to a Convention whose object would be to draw up an acceptable scheme of government for the country. Mahaffy offered the use of the Regent House for the meetings, and his offer was accepted. The Convention was in session there from July to the following April, but its deliberations became increasingly irrelevant as the polarisation between Sinn Féin and the Ulster Unionists intensified. In the end, the British government made no attempt to implement the Convention's majority recommendation of a home rule parliament for the whole of Ireland. From the front windows of their conference room, the delegates could look down on Foley's fine statue of Edmund Burke, and some of them may have reflected rather ruefully that he too had to grapple with intractable problems created by British conquest and colonisation.

Mahaffy died at the end of April 1919, the month in which Eamon de Valera,[14] who had been briefly on the books at Trinity as a student in the early 1900s, was elected President of Dáil Éireann, the new Republican Assembly that claimed to be the legitimate government of Ireland. The armed struggle against Britain was about to be renewed, and the final hour of the Ascendancy had come. It was a mercy that Mahaffy was spared sight of the destruction and bloodshed of 'the Troubles', mayhem that momentarily penetrated the College when a woman student was killed by a sniper's bullet while watching a cricket match in College Park on 3 June 1921.[15] But a stable Irish government eventually emerged from the guerilla warfare of these years, and a new epoch opened for the country and its oldest college.

Notes

1. McDowell and Webb, *History*, 347.
2. In 1883 the bishops made over the premises of 'Newman's University' to the Jesuits, and they ran the institution under the name of University College. The College prepared students for degrees of the Royal University, and developed into a successful if small academic centre where James Joyce was educated and Gerard Manley Hopkins worked for a time as a professor.
3. In partial extenuation of Trinity's attitude to the language, it may be recalled that when the National University was being constituted in 1908, the Irish Catholic bishops expressed their united disapproval of Irish being made a compulsory subject.
4. University College took over the Cecilia Street medical school, but not the College of Science, which continued as a separate institution until 1926, when the Free State government brought in legislation to merge it with UCD.
5. The first Junior Fellow to reach the Board by this route was E.J. Gwynn when he was appointed Senior Lecturer in 1926.
6. This provision resolved a long-standing controversy between the College and the General Synod of the Church of Ireland. Fawcett's Act initiated a process of laicisation in the fellowship body, and, not surprisingly, concern began to be voiced in Church of Ireland circles about the future control of the school that supplied the bulk of their clergy. Appointments and the curriculum were the main issues. The Church authorities regarded it as an anomaly that they no longer had any guarantee of the religious profession of those governing the Divinity School, though they admitted that instruction in 'scientific theology' was a function of the school as well as the training of ordinands. These apprehensions were crystallised in a synod resolution demanding the transfer of the school to the Church and the provision by Trinity of an endowment adequate for its maintenance, but to this the Board would by no means agree. The Fry Commission compromise of management by a separate council, including representatives of the bishops — a sort of *imperium in imperio* — , had originally been suggested by the University Council in 1879.
7. The development stemmed from a proposal by the elderly but very distinguished Senior Fellow Samuel Haughton (whose scientific interests ranged from meteorology to anatomy) for the establishment of a chair of pathology. The Board declined to go as far as this, but in 1895 agreed to create a lectureship in the subject, which was first held by A.C. O'Sullivan. O'Sullivan had been a Fellow since 1886, and was to hold the post for a long time, eventually becoming the University's first Professor of Pathology in 1922, two years before his death.
8. G.F. Fitzgerald was born in 1851, won scholarship in 1870 and fellowship in 1877, and held the chair of natural and experimental philosophy from 1881 to his premature death in 1901. He was an experimentalist and theoretician of near genius, being awarded the royal medal of the Royal Society (of which he was an elected member) in 1899 for distinguished contributions to theoretical physics, 'especially in the domain of optics and electrodynamics'. His name is immortalised in the 'Fitzgerald-Lorentz contraction', a postulated factor of contraction in moving bodies in the direction of their motion, which he was the first to suggest. Einstein made considerable use of the postulate in developing the theory of relativity.

   Fitzgerald built a flying machine remarkably like a modern hang-glider, and tested it in non-powered flight in College Park in 1895. A take-off ramp was erected against one of the balconies of the Pavilion, and the students assisted with towing ropes. The experiment gained him considerable notoriety in Dublin, and good photographs of is exist (see, for example, Bailey, *History*, 209), but it was not a great success. The glider hung for some years from the roof of the Museum Building (where Fitzgerald did most of this work), but was unfortunately destroyed when a thoughtless student put a match to one of its pendent cords.

   Fitzgerald showed equal enthusiasm in advocating the claims of educational theory as a university subject, and his persistence led to the institution of a diploma in the theory and practice of education (1896). The founding of the chair of education in 1905 (of which his brother-in-law E.P. Culverwell was the first holder) resulted from his campaigning. It only remains to record that this remarkable man was also an athlete of some note who played hurley and racquets, losing a championship final in the latter game to Traill in 1880.

John Joly FRS was one of the most able, versatile and distinguished scientists ever to work in the College. He acquired a worldwide and lasting reputation for his research work on the age and surface history of the earth, and he was also a notable pioneer in colour photography. He held the chair of geology from 1897 to his death in 1933.

9. Carson entered Trinity in 1871, as did Oscar Wilde. Wilde was elected to a scholarship in classics in his third year, but then transferred to Oxford, so is not technically a graduate, though he is now claimed by the College as a distinguished alumnus. Carson graduated in 1875 and went on to become 'one of the greatest advocates of all time', and 'the founding-father of Northern Ireland' — phrases used by G.L.Herries Davies when pointing out that he is nowhere commemorated in the College. See Davies's contribution 'hosce meos filios' in *Trinity College, Dublin and the Idea of a University* (Dublin, 1991), 317–38, an essay containing penetrating reflections on the vagaries of posthumous fame.
10. Gwynn had long been actively engaged in the provision of housing for Dublin's poor. He helped to raise the capital to found the Social Services (Tenements) Company, formed on 21 December 1900, with three Fellows (E.J. Gwynn, L.C. Purser, W.E. Thrift) and one Professor (John Joly) among its first directors. He also pioneered the scheme by which the company acquired houses in Grenville Street for its charitable purposes. These houses were made over to Dublin Corporation after World War II, but the company still survives as Trinity's only established charity, successfully running homes in Harold's Cross and Terenure for elderly people of limited means. Gwynn went on to become Professor of Biblical Greek in 1916, and Professor of Hebrew in 1920. In 1937 he stepped down from the chair in favour of his assistant Jacob Weingreen (whose eminent career fully justified this unusual switch in jobs).
11. Captain Clement Robertson BAI of the Tank Corps, who died in action at Passchendaele. Three other graduates had previously been awarded the V.C.: William Temple (1833–1919), James Henry Reynolds (1844–1932), James William Adams (1839–1903). Adams, the 'fighting parson', was the first clergyman ever to win the V.C. (on service in Afghanistan in 1897). I am indebted to my colleague G.L.Herries Davies for the above information.
12. Trinity's OTC was formed in 1910, and not disbanded until 1922. Full details of its activities and personnel are given in Roger Willoughby's pamphlet, *A Military History of the University of Dublin and its Officers Training Corps, 1910–1920*, published by the Medal Society of Ireland, Limerick, 1989. TCD MS. 2783 comprises various reports by individuals concerned in the Easter Week defence, notably the official one by the Adjutant, Major A.G. Harris. Although he was not a member, Professor John Joly volunteered his services, and an essay in his *Reminiscences and Anticipations* (1920) is a vivid diary-like account of the events of Easter Week as viewed from inside the College.
13. One of the men occupying Westland Row said later that his party were deterred by the sight of the sandbags and their belief that the place was strongly held.
14. After graduating in the Royal University in 1904, de Valera matriculated in Trinity with the aim of adding to his qualifications. He gained credit for his Junior Freshman year by examination, competed (unsuccessfully) for scholarship in 1905, and then found that the exigencies of earning a living prevented him from pursuing his course.
15. Her name was Kathleen Wright. For further details, see op. cit (n. 9), 336.

24 *Theobald Wolfe Tone (1763–98) graduated from the College in 1786, and was called to the Irish Bar in 1789. His uncompromising views and gallant death have ensured his position as the founder of the Irish Republican tradition.*

25 *George Francis Fitzgerald (1851–1901), perhaps the most outstanding Trinity scientist, graduated in 1871 with gold medals in mathematics and experimental science, and later became a Fellow (1877) and Professor of Natural and Experimental Philosophy (1881).*

26 *The Magnetic Observatory in the Fellows' Garden, by Frederick Darley (1838), with the Provost's House behind. The building was removed to Belfield in 1971.*

27 *Douglas Hyde (1860–1949), founder of the Gaelic League, graduated from the College with high honors in modern literature in 1884. From 1938 to 1945 he served as the first President of Ireland to be elected under the 1937 Constitution.*

28 *The Dublin University Hurley Club of 1880. The figure in the centre of the back row is J.H. Bernard, destined to become a Fellow (1884), Archbishop of Dublin (1915), and Provost from 1919 to 1927.*

29 *Maeve Kyle (106) winning the women's 100 yards at the College Races. Work in progress on the Berkeley Library (in background) indicates a date in 1965.*

30 *The tercentenary procession en route for St Patrick's Cathedral.*

31 *The first committee of the Elizabethan Society, 1905–06. From left, standing: L. Craig, R. Fitzgerald, O. Purser, S. Auchinleck. Seated: B. Stafford, Mrs Finegan, E. Tuckey, M. Weir Johnston, E. Maxwell, I. Shegog.*

32 *Spring sunshine in the College Park.*

33 *The Campanile in building* c.*1855. Rotten Row, later replaced by the Graduates' Memorial Building, is to the left.*

34 *A view of Botany Bay (completed in 1817), with tennis courts (first installed in 1955).*

35 *The Graduates' Memorial Building, by Sir Thomas Drew (1902). In foreground,* Reclining Connected Forms *(1969), by Henry Moore.*

36 *Riotous students under attack by the police. The disorders occurred on the occasion of the state entry of the new viceroy, Lord Eglinton and Winton, in March 1858.*

CHAPTER 12

Adjustment and survival 1919–1952

The task of selecting a successor to Mahaffy fell on Andrew Bonar Law, but there was no good candidate among the Senior Fellows, and the only possible choice among the Juniors was Professor Joly, who had recently been elected to a fellowship. Joly, however, did not command the necessary support within College, so, on advice from James Campbell and the Chancellor (Lord Iveagh), Law turned to John Henry Bernard. Bernard had resigned his fellowship seventeen years before to become dean of St Patrick's, and was now Archbishop of Dublin. His exceptional abilities as a scholar and administrator were not in doubt, but there was no great elation in College at his appointment. Many of his predecessors had gone out to bishoprics, but it was felt that there was something indecorous about a move in the opposite direction, and he was suspected (probably unjustly) of mercenary motives. His previous popularity had evaporated, and now, if he was not feared, he was certainly not well liked.[1]

The new Provost had to endure some offensive and unruly behaviour from undergraduates during his first day of official duties, which happened to be Trinity Monday (12 June 1919). When he was reading out the names of the new Scholars from the steps of the Public Theatre, some students threw pennies at his feet to emphasise his supposed desire for financial betterment, and the formal dinner in Hall that evening was marred by rowdiness. The previous Saturday Alcock and Brown had completed the first transatlantic flight when they landed their plane in a bog just south of Clifden, County Galway. When these heroes of the hour came up to Dublin by train on the Monday, an impromptu student reception committee managed to intercept Alcock, and made a late and boisterous entrance to the Dining Hall with the aviator in their midst. Reports that Bernard reacted coldly at first are plausible enough — the noisy irruption must have been very disconcerting — but he soon recovered sufficient poise to invite Alcock to sit by him at High Table and partake of a glass of wine.

Bernard at once set his mind to dealing with the serious financial problems besetting the College. The severe decline in fee income during the war years had combined with post-war inflation to produce a financial crisis, and help was sought from Whitehall. The British government responded by setting up a commission chaired by Sir Archibald Geikie. Geikie was well disposed to the College, and three of the other four members were Trinity graduates. The upshot of this final Royal Commission was a favourable report whose main recommendations were for an all-round increase in salaries and more lavish provision for science. The sums needed were stated to be a capital grant of £113,000, and an annual grant of £49,000 — the College's total annual income at the time being under £100,000.

A settlement on such a generous scale would have taken the College out of all its difficulties, but as the political scene changed, payment of the annual grant was deferred and in the end was not implemented.

Persistent lobbying by the Provost secured about half the capital sum in non-recurrent British Treasury grants between 1919 and 1923, but this money served only to make up the losses of the war years. The Government of Ireland Bill, enacted in December 1920, included a guarantee of an annual grant of £30,000 payable by the new government in Southern Ireland, but this legislation never took effect, being superseded a year later by the Treaty negotiated in London by Sinn Féin. Arthur Griffith, the leader of the Sinn Féin delegation, had told Bernard that he had no objection to the grant guarantee being carried over explicitly into the terms of the Treaty, but in the event this did not happen, and Griffith was dead by the time that negotiation was resumed between Trinity and the government of the Irish Free State in May 1923.

Not surprisingly, the attitude of the new Department of Finance was far less accommodating than that of Whitehall. The College was now a petitioner in a poor country that was trying to repair the ravages of a disastrous civil war. It also had to face the fact that it was widely regarded as the citadel of a discredited and outmoded unionism. All that could be secured after some tough bargaining was a non-recurrent grant of £5,000. This was also soon followed by a reasonable settlement of liabilities arising out of the compulsory reacquisition of College lands then in progress. The government made over a balance of £76,000 from the accounts of the public trustee, and agreed to pay an annual grant of £3,000 (which it still does) in final settlement of all land purchase claims. By the end of 1923, the immediate crisis was over, with inflation easing and rents and investments beginning to show a better return. By tight management and some modest increases in the scale of fees, the College managed to get through the inter-war years and the subsequent Emergency without running into debt, and without troubling the government with any more requests for assistance.

Within days of the signing of the Treaty, the Board went on record in support of the terms of settlement, affirming that 'the true interests of Trinity College can only be furthered by Irish peace', and urging Trinity men to play 'an active and sympathetic part in the building up of happier conditions in Ireland'. This was a magnanimous resolution, but it was not unanimous, dissent being recorded by the arch-conservatives T. T. Gray and G. L. Cathcart, and by the moderate and apolitical figure of H. H. Dixon, representing the non-Fellow Professors. The creation of the Free State left the southern Protestants as a very small minority in a partitioned country. They felt a strong sense of betrayal, and some apprehension that they might suffer repression and rejection in a predominantly Catholic society. The opponents of the motion were voicing this understandable if overemotional reaction, but its supporters were also sincere in their profession of loyalty to the new regime. Trinity's representatives in the Dáil included two Fellows who were destined for the provostship, E. H. Alton and W. E. Thrift, and their contributions to parliamentary debate and committee work gave clear proof of good faith. In the event, the College had no reason to complain of any government interference; it kept a low profile and was left severely alone by officialdom. So far as the Protestant community was concerned, no very heavy hand was laid on their liberties. They lost the right to divorce — not a practical issue for most of them — and they had to live under an increasingly rigorous censorship of films and publications, which, if somewhat irksome, at least provided a convenient target for liberal invective.

The new state was a self-governing dominion, but there were ambiguities in this status, and difficulties arose when loyalties came to be expressed on public occasions. What flag was to be flown, what toast drunk, what anthem sung? The compromise was soon worked out of flying the tricolour at one end of the West Front, the Union Jack at the other, and the College flag in the middle. This was a fair reflection of college sentiment, but when de Valera came to power in the 1930s the Union Jack was recognised to be a needless provocation, and it was no longer flown after the royal jubilee in 1935. A parallel custom prevailed for a time at

College dinners, when those present were asked to rise and raise their glasses to 'the King' followed by 'Ireland'. The transition to 'Ireland' only was made in 1946. It could be argued that 'God save the King' was the anthem of the Commonwealth as well as Britain, and on this basis it continued to be played at College Races and Commencements in the inter-war period, but wartime neutrality made this custom seem inappropriate, and it was quietly dropped. These issues aroused angry passions at the time, but in retrospect the College can be seen to have adopted a reasonably balanced attitude to the claims of tradition and the realities of the day.

In 1905 Arthur Aston Luce obtained his BA as an extern student in the pass course (though he went on to take a supplemental moderatorship), and when he gained fellowship in 1912 (in classics and philosophy), a candid colleague told him that his election would mark the end of recruitment by open examination.[2] The system had been under criticism for some considerable time. Its most serious defect was its limitation to mathematics, classics, Hebrew, philosophy, and physics. These traditional subjects no longer matched the expanded range of a curriculum in which history, modern literature, economics, and natural science had become popular options. Consequently, there was a severe shortage of Fellows qualified to teach these newer subjects even at pass level. There was the theoretical objection (which could be supported by examples) that a system which favoured a good examinee did not necessarily produce a good scholar, or even an outstanding teacher. Finally, there was a widespread perception, not altogether erroneous, that the strain of fierce and prolonged competition over a number of years — in 1902 and 1903 Goligher and Fraser respectively succeeded at their seventh attempt — was leading to intellectual 'burn-out'. The Fry Commission had underlined the need for change, but internal agreement was hard to secure, and the only pre-war modification was a provision in the King's Letter of 1911 enpowering the Board to elect professors to Fellowship without examination, provided the assent of a majority of Fellows was secured. This was an innovation that was to prove of considerable significance in the longer term.

A further window for change opened up when the examination was suspended from 1916 to 1919, and as a result the queue of candidates with a vested interest in the existing system disappeared. Mahaffy pressed the Fellows to take advantage of this opportunity and, when peace returned, the College was ready to accept an ordinance for a major reform. The

Board was given discretion to announce an election whenever it deemed fit, and not necessarily every year. The principle of open competition was retained, but now it became a competition in one particular subject specified in advance. If the Board thought there was not sufficient expertise in the College to examine in the chosen subject, it had the power to appoint external examiners. It could also vary the mode of examination to suit each case. In subsequent competitions the candidates were asked to submit their published or unpublished work, to attend for interview, and (occasionally) to take a written or *viva voce* examination. Their ability to communicate was tested by asking them to deliver a prelection on a subject of their choice. Under this system, evidence of ability to do original work soon became the most important criterion.

An earlier ordinance of 1916 allowed the Board to invite men with a distinguished record of research and publication to accept election without undergoing any competition, and this was used to secure the physicist E. T. S. Walton in 1934 and the pathologist R. A. Q. O'Meara in 1941. (Walton, a Trinity graduate, was awarded the Nobel Prize for Physics in 1951.) Otherwise, in the interwar years, the Board used its new and flexible powers to strengthen subjects where there was an obvious academic need or where there were local candidates of promise. The resultant broadening of expertise among the Fellows may be judged from the fact that from 1920 to 1939 fourteen Fellows were elected in subject competitions, four in mathematics, three in classics, and one each in biochemistry, Spanish, chemistry, physics, economics, medicine, and history. In the last subject, T. W. Moody, a graduate of London, made history by becoming the first Fellow who was not a graduate of Oxford, Cambridge or Dublin.

The outbreak of World War II meant that no competitions were held from 1940 to 1943. By then the number of Fellows had fallen to twenty-two, well below the statutory minimum of twenty-seven, and five of them were away on war work. There was an acute shortage of staff in some departments and a general shortage of tutors. The Board therefore decided to make three elections in 1944, one in the designated field of law (where J. A. Coutts was elected) and two more generally from among the existing lecturers. Published or unpublished work was to be the main criterion, but general usefulness to the College was also to count. It was specified that the successful candidates must accept tutorship, and this competition resulted in the election of G. F. Mitchell in geology and E. G. Quin in Irish and philology.

In the 1920s and '30s subject competitions resulted in some very good external appointments (Herbert Parke and Donald Wormell in classics, William Ditchburn in physics, and Theo Moody in history), but it was also clear that they had not infrequently been mounted with a favourite local son in mind. With a growing staff, and with funds for outside recruitment in short supply, it was a logical step to forego the luxury of contending candidates. In 1949 the College decided, in effect, to use election to fellowship as a way of rewarding and advancing its own most promising young lecturers. An ordinance gave the Board power to invite such candidates to submit their work to expert assessment, and to elect them to fellowship if they were pronounced to be of suitable calibre. This new method of recruiting non-professorial Fellows rapidly superseded the subject competition. Open competitions were held in history in 1951, leading to the election of F. S. L. Lyons, and in mathematics in 1953 (A. C. Allen), but otherwise all ordinary elections to fellowship in the second half of the century have been conducted under the 1949 ordinance.

John Henry Bernard died during the long vacation of 1927, and his successor, Edward John Gwynn (1868–1941), was admitted to office at the start of the following Michaelmas term. Gwynn was the son of the Reverend John Gwynn, who had been a Fellow from 1853 to 1864 and later a very distinguished Regius Professor of Divinity. Though not himself in holy orders, Edward was a quintessential Trinity man from a family rivalled only by those of Stokes and Purser in its contribution to the College.[3] He gained fellowship in 1893, and in his younger days was a noted advocate of constitutional reform. At the same time he proved a zealous and effective defender of Trinity's independence. His eminence as a Celtic scholar made him a good choice to head the College under the new regime, and he was the first Provost to be appointed by an Irish government (which had inherited the British Crown's prerogative in this matter). Until 1991 he was the only Provost to have received an honorary degree from the National University of Ireland, and he was also honoured by Durham, Glasgow, Wales and Oxford.[4] He presided for ten years with dignity and humanity until ill health forced him to retire in 1937.

Gwynn's retirement marks a suitable point at which to review the fortunes of the College since independence. According to F. S. L. Lyons, 'the twenties and thirties rank among the darkest periods of the College's history — it was poor, the buildings became steadily more dilapidated, and a great tradition of learning seemed destined for extinction'. Others describe the pleasures of student life in a 'very contented community' where one could 'play games, learn the art of politics in the College societies, take advantage of the first-rate theatrical fare which Dublin provided in those days, not to mention its myriad cinemas, have an occasional good steak at the Dolphin, do some work either in term or in the vacation as seemed most convenient, and above all talk, while walking round the squares or through the Wicklow mountains, or indoors over innumerable cups of tea — for alcohol was produced only for a birthday, an election to scholarship or society office or some similar occasion.'[5]

There are elements of truth in both pictures, though one is unduly pessimistic, and the other is suffused with the agreeable nostalgia that Trinity folk often feel for their *alma mater*.

The College was certainly much less affluent than it had been, but it lived within its means. It was able to offer improved salary scales to the junior staff, and in the twenty years from 1919 to 1939 the number of lecturers and assistants more than doubled, though the number of Fellows declined from thirty-one to twenty-six. Annual matriculations rose steadily, bringing the undergraduate population up from about a thousand to close on fifteen hundred by the end of the 1930s. Student rooms tended to become very shabby, and grounds and buildings maintenance slipped badly, but the major College societies were well supported and team games were played to a high standard.

In the development of College sport a major step had been taken soon after the war with the establishment of the Dublin University Central Athletic Committee. An ad hoc committee had been formed at the start of Hilary term 1919 to help the clubs resume their activities, and this committee asked the Board for financial support in the form of a levy of £1 per student. The Board would not agree to this, but took the helpful step of adding three Fellows to the existing committee — in effect recognising it as the central controlling body for sporting activities. The Board's nominees were R. M. Gwynn, H. Thrift, and W. E. Thrift, and the enlarged committee was instructed to 'reconstitute the athletic clubs, to take charge of the Pavilion, and to report to the Board'. The committee devised a constitution with student representation on the basis of four representatives each from the cricket, football, boat, and hockey clubs, and two from each of the other clubs. The Board had stipulated that one of its nominees should be chairman, and 'Willy' Thrift was elected at the first meeting. He continued as chairman of DUCAC until his appointment as Provost in 1937. His brother Harry, who succeeded him as chairman, had been a champion sprinter and a rugby international, and is mentioned in *Ulysses* as a competitor in a cycle race in College Park on Bloomsday (16 June 1904).[6] R. M. Gwynn had played cricket for Ireland.

DUCAC's first tasks were to renovate the Pavilion, to restore the playing fields, and to tackle the problem of finance. The Board gave initial grants totalling £420, and a central fund was instituted into which the clubs were to pay their receipts from gates and subscriptions, and from which they could claim certain team expenses. Otherwise, they were left free to manage their own affairs. DUCAC took a useful initiative in setting up a scheme of Pavilion membership, which the Board ruled should be open to women as well as men. The scheme proved very popular, and, at a guinea a head, brought in close on £400 in its first year. The formation of the TCD Association in 1928 was in part inspired by its success, and the distinctive colours of the Trinity tie and scarf were based on a design produced by the Pavilion members' committee in 1925. The programme of sporting and social events known as 'Trinity Week' was revived in 1920, and in the same year a wing was added to the north side of the Pavilion.

This was a good start, but at a time of rapidly rising numbers and costs DUCAC soon found that it could not meet all its commitments, which included the wages of the grounds staff and the provision of equipment. In June 1920 the Board accepted the case for an annual grant of £1,000, and this had to be further increased in 1924 when the Board agreed to share wages and machinery costs on a 50/50 basis, and to take over responsibility for pensions. The quid pro quo was DUCAC's agreement to the appointment of a College official, Captain J. H. Shaw, as its treasurer, but this turned out very much to DUCAC's advantage, for 'Jimmy' Shaw gave thirty-five years' efficient and dedicated service in this central administrative role in College sport.

The most unhealthy aspect of the College's situation was its growing isolation from the main currents of national life. While UCD was making significant contributions, TCD retreated into its shell, and let events pass it by. In this it was reflecting the ghetto mentality that was tending to envelop the Protestant community in the South. It has been well said that the College in the centre of Dublin took on 'a striking resemblance in social terms to the Big Houses of the countryside — each symbolising a ruling caste in the aftermath of its power'.[7]

Fortunately, however, the College's social and political isolation did not mean that it became intellectually moribund. There was considerable innovation in the range of subjects and courses offered, with the College providing systematic teaching in geography, commerce, social studies, and public administration for the first time. All these courses had the potential, later realised, for major development, and the evening classes in public administration proved very popular with civil servants, and went some way towards breaking down barriers.[8]

Most departments continued to teach their honor students to a high level, though standards were declining in the pass course. The Fellows produced some efficient administrators, notably M.W.J. Fry as Senior Lecturer (1927–43) and W.A. Goligher as Registrar (1930–37), but as a group they fell far short of the brilliance of their Victorian and Edwardian predecessors. Professors of real distinction were rare, but men like Edmond Curtis and Alison Phillips in history, Henry Stewart Macran in philosophy, Henry Dixon in botany, and Brontë Gatenby in zoology had a more than local reputation.

When Gwynn resigned the provostship in April 1937, the Junior Fellows invited the non-Fellow Professors to join them in nominating a successor. The name of William Edward Thrift (1870-1942), then Vice-Provost, was put to the meeting and adopted *nem. con.*, and the government duly appointed him. Of English birth, Thrift had made Dublin his home, and had served the College conscientiously but without special distinction as a Fellow and Professor of Physics. Perhaps his most remarkable achievement was to gain appointment as Deputy Speaker of the Dáil (where he represented the University from 1922 to 1937) — a well-deserved tribute to his fair-mindedness and skill as a committee-man. Thrift possessed a quick and incisive mind and considerable financial acumen, but he was not a particularly happy choice as Provost. He lacked leadership quality, and during his short term of office — he died on 23 April 1942 — power tended to pass into the hands of his Vice-Provost, William Alexander Goligher, a tough and abrasive northerner from Derry.

The meeting of senior staff, convened after Thrift's death, was faced with a choice between two candidates only, a somewhat elderly humanist and a comparatively junior scientist. Ernest Henry Alton (1873–1952) had held the chair of Latin since 1927 and was now Vice-Provost. His expertise as a textual critic of Ovid was widely known and respected among classical scholars, but he had never brought his work to full fruition in a major publication. Kenneth Claude Bailey was Alton's junior by twenty-three years. He had put to use his classical training in a commentary on the Elder Pliny's account of chemical subjects, and, as Professor of Physical Chemistry since 1935, had gone on to establish a solid reputation by research and publication in the field of chemical reactions. He was also well known in College as a hard-working and efficient Junior Dean. Seniority, however, triumphed: Alton secured a handsome majority in the ballot, and his nomination was duly accepted by de Valera's government.

Alton was no stranger to public life, having served continuously as one of

Trinity's four representatives in the Dáil from 1922 to 1937. When this representation was terminated under de Valera's 1937 Constitution, he was returned as one of the University's three representatives in the new Senate. His friendliness and good nature made him an effective presenter of minority views in the new corridors of power, and helped to inform and conciliate opinion outside the walls. Inside College, his warm and outgoing personality endeared him to his colleagues, as did the aura of genial inconsequence that often hung over his activities. As Provost he devoted much of his leisure time to productive work on the archives, but it was his destiny to elucidate rather than make College history. For the first three years of his tenure, the war shackled all progress, and then a serious illness put him out of action for six months (in the summer of 1947) and sapped his ability to take major initiatives. On entering office, he did well to appoint Bailey as Registrar, and the day-to-day running of the College largely devolved into his capable hands. From 1946 on, his old friend A. A. Luce was Vice-Provost, and it was he who had to bear the brunt of the mounting agitation for constitutional reform.

World War II (1939–45) was not as traumatic a time for Trinity as the Great War. Ireland remained neutral, and the College was able to maintain its routine despite shortages of supplies and fuel. Four Fellows, two professors, and half-a-dozen lecturers took leave of absence for war work in Britain or further afield, and there was a small decline in student numbers, but no mass exodus. Over 1600 graduates and undergraduates joined the fighting forces on the Allied side. The percentage of those killed was mercifully far lower than in World War I (6.5% as against 15%), but Trinity men, and women too, lost their lives in Europe, North Africa, and the Far East.[9]

When air attacks on the British mainland intensified towards the end of 1940, German planes began to be heard over Dublin too, and in 1941 some bombs fell in Dun Laoghaire, Terenure and the North Strand area, causing damage and casualties. The threat to College, and especially to the Library, led to the establishment of a roster of volunteers to maintain a nightly watch on the buildings. The Junior Dean, K. C. Bailey, and G. F. Mitchell were active in leading this effort and giving instruction on how to tackle incendiaries. The College acquired a fire engine, and a large static water tank was constructed in the Fellows' Garden. The devastating blitz on Belfast on Easter Tuesday 1941, in which close on 750 people lost their lives, brought home the grim realities of the war.

To meet the threat of invasion, the government had called for volunteers for a Local Defence Force and a Local Security Force. Trinity had already provided a successor to the old OTC in the shape of a Volunteer Sluagh (Company) in the Irish Army, part of the Regiment of Pearse, formed in November 1935 under de Valera's administration. The regiment was a training corps for all the Irish university colleges, and one of the Fellows, a northern Presbyterian named James Bell, held a commission in it as a lieutenant.[10] Recruitment for the LDF in 1941 was on a different basis, and enough volunteers came forward within Trinity to form a separate Company, I Company in the 42nd (Dublin) Rifle Battalion. This company, which included lecturers, students and College employees, paraded in strength through the Front Square on Trinity Monday 1942, a muster reviewed by Provost Alton from a stand outside the Graduates Memorial Building. It was ready, if the need arose, to play an active part in the defence of the state.[11] Night patrol continued for some years, but the danger receded after the Allied invasion of Europe, and the fire engine was only once called into action, and that for a fire outside College.

The dreary watching and waiting of the war years ended with a riotous incident on 7 May 1945 when news of the unconditional surrender of Germany was received. The routine of night patrols had familiarised the students with ways of access to the roof spaces, and a group of them now made their way up to the central flagpole on the West Front, and began to hoist a miscellaneous array of flags, including the Union Jack, the Stars and Stripes, and the Hammer and Sickle, in honour of the victorious Allies. The Irish tricolour was also flown. A large crowd in College Green watched these antics benevolently at first, but feelings became more enflamed when a group of Ailtiri na hAiseirghe supporters arrived and staged an anti-Trinity demonstration, during which a Union Jack was burnt. This action roused anger among the students — about one in four at the time was from the North — and some of them responded by setting fire to an Irish flag in full view of the crowd below. Anti-Trinity feeling now boiled over, and the situation became so threatening that the Gardai felt obliged to clear the streets with baton charges. Meanwhile the College authorities had succeeded in securing the gates and getting all flags and students down and out of sight. For several successive nights the College community came under siege, with windows in Botany Bay broken by stone-throwing and rumours of shots fired into the grounds. But the crisis soon eased and no lasting damage was caused. The main casuality was the Junior Dean, J. M. Henry, who was removed from that office a month or two later. It was felt, with reason, that his handling of the situation had been less than adequate, but in extenuation it must be said that Henry was no disciplinarian. He was always more noted as a conversationalist than as a man of action, and had been a reluctant incumbent of the post.

The most significant event of Alton's provostship was the introduction of regular state support for the College in the form of an annual grant, first paid in the year 1947/48. Early in 1946 the College was in a position to make a good case that such support was urgently needed to bring its salary scales up to a competitive level and to cope with arrears of maintenance. But the Board was reluctant to approach the government; some of the older members remembered how the Geikie recommendations had failed to materialise, and feared another rebuff, while others were apprehensive about the strings that might be attached to any subvention. Meanwhile, one of the Junior Fellows, A. J. McConnell, was informed by his friend Monsignor Browne, then President of University College, Galway, that the government had asked the colleges of the National University to prepare a statement of financial needs with a view to a general and substantial increase in their grants. No such request had gone to Trinity, which was then regarded by the civil service as a private institution. With Browne's permission, McConnell reported the matter to a meeting of the Junior Fellows, who decided that the issue must be forced, and sent an urgent resolution to the Board to this effect. Reflecting that 'if anything goes wrong, we'll know who to blame', the Board agreed to act in the desired way.[12] A well-documented request for assistance was forwarded to the government, and an interview sought with the Taoiseach.

On 20 February 1947 the Provost and Registrar were received by Eamon de Valera and his Minister for Finance, Frank Aiken, and the following day word came through that the government had agreed to meet the College's request in full, and that the sum of £35,000 would be included in the Exchequer estimates for 1947/48. The grant was given for 'general purposes' and without any conditions, apart from a personal request by de Valera that the money should not be used to raise salary scales above those current in the National University or to augment emoluments that were already above the norm. Eamon de Valera and his ministers deserve much credit for this generous treatment of the College. They lived up to the spirit of the guarantees embodied in the 1916 Proclamation, and opened the way for Trinity to come out of its shell and move towards full integration in the country's system of higher education.

This happy augury of external reconciliation came at a time when internal dissensions were building towards a bitter rift between Senior and Junior Fellows. The course of the quarrel has been chronicled in detail by two who were intimately involved, and only a summary of the main factors and events will be given here.[13] There was a serious 'generation gap' between seniors and juniors — in June 1951 the average age of the former was seventy-three while of the latter only one had even turned fifty — and with this went fundamental divergences of attitude and expectation. One side tended to be conservative, authoritarian, and complacently content with Trinity's traditional ways and practices. The other side was headed by reformers inspired by democratic principles and pressing hard for a more representative governing body (which would naturally include themselves). It was in many ways a typical struggle for power, but there was also a real need to modernise the College in a rapidly changing world.

The frustration of the juniors was exacerbated by the secrecy with which the Board conducted its business, and also by shortcomings in two key administrative posts, which by tradition were held by Senior Fellows and so by amateurs doing jobs that increasingly demanded professionalism. The Bursar, Harry Thrift, was responsible for the finances of the College and also for the upkeep of its grounds and buildings. In the former sphere he lacked foresight, and in the latter he was oversensitive to criticism. The office of Senior Tutor had been revived to help the tutors, who were now burdened with pre-matriculation correspondence from five continents, and R. M. Gwynn had been put in charge. In a College short of secretaries and ill-provided with telephones, his office did in fact furnish useful assistance in tutorial chores, and was better run than it appeared on the surface. But the real need was for a professionally organised admissions office, and it is not surprising that a scholarly septuagenarian with an ear-trumpet did not satisfy everyone.

The battle was first waged on administrative matters, when a request from the Junior Fellows for a 'House Committee' was turned down by the Board, and the tutors' demand for more secretarial assistance was conceded grudgingly and only partially. Labouring under an acute sense of grievance, the Junior Fellows then brought the constitutional issue to the fore. By the end of Trinity term 1951 they had secured widespread agreement that 'a more representative Board, consisting mainly of elected members' was necessary for the welfare of the College, and a resolution to this effect, signed by the great majority of the academic staff, was forwarded to the Board. In the following Michaelmas term, the Board asked the Junior Fellow representatives to elaborate on the reasons for the discontent. While this was being done, the Inter-Party government, which had not treated the College's financial problems with much sympathy, fell from office, and Fianna Fáil returned to power.

A truce was called while a statement on financial needs was prepared for the new government. It is a pleasure to be able to record that Alton's last hours were cheered by the good news of a substantial increase in the annual grant, which de Valera conveyed to him a few days before his death (on 18 February 1952). An obituary in the College Record (*Trinity*) summed up his personality and the deep sense of loss felt at his passing: 'He was tolerant of opposition, rarely ruffled in debate, and at all times he was considerate for the feelings and interests of others. We repaid him with loyalty and love. Greater Provosts there have been, but none more loved.'[14]

The constitutional conflict reached its climax early in the provostship of his successor, Dr A. J. McConnell, so it will be convenient to describe the outcome here rather than in the next chapter. Voting strength on the Board was now very evenly balanced since Sir Robert Tate had died shortly before Alton, and one of the leading reformers, Herbert William Parke, had been co-opted to senior fellowship in his place. The reformers could count on five votes, one from the Provost, one from Parke, one from Duncan (who had been elected Registrar in place of McConnell), and two from the Junior Fellows' representatives (Wormell and Webb). Arrayed against them were the five pre-1920 Fellows (Gwynn, Thrift, Luce, Johnston and Godfrey), who were rigidly opposed to any alteration in the constitution of the Board and the status of senior fellowship.

Two crucial resolutions were due to be put to the vote on 24 May, one imposing an age limit of seventy-two for Board members, and the other proposing an increase in Junior Fellow representation from two to four. If carried, these resolutions would have had the effect of tilting the balance of power away from the conservatives, but the outcome was uncertain since it was not clear how the remaining senior Fellow (W. R. Fearon) and the two Professors' representatives (L. B. Smyth and D. S. Torrens) would vote. A few days before the meeting, Smyth had been told that was terminally ill, and he did not attend. Torrens voted for the motions, but Fearon voted against, so the voting was equal, and consequently the resolutions failed to pass.

An unforeseen solution of the impasse became apparent within a few weeks, when the Provost tabled his nominations for the annual offices. Since 1911 the offices of Bursar, Senior Lecturer and Registrar had been open to Junior Fellows, but not more than one of them (usually the registrarship) had been so held at any given time. By the simple expedient of nominating Junior Fellows to all three offices, McConnell could open the way for two more reformers to join the Board, and this he duly did. A number of the Junior Fellows thought that this calculated breach with tradition was too extreme a measure, and there was a strong sense of grievance among the Seniors at the coming loss of their perquisites, but the only course open to the opposition was to challenge the nominations at the Board table. This happened on 28 June when the Seniors proposed their own 'no-change' team.

The voting followed the same pattern as in May, but this time there was no deadlock since, in the matter of nominations, the Provost had a casting vote. So the so-called 'palace revolution' went through, and the long-continued dominance of the Senior Fellows in the administration of the College was brought to a decisive end. No statutory change in the constitution was needed, and none was implemented until 1958, a fact that may throw some light on the basic motivation of the reform party. The convention of having Senior Fellows in the major annual offices was simply replaced by the opposite convention of having Juniors. With Duncan as Bursar in place of Thrift, Wormell as Senior Lecturer in place of Godfrey, and Mitchell as Registrar, the Provost was in a position to institute and carry through a major programme of reform.

Notes

1. McDowell and Webb give a full and penetrating account of his character and its development, *History*, 307f and 424f. They also record valuable eye-witness evidence on the Alcock incident.
2. Three more candidates were elected under the annual examination system: Joseph Johnston in 1913, James Maxwell Henry in 1914, and Francis La Touche Godfrey in 1915.
3. Gwynn took the chair at the meeting of graduates on 11 June 1928, at which the Trinity College (Dublin) Association was formed, and remained one of its firmest supporters. Bailey (*History*, 200) characterises him as 'a man of clear and unhurried judgment'; McDowell and Webb (*History*, 441) describe him as 'a master of the felicitous phrase, based often on understatement, which made him an excellent, and mercifully brief, after-dinner speaker'.
4. Provost Watts received an honorary DSc on 9 May 1991.
5. F. S. L. Lyons in F. MacManus (ed.), *The Years of the Great Test* 1926-39, 98; McDowell and Webb, *History*, 445.
6. A recent proposal to read 'Shrift' is 'yet one more example of Joycean Scholars ignoring the local context of Dublin which Joyce knew so well.' (Senator David Norris, in a personal communication to the writer).
7. Terence Brown, *Ireland, A Social and Cultural History*, 115.
8. Newly instituted were: a moderatorship in economics and political science (1932); a School of Commerce in which the qualification of BA, BComm could be obtained (1925); Diploma courses in religious knowledge (for women: 1919), geography (1930), The history of European painting (1934), social studies (1934), biblical studies (1936), public administration (1941).
9. Lists were published in the 1950 and 1955 editions of the *Register of the Alumni of Trinity College Dublin* (compiled for the TCD Association).
10. Bell was struck down in his prime by a fatal illness and died early in 1941.
11. Professor E. Fahy was company leader; S. Victor Crawford was assistant leader, and the platoon leaders were J. F. Murtagh, B. E. Booth, G. H. McCutcheon, and F. W. Pierce (a Lecturer in Spanish). Mr Basil Booth kindly supplied me with this and other information about I Company and the Regiment.
12. This account is based on information given by A. J. McConnell in a radio interview on RTE on 9 October 1989.
13. See McDowell and Webb, *History*, 480–497.
14. From an obituary notice by A. A. Luce in *Trinity* 4, 1952, 31.

CHAPTER 13

Change from within: modernisation and reform 1952–1967

In the four decades from 1952 to 1992 Trinity College probably saw more changes than in the previous three and a half centuries. A comparison between the College's vital statistics at the beginning and end of the period will indicate the scale of the transformation. The rest of the chapter will be devoted to a survey of the first fifteen years of A. J. McConnell's provostship down to the day in April 1967 when Donogh O'Malley announced his scheme for a 'merger' between Trinity and University College, Dublin. That date marks a significant watershed in the affairs of the College. Before it, Trinity had complete freedom to reform and modernise itself from within; after it, the pace and shape of development came to depend more and more on the scope and scale of government planning and provision for higher education.

By 1990/91 Trinity was sustaining a range and complexity of activity that makes the College of 1951/52 seem charmingly small, delightfully uncomplicated, and quaintly archaic. Then the full-time academic staff comprised 7 Senior Fellows, 22 Junior Fellows, 26 non-Fellow Professors, and 68 Lecturers and Assistants. The administration of the College was still entirely in the hands of the Senior Fellows, with full-time 'professionals' at middle management level only. There was no post of Treasurer or Secretary. The Professor of Ancient History presided over the Library, whose day-to-day running was in the hands of an Assistant Librarian and a staff of nine. Harry Thrift, as Bursar, still signed all cheques drawn on College accounts. The Accountant, C. B. Kennedy, took in the fees. Captain J. H. Shaw, as secretary of the lecture committee, could use the recently installed internal telephone system, but it was not so long since the beating of Senior Lecturer Matty Fry's stick on the floor overhead had summoned him to render clerical assistance. The College's panel of secretaries had grown to ten.

In 1990/91 there were still 7 Senior Fellows (as required by statute), but the 1991 elections increased the list of Junior Fellows to 153. There were 400 full-time academic staff (Fellows included), of whom 62 were Tutors. A professionally qualified Librarian administered a vastly expanded and computerised library complex with the aid of a Calendar-listed staff of over a hundred. In addition to a Treasurer and a Secretary, there was a Buildings Officer, a Director of Accommodation and Catering Services, a Finance Officer, an Academic Secretary, and a Staff Secretary, all managing important areas with staffs to match. The secretarial (and related) staff of the College numbered 159.

In 1951/52 the teaching departments, professional and non-professional, were organised in twenty schools, each with its own school committee. In the late 1960s this organisation was subsumed under a faculty structure with Deans heading six main subject areas: Arts (Humanities); Arts (Letters); Business, Economic and Social Studies; Engineering and Systems Sciences; Health Sciences; and Science (including Mathematics). By 1990/91 the Faculty Deans had come to play a major part in the evolution of academic policy. All the Schools of forty years before (with the sole exception of Agriculture) still found a place in the new structure, but the University had also instituted instruction in many new subjects, and had greatly extended teaching in some formerly marginal disciplines. The list of new departments included history of art, psychology, drama and theatre studies, language and communication studies, business studies, sociology, mechanical and manufacturing engineering, microelectronics and electrical engineering, computer science, statistics,[1] clinical speech and language studies, dental science, occupational therapy, community health, pharmacology and therapeutics, psychiatry, physiotherapy, genetics, and pharmacy.

The great increase in staff numbers, not to mention the many new chairs, was partly related to this major expansion in the scope of the University's teaching, but even more to the relentless pressure of ever-increasing student numbers over the previous three decades. An analysis of the figures for full-time students (including those registered for higher degrees) shows that in 1949 these totalled 2236 (of whom 712, or 32%, were women). In 1950 the immediate post-war bulge reached its peak with a total of 2351. Then there was a drop each year until 1956 — years of economic stagnation in Ireland — when the full-time student population had declined to 1651 (with women holding at 33%). The 1956 figure was much the same as that for 1939 when the College had 1543 students (women 23%).[2]

Then began the longest and largest expansion in the College's history. It is a remarkable fact that from 1957 to 1990 the population curve rose in every year but four. This happened despite a sharp rise in admission standards, particularly in the more popular schools. In 1964 there was a statistically insignificant drop of 78, but the upward march was then resumed for the rest of the decade until 1970 when there were over 4000 students in the College. The next three years saw small fluctuations just below this peak — 3915, 3944 and 3879 are the figures. This temporary plateau was partly due to the raising of the minimum matriculation standard (to 'good' marks in three subjects) with effect from 1969–70, and partly to the limiting of the non-Irish intake to ten per cent.

From 1974 onwards, the admission figures surged continuously upwards, sometimes by as much as 400 in one year, until in 1990/91 the grand total of registered students (7620 full-time and 1628 part-time) stood at 9248. Just over half of the full-time students were women. Until the mid-1980s full-time male students always outnumbered female, but it has been the other way round since 1986.

Such sustained growth over thirty-three years finds no parallel in the previous history of the College. In the post-war epoch, increasing demand for university places was a worldwide phenomenon, and in Ireland the pressure was further augmented by a number of special factors: the development of free second-level education, the introduction of a third-level grants scheme, population growth in the 1970s, the general increase in prosperity brought on by membership of the European Community, and enhanced career opportunities for women.

Analysis of the home residence of full-time students since 1939 reveals major changes in the composition of the student body. In 1939, 1017 students (66%) came from the Republic, 379 (25%) from Northern Ireland, 81 (5%) from Britain, and 66 (4%) from elsewhere. Twenty years later the proportions were markedly different: 981 (43%) from the Republic, 320 (14%) from the North, 600 (26%) from Britain, and 365 (17%) from other countries. The number of students from outside the British Isles peaked at 415 (16%) in 1961, and then fluctuated round a mean of 300. In 1990 it stood at 387, which was only just over 5 per cent of the total. By contrast, the number of Southern Irish students then stood at 6417 (90%), of whom somewhat more than half were living in Dublin city and county. The percentage of students from Britain remained high during the 1960s, reaching a peak of 34 per cent in 1963. Then it declined along an ever steeper gradient to a figure not much over 1 per cent. There was also a marked and much to be regretted decline in the proportion of students from Northern Ireland. The figures here peaked at 1023 (26%) in 1969, the year when the 'Troubles' started; they then fell away steadily in both absolute and relative terms to the 1990/91 figure of 255 (3%).

The centralised admissions scheme operating throughout the United Kingdom has made it easy for school-leavers in Northern Ireland to look outside Ireland for their university training. In the Republic in the early 1970s, the ending of the Catholic hierarchy's 'ban' brought a big influx of students from the South. This trend continued, helped by the institution of admission through the Central Admissions Office (CAO), which began in the academic year 1977/78. The CAO does not include the religious denomination of students in its statistics, and by 1970 Trinity had ceased to ask a question about this on its entry form, so it is no longer possible to give precise figures on this point. However, it will probably be not too far from the mark to suggest that the proportion of Catholic students in the College in 1991 was about 80 per cent. In 1950 it stood at 23 per cent, in 1960 at 29 per cent, and in 1970 at 34 per cent.

Until the 1950s Trinity remained very set in its ways, and it is a measure of its vitality as an organism that it managed to adapt successfully to a rapidly changing world under a structure of government and administration that was progressively modified and enlarged, but never fundamentally altered in its constitution. Until the 1930s, the great majority of the staff were Irish by nationality and graduates of the College. After the war the pool of choice widened, and many of those appointed were trained in other Irish or British universities. They brought in new ideas, and their influence was a significant factor in the accelerated pace of change. But the English had no monopoly in the reform movement. Irishmen Mitchell, Moody and Ryan were just as active and forward-looking as the Englishmen Wormell and Chubb and the Scotsman Howie.[3]

Nominations for Alton's successor were considered at a meeting of Fellows and Professors on 11 March 1952. The government had asked the College to submit three names, and when the voting concluded the mathematician Albert Joseph McConnell headed the list, with the classicist Herbert Parke second, and the biochemist William Fearon third. Eamon de Valera at once approved the College's first choice, and McConnell was duly admitted Provost a week later. A Presbyterian from Ballymena, he was the first 'dissenter' to hold the office. McConnell was much younger than either of his immediate predecessors, being only forty-eight at his appointment, and he presided for twenty-two years until his retirement in 1974.[4] This made his provostship the second longest, after Baldwin's, in Trinity's history.

McConnell took office as a reformer determined to curtail the influence of the Senior Fellows, and very conscious of the need to modernise College practice and administration. In this he could count on effective support from his new team of annual officers, with Junior Fellows Frank Mitchell and Donald Wormell in the key posts of Registrar and Senior Lecturer, his contemporary and fellow-northerner George Duncan as Bursar, and the scholarly Herbert Parke as Vice-Provost and Librarian. Convinced that it was high time to give up the policy of low profile, McConnell began to look for opportunities to bring Trinity more into the mainstream of Irish life. The fact that the College was now in receipt of an annual grant had opened the door to regular contact with the government, and through his personal friendship with de Valera — a friendship that arose from shared mathematical interests — McConnell was well placed to cultivate ministerial relationships at a time when Fianna Fáil had recently returned to power.[5] The Dining Hall now became the focus for a policy of more active and systematic entertainment of public figures, and good relations with the state were further promoted when President Seán T. O'Kelly accepted an honorary degree in 1956.

At his first Board meeting on 19 March 1952, the new Provost showed that he was in earnest in seeking practical ways to counteract Trinity's comparative isolation from Irish public life. He secured agreement that the Senior Tutor (R.M. Gwynn) should write to the particular local education authority whenever it was excluding students or would-be students of the College from the benefit of its grants. George Duncan had prepared a dossier on the matter and the issue was vigorously pursued by Frank Mitchell when he became Registrar the following July. He wrote to all local authorities requesting a copy of their current scheme of university awards. When Roscommon County Council, for example, replied that their scholarships were tenable at Galway and Maynooth, and, 'in the case of non-Catholic students, Dublin University', Mitchell wrote back quoting a clause from the Irish University Act of 1908 forbidding discrimination on religious grounds, and adding, pointedly enough: 'It would seem that the conditions of your scheme do introduce a religious qualification.' In the case of Louth, where Dublin University was excluded from the scope of the scheme by managerial practice, Mitchell wanted to know whether this was the result of a County Council decision and, if so, whether it could be reversed. This unexpected offensive by the College generated much local debate, and some hostile and bigoted remarks were reported from Council meetings, but eventually most of the local authorities came to see that they could not easily and decently maintain a sectarian policy in relation to public funds. In 1954 only fourteen of them offered scholarships tenable at Trinity. By 1960 the number had risen to nineteen, and by 1967 to twenty-five. In 1968 a more centralised scheme of grants under the control of the Minister for Education was brought in by legislation.

The College itself was faced with a somewhat similar problem in regard to the Divinity School. Formal notification of an increase in the government grant from £45,000 to £85,000 had been received in March 1952, and public money now formed a substantial part of the annual income. Clearly the College could not risk being accused of using such money for the support of the Church of Ireland. Accordingly, on the recommendation of the Finance Committee, the Board at the end of April agreed to establish a new and separate account to finance salaries in the Divinity School and in relation to the College Chapel. Stock to the nominal value of £140,000 was transferred from the College endowments, and it was stipulated that any annual surplus accruing on the account should be transferred to a Chapel maintenance fund.

These measures represented a firm grasping of two thorny issues. A substantial break with academic tradition was made in 1953 when revised regulations for the pass course came into effect. Freshmen were offered a wider choice of subjects, and were relieved of the necessity to take Latin unless they so wished. It was an inevitable consequence of this change that Latin soon ceased to be a compulsory subject for matriculation. The regulation requiring honor students to pass the Final Freshman examination ('Little-go') was also considerably modified. Such students were no longer required to take the whole examination, but to pass in two subjects only (not cognate with their honor course). This meant an end of compulsory logic, a custom as old as the College, and its dropping as a universal discipline was felt by many to be an impoverishment of the undergraduate course. Standards in the honor courses, however, were strengthened and further secured by the adoption of a system of external examiners for moderatorships.

On 7 May 1953 the Moyne Institute of Preventive Medicine was opened by the Marchioness of Normanby in the presence of the President, the Lord Mayor, and other distinguished visitors. This major addition to the College buildings was the gift of the Marchioness in memory of her father, Walter Edward Guinness, Baron Moyne, who was assassinated in Cairo in 1944 while serving as British Minister Resident. Lady Normanby had approached the College some years before with the offer of a memorial building, and the form and detailed planning of the Institute owed much to the drive and initiative of J.W. Bigger, then Professor of Bacteriology and Dean of the Medical School.[6] The site on the corner of College Park below the Pathology Building was allocated by the Board in 1949, and a leading Dublin architect, Desmond FitzGerald, was chosen by Miss Grania Guinness (as she then was) to design the building. The Board authorised her, Mr FitzGerald, and Professor Bigger to proceed with the project. Bigger was present at the laying of the foundation stone in the autumn of 1950, but did not live to see the building completed. The Department of Bacteriology, under his successor, Professor Stanley Stewart, moved out of the Pathology building to occupy one wing. The other was allocated to a new Department of Social Medicine (hygiene and nutrition), the first of its kind in Ireland, under Professor W.J.E. Jessop. The Y-shaped building was well adapted to its site, and made a quietly dignified addition to the ensemble of the East End. The full cost of the building (estimated at £50,000, but later rising to £85,000) was borne by Lady Normanby, while her brother, Lord Moyne, established a capital fund for its maintenance. Shortly before the opening, Lady Normanby was honoured by the degree of LLD, which was conferred on her by her uncle, Lord Iveagh, as Chancellor. The Provost praised her with her grandfather, the first Earl of Iveagh, as 'one of the two greatest private benefactors of the College'.

While the Moyne was coming into use at one side of the Park, the Engineering workshops on the other side were being extended with the aid of a grant of £4,000 from the TCD Educational Endowment Fund. The Endowment Fund had been set up by deed of trust dated 19 December 1927. Started by the initiative of a number of graduates headed by Sir Robert Woods, its object was to re-endow the College with sums of the order proposed by the abortive Royal Commission of 1920.[7] An initial target of £250,000 was set, but only a tenth of this sum had been raised by 1950, and when post-war inflation was taken into account, it became clear that the aim of a major re-endowment would never be realised. With T.C. Kingsmill Moore as chairman, D.A. Webb as treasurer, and J.V. Luce as secretary, the policy was altered in the early 1950s to allow for considerable annual spending on a range of projects, although the need to build up capital was also kept in mind. Wider powers of investment were soon felt to be necessary, and there was some doubt whether tax could be recovered on covenanted subscriptions. Since it was not possible to modify the original trust deed, a parallel fund, the Trinity Trust, with a more flexible deed, was established in 1955. It was intended that the Trust would continue the work of the Endowment Fund, and eventually replace it as the main source of funding. The new policy worked out well; graduates could see some return for their contributions, and as spending increased, so did the income. Building projects supported by the Trusts between 1955 and 1961 included the provision of three hard tennis courts in Botany Bay, a remarkably innovative reconstruction of the Anatomy Theatre masterminded by Professor Cecil Erskine,[8] the refurbishment of the Debating Hall in the Graduates Memorial Building, the insertion of a new floor in the Gymnasium, and the addition of a new wing to the Pavilion.

Since 1947 the College had been setting aside an annual sum of £10,000 for new building, and a decade later it was estimated that close on £400,000 had been allocated for work completed or under contract. This sum included over £100,000 received in benefactions, the major donation being that for the Moyne Institute. Extensive modernisation was carried out in ten departments, most of them in the science faculty. The most striking of these schemes were in geology (in the Museum Building), where horizontal and vertical partitioning produced badly needed new space for staff rooms and laboratories, and in the Chemistry Building, where a new wing, designed by the College architect, Ian Roberts, and built with the aid of a contribution from Imperial Chemical Industries, was opened in October 1958.[9] An extensive programme for the repair and restoration of the historic buildings was also put in hand with the aid of an annual government subvention of £10,000, first received in 1952. The programme was completed in 1967.

An elegant piece of renovation was carried out in the Magnetic Observatory in the Fellows' Garden, and the building was reopened as a Manuscript Room by the Taoiseach, Eamon De Valera, in Trinity term 1957. Twenty years before, acting in the same capacity, he had opened the 1937 Reading Room. The new facility remained in use through the 1960s until the site was requisitioned for a projected wing of the Arts Building. A new Manuscript Room was then created in the west pavilion of the Old Library, and the Observatory was donated to University College. It was dismantled in 1971 and removed stone by stone to the new site at Belfield, where it now stands as a 'garden temple' in a secluded corner of the grounds.

Student amenities were not neglected. In the first few months of McConnell's reign, the Dublin University Players were installed in a new theatre in No. 4. This was the scene of a memorable series of productions through the 1950s, and the nursery of some exceptionally talanted actors and producers.

Adaptation, extension, and new construction continued apace throughout the 1960s. In 1959 a start had been made on a programme for the modernisation of student rooms. The sets in No. 30 were converted to single 'bed-sits' which were then let fully furnished. This pilot scheme was so successful that it was extended to No. 28. The east range of Botany Bay was tackled on similar lines in the long vacation of 1961, and the north range a year later. The turn of the Front Square houses came in 1963–66.

A major extension to the Physics building, estimated to cost £50,000, was financed out of a science development fund which, under the effective chairmanship of Sir Hugh Beaver, had reached £100,000 by the beginning of 1960. The fund also paid for the renovation of a research laboratory in chemistry, and equipped a laboratory for the Engineering School in newly acquired accommodation in 21 and 22 Lincoln Place. Further space was gained for departmental accommodation with the purchase, on 22 November 1961, of 29–31 Lincoln Place, previously occupied by J.J. O'Hara and Company, which was used to provide a home for the new Department of Genetics. This was the start of a major reacquisition of perimeter properties which continued vigorously in the 1960s in Westland Row and Pearse Street.

In January 1960 stage one of the 'Catex scheme' was put in hand. The scheme was for an extensive reorganisation of the catering facilities in the area of the Dining Hall, and included the construction of new kitchens, and the horizontal partitioning of the old kitchen to give storage space below and a new hall above. It also involved the adaptation of the cellars below the old hall for a student buttery. The whole project was completed by the end of 1963, and the buttery opened as planned on 14 October in that year.

Development was not confined to the central site. Since 1957 DUCAC had been pressing for additional sports grounds, and its needs were well satisfied by the purchase, in October 1960, of a 34-acre lot at Santry Court in the 'green belt' between Ballymun and Dublin Airport. The land was acquired for £10,000, and 20 acres were allocated for athletic purposes, with the Board giving a grant of £1000 and undertaking to erect and maintain boundary fences. The rest of the development became the financial responsibility of DUCAC. Over the next three years a pavilion was built and seven pitches laid out, including Trinity's first Gaelic games pitch. The financing of such an ambitious project would have been beyond DUCAC's capacity to sustain but for the institution, in the academic year 1957/58, of a system of centralised support for clubs and societies through a capitation fee paid by all students. Rising numbers made revenue from this source buoyant, and DUCAC was able to arrange the necessary loans from the *cista communis* (interest free, and all duly repaid) through the standing committee that managed the capitation fund. The Board reserved the balance of the site for other development, and its main use to date has been as the location of a book repository annexe for the Library.

The completion of the Library Extension (now the Berkeley Library) was the main achievement of the decade, but there was also a significant addition to the science facilities in the shape of the Biochemistry building. This project, completed in 1967, owed much to the drive and vision of Brian Spencer, who became Professor of Biochemistry in December 1960. A grant of £119,000 was secured from the Wellcome Trust, and the balance of the £175,000 needed was made up from College funds.

From the spring of 1966, forward planning for the development of the College site received a significant contribution from an outside expert, Professor Myles Wright of the University of Liverpool, who had been employed by the state to advise on plans for greater Dublin. Myles Wright was appointed planning consultant to the College, and under his guidance the Site Development Committee soon agreed that the College might be made to accommodate 6,000 students. This decision set the scene for the expansion of the 1970s, with the new Arts and Social Sciences Building as the major project.

On 5 December 1956 the Board directed that, 'in order to permit the development of the School of Agriculture, the College take steps to acquire a farm of less than three hundred acres located not more than thirty-five miles from the College'. This somewhat cryptic decision was not unanimous. The Provost endorsed the proposal, and Frank Mitchell was an enthusiastic protagonist, but the Bursar and some of the Senior Fellows had doubts about the wisdom of deploying substantial resources in this way. Trinity did not then, or later, receive any state grant for agriculture, but the case for its more active involvement in the country's chief industry had a certain appeal, and the time seemed ripe.

The School of Agriculture dated back to 1906, but had never attracted more than a handful of students. Until 1912 practical instruction was given on a farm at Kells, County Meath, and, in conjunction with the College of Science technical training was centred in Glasnevin. When the College of Science was handed over to UCD in 1926, the arrangements continued much as before. After doing two years of basic science in Trinity, students of agriculture completed their course at the Albert College in Glasnevin under UCD auspices. In 1954 the United States government made a grant of nearly £2 million to the Irish government to found a research institute, and Seán Moylan, the Minister for Agriculture, invited the College to take part in its work. The Board was considering how best to respond to this invitation, which it welcomed, when, by a remarkable coincidence, the opportunity arose to acquire the property of Townley Hall.

The Townley Hall estate, situated on the north bank of the Boyne a few miles upstream from Drogheda, contained 500 acres of farmland and 350 acres of woodland. The house, built early in the nineteenth century, was a fine specimen of the work of Francis Johnston, architect of Dublin's General Post Office and St George's Church. There was a family link with the College in that Mrs Balfour, the last resident owner, was a daughter of the illustrious John Kells Ingram, a Fellow of Trinity from 1846 to 1899. She had long been a widow, and after her death in 1955 the estate passed to a distant cousin, David Crichton, who offered it to the College on favourable terms. At about the same time the last surviving member of the Kells Ingram family, Captain John Kells Ingram, died in South Africa, leaving the bulk of his estate to Trinity, and money from this bequest provided part of the purchase price.

The newly acquired property was renamed the Kells Ingram Farm.[10] The intention was to run it as a commercial undertaking which would generate a useful return on capital and would also provide Trinity students with a practical demonstration of efficient farm and forestry management. A Farm Management Committee was set up with Frank Mitchell as its chairman, and Patrick McHugh was appointed manager. Steps were also taken to turn the house, which was found to contain a valuable collection of books, into a suitable venue for study groups and conferences.

At the same time strenuous efforts were made to develop the School of Agriculture by the institution, in 1959/60, of a moderatorship course in agriculture leading to an honors BA after a four-year course centred in the College and on the Farm. There was considerable emphasis on agriculture economics, and the course was designed to run in tandem with the older 'professional' course, leading to the degree of Bachelor of Agriculture.

With the aid of a Board loan of £20,000, the Farm made a modest surplus in 1959/60, but a deficit the following year indicated a serious shortage of working capital. This was to some extent remedied when, in 1960, Mitchell managed to secure a grant of $112,500 from the Kellogg Foundation, of which $50,000 was allocated for management capital, $50,000 for the repair and rehabilitation of the house, and $12,500 for reconstruction of the estate roads. A project for an applied genetics unit at the Farm was also initiated with the installation of a cobalt irradiation source.

Unfortunately, a number of factors combined to dash the high hopes with which the whole imaginative scheme had been undertaken. The soil, on slate not limestone, was not rich enought to generate the profits needed. Dry rot was discovered in the house, and efforts to interest outside bodies in its use failed. The Department of Agriculture would give no indication of any intention to support Trinity's teaching in the subject, while the Agriculture Institute continued to develop its own centres, and made no effort to use the laboratory at Townley Hall. The total number of students went up from 22 in 1956 to 41 in 1961, but only about half-a-dozen were coming forward each year for the moderatorship course. The winding-down of the project began with a direction that no more honor students were to be enrolled after 1963/64. By the end of 1966 the Board was instructing the officers to examine opportunities for the realisation of its investment, and the sale of the Farm to the Department of Lands was completed in November 1968.

Early in McConnell's provostship, Dr Parke, the Librarian, informed the Board that storage space in the Old Library would run out in six to seven years' time. Given that the copyright privilege was likely to be renewed — legislation to this effect was passed in 1956 — the Board accepted that a major development of the Library was urgently needed. In the autumn of 1953 the Provost was able to tell graduates at the TCD Dining Club dinner in London that an extension comparable in scale to the existing building had been approved in principle. Such a building could not be provided out of the College's existing resources, and funding would have to be sought from trusts and individuals. At the same time the Provost was able to announce that Lord Iveagh as Chancellor fully supported the project, and that he and his daughters had opened the subscription list with a gift of £45,000, one-tenth of the estimated sum needed.

Progress over the next three years was slow, chiefly because the Librarian was exploring ways in which the National Library might become involved. Eamon de Valera was known to favour closer links between the two Libraries, and a project for joint expansion seemed to hold out hope of financial support from the government; but, with nothing definite emerging, Trinity decided to press ahead with its own plans. The text of an appeal to graduates was approved in the summer of 1957, and a project for a film, first suggested by a committee in London (of which R.E. McGuire, brother-in-law of the Provost, was a most active secretary) was put in hand. The first outdoor sequences were shot in a brilliantly fine Trinity Week, with indoor work scheduled for the autumn. The film, entitled 'Building for Books', turned out to be a great success, with the camerawork ably directed by Vincent Corcoran, and a lively and sensitive script written by R.B.D. French.[11] It won a certificate of commendation at the Cork Film Festival, and was later taken up for general release by the Rank Organisation. Cinema audiences all over the British Isles and further afield were given an impressive glimpse of Trinity and its great Library, and the film, when shown at graduate gatherings, had remarkable power to evoke happy memories and to open purse strings.

In mid-November 1957 the Board reorganised the Library Extension Committee, establishing an appeal section and a building section, and appointing J.V. Luce as Executive Officer. The appeal went public on 15 July 1958 at an evening reception in the Long Room. The Vice-Chancellor, Lord Rosse, as Chairman of the Extension Committee, addressed a distinguished gathering that included the copyright librarians from Britain and representatives of the Carnegie Trust. An approach to Irish banks, insurance companies, and industrial and commercial firms was organised through a subcommittee that included Trinity graduates prominent in Dublin business life, and a gratifying measure of support was forthcoming.[12] A similar campaign was mounted in Britain through a working group that R.E. McGuire had organised in London.

The plan was to seek contributions first from staff and graduates, then to move out into the wider business world of the British Isles, and finally, armed with good evidence of support from nearer home, to approach the big American foundations. The campaign was devised and carried through with only marginal assistance from fund-raising firms, but in October 1958 it was thought advisable to secure some professional help in tackling corporate America, and the services of a fund-raising consultant, John Holmes, were secured to act as paid secretary to an American Council of the University of Dublin. A year later the Board authorised the Extension Committee to engage a professional firm in England, Brewster Owen, to promote the appeal there. Their services were particularly useful in organising the arrangements and publicity for the major venture of an exhibition in London, early in 1961, of the Book of Kells (the St Matthew volume) and other early Celtic MSS, together with some choice items from the College's silver and pictures.

The exhibition was mounted in the main gallery of the Royal Academy in Burlington House, Piccadilly. It was the first time that even part of the Book of Kells had left Ireland, and the Librarian, escorted by members of the Special Branch, took personal responsibility for its transport, carrying it on the journey via Holyhead to Euston in a 'battered suitcase', as the press reported with some glee.[13] It was displayed side by side with the Gospels of Lindisfarne, kindly loaned by the Trustees of the British Museum. The two great manuscripts made a very memorable centrepiece for the exhibition, which was seen by close on 60,000 people, and which covered its expenses. The College's enterprise was commended by Lord Kilmaine when forwarding a donation of £10,000 from the Dulverton Trust. This was the first gift from a Foundation, and brought the Appeal Fund up to £212,000.

Meanwhile, plans for the new building received much more definition with the appointment of assessors for an international competition. The panel was headed by Lord Rosse, and included three distinguished architects, Sir Hugh Casson from London, Signor Franco Albini from Milan, and Raymond McGrath, chief architect of the Board of Works in Dublin. The team was completed by an American library consultant, de Witt Metcalf, but he had to drop out later through illness, and his place was filled in the concluding stages by Ralph Esterquest, Librarian of the Harvard Medical School. Together they constituted a very weighty and experienced team, with Casson's flair well balanced by McGrath's practicality, and Rosse in no way behind the rest in his feeling for good design.

The assessors began their work with a crucial recommendation about the extension. The College's first thought had been to build in three stages as funds permitted, and there was already enough money for the first stage. But the assessors advised against this approach as inadequate even for immediate needs; so the decision was taken to go ahead in faith and seek a design that would match the Old Library in its scope and satisfy all needs for the foreseeable future. The stretch of tree-covered ground between College Park and the Fellows' Garden had long been envisaged as the appropriate area for the development, but there had been much discussion on the extension committee about whether to risk putting up a modern building on such a key site. Some were for playing safe with a neo-Georgian pastiche. But it was pointed out that the Museum Building was as representative of the nineteenth century as the Old Library was of the eighteenth, and that modern architecture could be good as well as bad. In the end no restriction was placed on exterior design or materials. The key parameters were provided by an upper limit on cost, by the detailed schedule of accommodation, and by the need for an elegant and functional connection between the old library and the new. However, the committee realised that entrants for the competition would be likely to favour a modern solution to the problem. John Luce as Competition Registrar and

Ian Roberts as College Architect were responsible for preparing and circulating the necessary documents.

The competition was launched on 15 June 1960 and concluded with the public announcement of the prizewinners on 8 June 1961. Eleven hundred copies of the competition conditions had been sent out all over the world, and any fears that a new building in Trinity College would not attract international interest were soon dispelled. Nearly 500 competitors registered, and 218 completed entries were received by March 1961. The competition was run under the rules of the International Union of Architects, based in Paris, and Luce was responsible for their application. The rules required absolute anonymity, and each entry was unpacked and numbered by him personally in a small room assigned for this purpose in the New Square. The corresponding number was placed on the enclosed sealed envelope containing the competitor's signed entry form, and these envelopes were then deposited with the Bank of Ireland in College Green.

When the time came for judging, the entries, each of which ran to several large sheets, were set up on wooden easels especially constructed for the purpose, and the display filled the floor of the Exam Hall. The judges went round marking entries they had rejected with a cross, and entries with three or more crosses were then removed from the stands. The pace slowed and deliberation intensified as a shortlist emerged and Esterquest was asked to assess these entries from a librarian's point of view. Three-and-a-half days had elapsed before the assessors finally agreed on the winning design, the two runners-up, and some commended entries. The following day, 3 May, the sealed envelopes with the corresponding numbers were opened by the Lord Mayor in the presence of witnesses (as required by the rules), including the Secretary of the Department of Education and the City Architect. The first prize of £1500 went to Paul George Koralek, a young architect of British nationality temporarily attached to the firm of Marcel Breuer and Associates in New York. The second prize of £1000 was won by Al Mansfield from Haifa, and the third prize of £750 by a team of five architects from the USA. Those commended included a team of four Turkish architects.

Koralek had been born in Vienna on 7 April 1933, and was brought to London the following year by his parents. He held a diploma with honours from the Architectural Association School of Architecture in London. It had for some time been his intention to return to England to go into partnership with Peter Ahrends and Richard Burton, also honours diploma holders of the AA, who had recently opened an office in London. On the recommendation of the assessors, the Board, as promoters of the competition, agreed to appoint him and his firm as architects for the work. The assessors felt that some modification of the design might be needed, but agreed that it could be built within the prescribed cost limits.

The competition had cost £9000 to run, and must be regarded as having had a very satisfactory outcome, particularly when news came early the following Michaelmas term that the government had agreed to augment the Appeal Fund on a pound for pound basis up to a maximum of £368,000. If this sum proved insufficient, a further loan would be provided by the Minister for Education. In return for this recognition of its Library as a national asset, the College agreed to implement its offer to extend specialised library services to departments of state and commercial firms, and also to allow members of the public reasonable access to copyright material not available elsewhere. The College also agreed to co-ordinate its acquisitions programme with the National Library of Ireland, and to continue its appeal for funds.

As Koralek's design was being developed to its final stage, it became clear that College numbers would soon exceed the limit envisaged when the new building was first planned. Accordingly, increased space was provided for readers, and 7000 square feet of the basement storage space was adapted temporarily to provide additional lecture and seminar rooms. Provision was also made for an Exhibition Hall which, thanks to the efforts of George Dawson, was financed totally by benefactions, chiefly from the Gulbenkian Foundation, but also from Lady Mayer, the Chester Beatty Trust, and Dawson himself. With these modifications, the final drawings were approved in October 1962. As the building was going up, two more major donations were received. Jack Morrison, a London businessman, gave £30,000; his generosity was commemorated by the naming after him of the main reading room. Early in 1964 the Ford Foundation topped off the appeal with a donation of £100,000. This brought the total up to £815,000, sufficient to cover the expenditure without recourse to any loan.

The building was completed in the summer of 1967, and was formally opened by President de Valera on 12 July. Though strikingly modern in idiom, it stands in harmony with the spaces and masses of the older squares. Much of its bulk is below ground. A large double basement, extending well forward of the entrance façade, allows for an efficient underground connection with the Old Library — a problem not well solved by many of the competition entries. The elevated podium forms an interesting feature in itself, and serves to link the building with its older neighbours. The interior avoids the monumental, and provides an environment for readers that is both elegant and cosy. The high standard of the work in concrete done by the contractors, G. and T. Crampton, is a notable feature. All in all, Koralek's Library was adjudged to be a strikingly successful addition to the architecture of the College and the city.

The long planned increase in the number of Junior Fellow representatives on the Board from two to four was finally effected by an ordinance passed on 23 April 1958. The measure went through at a time when an enlargement of the fellowship body by the regular election of full-time Professors was also about to be undertaken, and this latter move was a more significant innovation. The way had been opened by an ordinance passed the previous year, and on Trinity Monday 1958 seven Professors became Fellows: E. J. F. Arnould in French, W. Cocker in chemistry, W. D. Gill in geology, D. W. Greene in Irish, W. J. E. Jessop in social medicine, J. H. J. Poole in physics, and J. Weingreen in Hebrew and oriental languages.

The election was a recognition of the services and scholarly eminence of the seven, but it was also part of a long-term strategy to heal the old rift between Fellows and non-Fellow Professors. It might once have been the case that some 'professors' were little more than junior lecturers hired to teach a special subject for a limited period. But the status of the post had risen steadily since early Victorian times, as had the academic distinction required for appointment, and given the responsibilities attaching to headship of a large modern department, it was no longer defensible to exclude professors from the body corporate. The election of professors to fellowship within two years of their appointment is now routine practice. As a result, the number of non-Fellow professors has become very small in relation to the Fellows, and their retention of two seats on the Board (under the entrenched clauses of the 1911 constitution) something of an anomaly.

Another major change was made in April 1959 when life tenure of fellowship, first instituted in 1637, was finally abandoned in favour of compulsory retirement at the end of the academic year in which the Fellow reached the age of seventy. The change was to apply to all subsequent elections, and the following month T. B. H. McMurry became the first of a new generation of Fellows no longer appointed *ad vitam aut culpam.* A similar regulation had recently been decreed by Council for all future professorial appointments. The change was made feasible by the previous introduction of a new and better pension scheme for full-time academic staff. Existing Fellows were not compelled to accept this modification of their contract, but Frank Mitchell, Basil Chubb and Louden Ryan did so at once, and all in time were induced to do so, partly by the feeling that the measure was in line with the times and in the best interests of the College, and partly by the offer of improved pension terms, with better provision for dependents. The institution of the category of Fellow Emeritus was a consequential change. Emeritus Fellows continue to enjoy the privileges of free Commons and rent-free accommodation, but cannot exercise any voice, vote, power, or authority in College or University, nor claim any dividend or emolument apart from their agreed pension, unless they accept an invitation from the Board to perform specific duties. The ordinance also contained new disciplinary provisions, under which a Fellow negligent or inefficient in the performance of his duties, and receiving an official reprimand, could be deprived of his fellowship after two such reprimands.[14]

The traditional pattern of fellowship was further altered in May 1958 when an ordinance, opening tutorship to non-Fellows, was sent to the Fellows for approval. Fellows had long ceased to give any actual tuition to their pupils. Their main tutorial function was to stand *in loco parentis*, offering general direction and encouragement, and dealing with specific problems in matters such as health, discipline and finance, as they arose. Tutorial payments were no longer on a *per capita* basis, but consisted of a small addition to salary; and the consolidation of academic salary scales effected some years earlier meant that tutorial remuneration had ceased to be a significant element in a Fellow's total emoluments. Increasing specialisation and the rise in student numbers also meant that tutorial needs could no longer adequately be met from the fellowship body alone. The combination of all these factors made a widening in the panel of choice inevitable, and the first appointments of lecturers to tutorship were made at the start of Michaelmas term 1958, with Gerald FitzGibbon in engineering and Edward Stuart in chemistry being assigned full chambers and George Dawson in genetics and Frank Dowrick in law, half chambers.

Another significant change in constitutional practice came towards the end of 1961. The Board directed that, from the beginning of Hilary term 1962, one representative of the Association of Readers, Lecturers and Assistants (first formed in 1948) should be permitted to attend Board meetings with speaking, but no voting, rights. The RLA's first nominee was Owen Sheehy-Skeffington, a Reader in French, who was much in the public eye as a champion of liberal causes, and had represented the University as a Senator since 1954 (though he unexpectedly lost his seat in December 1961, and did not regain it until he topped the poll at the next election in 1965).

The following year witnessed protracted discussion on the remodelling of the University Council. The intention was to increase its powers and to reconstitute it on a more representative basis. It was hoped to give professors an increased say in the running of the University and to share business more equally between Board and Council. When the new Council began its work in Michaelmas term 1964, this latter object was soon seen to have been achieved. Previously the Board had been meeting every week, and the Council about seven times a year. Now the pattern was established of Board and Council meeting on alternate weeks.

Membership of the Council was raised from nineteen to twenty-two, with the Senior Tutor joining the Provost, Registrar and Senior Lecturer as an *ex officio* member. Representation from the Board (previously at two) was abolished, and Senate representation was reduced from four to two. Previously there had been six members representing arts subjects and four representing professional subjects. Now there were to be twelve members elected from among their own number by the professors and other heads of department, divided for this purpose into four major fields of scholarship: literature and the arts, social studies, natural sciences and engineering, and medical sciences. The count was completed by four members elected from those members of the academic staff who were neither professors nor heads of department.

The powers of the new Council were considerably extended. Previously, the Council had nominated to professorships; now it became the nominating body for readerships, lectureships, and other academic posts as well. It was specifically given the duty of regulating conditions for postgraduate study. The earlier statute stated that the Council 'legislates on all matters relating to courses and examinations' (except those in the Divinity School). The revised statute put the Council 'in charge of the academic functioning of the University'. Previously, the consent of the Board was required for all acts of the Council. This requirement remained, but was now to be taken for granted unless the proposals implied increased expenditure. The division of powers along 'academic' and 'financial' lines has worked surprisingly well in practice, with the new Council taking over the general direction of educational policy and handling individual staff appointments, and the Board remaining responsible for general administration, including budgeting, fee and salary levels, site development and discipline.

Among other responsibilities, it fell to the new Council to supervise the new course in general studies introduced in 1959/60. A radical revision of the old pass course had been effected. The objective was to improve standards by prescribing a shorter list of subjects to be studied in greater depth, while stopping some way short of honor course specialisation. Three subjects had to be taken in each year. Students could change one subject at the end of their first year, but at the degree examination they were required to present at least two subjects that had been studied over the four years. Subjects were divided into two groups, with languages and history in group A, and mathematics, philosophy, geography and economics in group B; not more than two subjects could be taken from one group. There was a single annual examination held in June, with a supplemental in September. This reduction in the number of examinations signalled an end to the possibility of proceeding to a BA by examination only, a consequence confirmed by new attendance requirements introduced in 1963/64. If one believed that there was a place for the 'pass' man or woman in a modern university, general studies represented a satisfactory arrangement, allowing students to reach a respectable standard over a reasonable range of subjects. The course continued into the 1970s, and was not abolished until the introduction of the scheme of two-subject moderatorships in October 1978. Its passing marked the end of a process that had begun a century-and-a-half before when Provost Lloyd first introduced an honors level into the basic undergraduate course. Specialisation had finally triumphed over the mediaeval concept of a common curriculum in the liberal arts.

The 1959/60 reform affected the traditional structure of the undergraduate courses in other ways too. It saw the end of 'Little-go', in the sense of a common examination taken in whole or part by all students before entry to their Junior Sophister year. Honor and professional students were still required to choose a subsidiary subject taken from the general studies list, but this marginal concession to the ideal of a broader cultural training was soon relinquisted. The subsidiary subject requirement for honor students was abolished in 1964, and the heading 'Arts requirements for professional students' last appeared in the 1967 Calendar.[15]

Early in 1963 the Board received with much regret Lord Iveagh's resignation from the chancellorship, which he had held since 1927; this took effect at the end of Trinity term. His successor, appointed early in 1964, was Frederick Henry Boland, a graduate and former Scholar in classics, who had gained great distinction as a diplomat and had risen to become President of the General Assembly of the United Nations. At the same time the Board proposed and the Senate accepted the abolition of the office of Vice-Chancellor, and its replacement by a panel of three Pro-Chancellors, who would hold office in their own right and not just as deputy for the Chancellor. Previously the Vice-Chancellor had standing or function only when the Chancellor was absent from Dublin, but under the new system a Pro-Chancellor could take the place of the Chancellor on any public occasion when the latter could not be present. The first three Pro-Chancellors to be appointed were Lord Rosse, Lord Moyne and Professor G. A. Duncan.

While these developments were taking place the Fellows also moved to relinquish their exclusive control of the administration of the College through the annual offices — the bursarship and the registrarship being the key posts in this connection. The crucial decisions were taken in the late 1950s and early '60s, and essentially consisted of the establishment of new top-level and full-time administrative posts in the areas traditionally overseen by Fellows.

The sphere of grounds and buildings was the first to be tackled. In 1956 the Fellows had sent the Board a document proposing an office of Agent, and the appointment of F. B. Chubb as Bursar in July 1957 brought some radical new thinking to bear on the problem of general College maintenance. Towards the end of Trinity term 1958, the Board, on a division, agreed to proceed with the appointment of an Agent. The duties of the post were to include the upkeep and repair of all College buildings and grounds (including Trinity Hall), with responsibility also for the preparation of plans for any major reconstruction or development. The Agent was also to supervise 'the minor officers and servants of the College', to negotiate with trade unions, and 'to have general responsibility for the functioning of the kitchen'. In effect, the new officer was taking over a substantial part of the duties previously vested in the Bursar, leaving that functionary freer to concentrate on financial affairs.

It was a demanding job, and the College was lucky enough to secure a man with an exceptional talent for organisation to fill it. On 8 October 1958 Lt Colonel John M. Walsh was appointed for an initial period of four years. The experimental nature of the appointment was stressed when the Board minuted that 'it is not propposed to give the Agent any place in the Statutes, at least for the time being'. However, John Walsh soon made himself indispensable by his willingness to shoulder a wide range of responsibilities, by his precise ordering of committee business, and by his patience and resilience in the face of criticism. During his twenty-two-year tenure, he could claim credit for many improvements, including the conversion of cellar space under the Dining Hall to a student buttery complete with bar, and the development and implementation of unpopular but badly needed traffic regulations. He also had to bear the brunt of student boycotts of catering. When he retired in 1980, the extent of his contribution was in effect recognised by the reallocation of his functions to the directors of two major departments, Buildings, and Accommodation and Catering Services.

The institution of the office of Steward may appropriately be noticed in this context since the original proposal from the Junior Fellows stressed the close relationship which the Steward should have with the Agent in regard to catering. The proposal was accepted by the Board on 9 March 1960. The Steward is appointed by the Board on the nomination of the Common Room. The functions of the office tend to be aesthetic rather than administrative. The Steward's role is to be the mouthpiece of the academic staff about standards and amenities in the service of meals, and to voice views and suggestions on matters like menus, table wines, cutlery and glassware. The Steward also bears a special responsibility for the planning of major College dinners.

The next substantial addition to the administrative network was made early in 1961. The Junior Fellows had again taken the initiative in pressing for the appointment of a fully qualified professional officer to manage and supervise all the College's financial business, and their proposal, in a somewhat modified form, was accepted by the Board. The relevant minute expresses well the functions proposed for the new post:

> That an officer experienced in accountancy and budgeting and in the management of property and investments be appointed Treasurer; the Treasurer will have charge of all financial business, and will carry out research and planning in the College's finances at the request of the Board or Finance Committee, or as he himself thinks necessary in the interests of the College.[16]

The Treasurer was to be secretary to the Finance Committee and would attend meetings of the Board 'when requested' — a request that soon became a requirement. Even more than in the case of the Agent, the relation between the new officer and the Bursar needed definition. It was accordingly minuted that the Bursar should act as 'consultant and adviser to the Treasurer on executive decisions and financial measures which may have repercussions on the academic community, and will advise on the broader aspects of financial policy'.

This formula encapsulates the principles by which the College has grafted the new administration on to the older stock of the body corporate. Fellows holding major annual offices, like the bursarship and the registrarship, no longer administer their bailiwicks directly, but are charged with a significant consultative and advisory role in relation to those appointed to do so. In this capacity, they bring the feelings and wishes of the academic staff to bear on the executive, and influence the formulation of policy as well as its implementation. Friction tends to develop between academics and administrators, and Trinity has had its share, but on the whole the transfer of executive authority to a new class has generated less tension and opposition than in many universities where the administration has tended to become too dominant. The older College offices have retained their traditional prestige, and relations between their occupants and the professionals generally have been harmonious and constructive.

The new Treasurer, Franz C. W. Winkelmann, took up his duties on 1 March 1962, and at the time of writing the College still enjoys the benefit of his skilled supervision of its finances. With the aid and advice of external auditors (Craig Gardner), the College accounts were recast in a suitably professional format.[17] Winkelmann devoted particular attention to the maintenance of the pension arrangements on a sound basis — they are now administered in conjunction with the Irish Pensions Trust. He also put through a successful programme for recovering possession of the leases of perimeter properties in Pearse Street and Westland Row. His skills in investment management and in budget negotiation with government or the Higher Education Authority were major assets to the College during three decades of growth, inflation and (latterly) cutbacks.

On the basis of a report from management consultants, presented to the Board on 22 May 1963, the need to institute a new post of College Secretary was accepted. It was intended that the Secretary would be generally responsible for administration in the same way as the Treasurer for finance. The following October, Robert Brownlow Pyper, a graduate of the College in history, took up duty, but did not find the post much to his liking. He was succeeded on 1 January 1966 by Gerald H. H. Giltrap, also a Trinity graduate in history and political science, who came from a top administrative post with Aer Lingus. 'Gerry' Giltrap remained at the centre of College affairs for a quarter of a century until his retirement as Secretary at the end of September 1990. His experienced hand was then employed as Provost's adviser in making the final preparations for the celebration of the quatercentenary. The University testified its appreciation of his services by the award of the degree of LLD *honoris causa*, which was conferred on him in July 1991.

The principle of professionalism was extended to the librarianship at the end of Trinity term 1965. Since 1949 Herbert Parke had been the traditional amateur scholar in the post, giving good service with the assistance, from 1952 on, of deputy librarians with high professional qualifications. R. O. Dougan left in 1958 to take up appointment as Librarian of the Huntington in California, and was succeeded by F. J. E. Hurst. The Board now accepted Parke's resignation, expressing its appreciation of all his work for the Library, and appointed Hurst in his place. Parke was given the new post of Curator (without stipend) and was appointed chairman of the library committee. John Hurst moved to Coleraine in 1967 and as Librarian played a key part in the development of the new university there. Under his successors, Denis Roberts, Peter Brown and Peter Fox, the Trinity Library was kept in the forefront of computerised development. Reader services were greatly extended, and large undergraduate reading areas in arts and science were provided in the Arts Building and the Luce Hall. The Berkeley Library became the main centre for research, and storage space was considerably extended by the building and subsequent extension of the Santry book repository. The idea of a conservation laboratory was first mooted by the Keeper of Manuscripts, William O'Sullivan. Advice was sought from Roger Powell (who had repaired and rebound the Book of Kells in 1953), and, with enthusiastic support from Peter Brown, the project came to fruition with the grand opening of the laboratory in May 1974. Since then the laboratory has established itself as a major centre of expertise under the able direction of Anthony Cains.

The end of an era was symbolised when Captain J. H. ('Jimmy') Shaw retired from the assistant registrarship in July 1966 after forty-seven years of efficient and devoted service. His ground-floor room in East Theatre, with its comforting coal fire, had long served as a supplementary 'common room' where friends dropped in to exchange gossip or receive a discreet briefing on the latest College news. Now many an old-stager felt that this warmly personal service had been replaced by a faceless bureaucracy with which they were less than comfortable. In the rapidly growing University, the centrally heated office and the typewritten directive had to come, but such intimations of progress did not receive a very cordial welcome in the more conservative corners of the Front Square or the Rubrics.

Plato's belief that changes in music are inevitably the prelude to more fundamental changes in society seems plausible enough when one reflects on the rise of rock, on Beatlemania, and the 'swinging sixties'. A more relaxed attitude to association between the sexes began to characterise the 'permissive' society. Those who insisted that the 'new morality' was simply the old immorality in a new form were forced on the defensive as more tolerant attitudes gained ground.

The progress of the sexual revolution, and the reactions it caused, are well illustrated by an incident involving the weekly student magazine, *T.C.D.*, early in 1964. The first issue of Hilary term contained an article on student pregnancy and marriage that would hardly raise an eyebrow today, but created a furore at the time.[18] Conservative opinion was so outraged that the Provost felt obliged to take the drastic step of dismissing the editor and suspending the magazine for two issues. No attempt was made to appeal the sentence, but the student body as a whole reacted unfavourably to the banning, and the 'Hist' by an overwhelming majority expressed its 'deep regret' at the Provost's action. The new editor had the last word in his Valentine's Day issue when he made a dignified rejection of the imputation that his predecessor had acted irresponsibly, and there the matter rested. The Board was not totally opposed to free speech. The year before, it had allowed the 'Phil' to debate homosexuality, provided it did so *in camera* and without advertising the meeting outside the Society's rooms.[19] *Autres temps, autres moeurs!*

A symbolic blow for feminine equality had been struck when Frances Moran joined the Board in Michaelmas term 1958 as an elected representative of the non-Fellow professors, the first woman to achieve this eminence. By so doing, she became (temporarily) a member of the body corporate. The day when women would achieve this permanently was not far off. The status of women members of staff had been somewhat grudgingly improved earlier in the year when the Common Room decided to admit them as associate members. They paid a half subscription and were permitted to use the premises until 5.30 pm. With a male chauvinist aplomb that would be unthinkable today, the Committee retained the power 'to arrange such dinners or other entertainments for men only as it shall think fit'.

But the climate of opinion was altering fast. In the 1960s the 'six o'clock rule' (which had been 'seven o'clock' since 1955/56) was progressively extended to midnight. In Trinity term 1962 women students were given limited access to the lunch buffet — they had to avoid the peak hour between 12.30 and 1.30.[20] In 1965, after Iris Murdoch had dined on high table as the guest of a student society, the Board was shamed into admitting women staff to the College's evening meal.

In December of the same year, the Board received a proposal from the Junior Fellows that statutory steps should be taken to admit women to fellowship, and that, pending such a revision, a category of non-foundation fellowships should be established. The Board referred the question to a meeting of all the Fellows, at which a substantial majority opted for their full admission, provided that any legal problems could be overcome. Alleged difficulties, like the phrase *pro virili parte* in the fellowship oath, wilted before the commonsense view, based on the spirit of Fawcett's Act, that discrimination in such matter on grounds of sex must be unfair. And opposition collapsed when McDowell and Webb found an obscure British Act of 1919, relating to civil service appointments, but also containing a reference to universities, which legitimised the substitution of 'she' for 'he' in statutory regulations of this nature. So on 4 October 1967 the Board decided by 13 votes to 1 in favour of the admission of women to fellowships and foundation scholarships, and an appropriate ordinance was approved before the end of the year. The following Trinity Monday saw the election of three women lecturers (Mary Ita O'Boyle, Catherine Brock and Barbara Wright) and one professor (Jocelyn Otway-Ruthven). At the same time Professor Moran was elected to honorary fellowship. Women had long been elected to non-foundation scholarships, so their election on this occasion to foundation scholarships also did not seem such a striking break with tradition.

As Fellows and Scholars on the Foundation, women became entitled to free Commons and rooms in College. There was never any attempt to deny them these rights, but the problem of access to toilet and bathroom facilities at once became a subject of discussion at Board level. With a nice irony, the Board envisaged that, with women in residence, the twelve o'clock rule might have to be extended to men. There was no difficulty about Commons, but the practicalities of accommodation took longer to arrange. The authorities realised that it would be futile to attempt to confine residence opportunities to women Scholars only, and in 1972/73 all women students became entitled to apply for rooms in College on the same terms as men.

There were other straws in the wind of social change. By a majority of one vote (and not all the Senior Fellows voted against) the Board allowed the Trinity Week Ball of 1959 to be held in College. A fine night, a full moon, and the piquancy of doing the 'twist' under the eye of Swift or Grattan conspired to make the evening a memorable success. In October 1960 the Board again divided, this time on an application from DUCAC for a club bar in the Pavilion. The request was approved in principle, provided that only beer, cider and soft drinks were served, and that there was a match or athletics fixture in the Park. This was the thin edge of quite a big wedge. Before long the Pavilion bar was operating daily on regular hours with a full range of drinks and snacks and a professional barman. In January 1964 the Board accepted the rules and constitution of a Societies Club organised by the Agent to provide a similar service in the buttery. That year the rules on student lodgings were relaxed to the extent of allowing Sophisters to live in flats.

There was also a progressive lifting of the ban on Sunday games, with leave being given to the Cricket Club (in 1963) to arrange away fixtures on a Sunday, and permission granted (in December 1964) for Gaelic football to be played at Santry. At the end of 1967 the Board gave DUCAC leave to use College Park for Sunday games on the understanding that no fixture would begin before noon.

A major advance in student welfare came in Michaelmas term 1964 with the introduction of a College health service for all students on the books. Consulting rooms were fitted up in No. 11 with daily attendance by a doctor. Obstetric care, dental care, and the provision of glasses were not covered, but arrangements could be made for a doctor to attend students at their place of residence in the city in case of real need.

Relations with the wage-earning staff now began to occupy more of the Board's time. Vestiges of an older paternalism can be glimpsed in a report from the Agent in October 1963 on the first five years of his office. In detailing more business-like arrangements that he had instituted for the payment of workers who were absent because of sickness, he remarked: 'Until comparatively recently there had been no fixed policy. . . . The College custom had been — with characteristic but sometimes costly generosity — to continue to pay a sick employee at his full rate, the College being reimbursed only to the extent of his social welfare sickness benefit.'[21] Now an era of hard bargaining with unions was at hand. In October 1965 a serious dispute arose with the porters over manning rosters and night patrol duties. The changing scene is well characterised in the following extract from a report on the dispute made by the Agent and Junior Dean, Dr McDowell:

> In the past the porter's life was one of simple and traditional routine duties diversified by the need to cope occasionally with simple instances of undergraduate exuberance. Now the motor car, the telephone, a continuous and increasing flow of 'strangers', a far longer College day, ending not at six but at nearly midnight, and a vast growth of activity in College at all levels, make increasing demands on the porters' intelligence, initiative and tact.[22]

The dispute was resolved by the institution of a 40-hour week, but this soon led to a similar demand from the Workers' Union of Ireland on behalf of the gardeners and groundsmen.

Towards the end of Trinity term 1964, a major clash over the organisation of Commons developed between the Treasurer and Agent on the one hand and the academic staff on the other. The Treasurer queried the subsidy needed to keep Commons in its traditional form, and the Agent wanted to encourage non-residents to take an evening meal in the new hall that had been constructed over the old kitchen. All students in residence were still required to dine in Hall at least five times a week, Commons being served every day including Saturday and Sunday (and twice an evening from Monday to Friday during lecture term). The Agent now proposed a move to a single voluntary Commons in the old Hall, together with a cheap self-service meal in the new Hall, and the Board accepted this radical break with tradition without much argument or consultation. A storm of protest followed, and at its meeting on 8 July the Board, after noting letters from the Junior Fellows and the Tutors, rescinded its decision to make Commons optional. However, the basic price was raised from 4/6 to 6/-, with a higher price of 8/6 charged for second Commons at High Table.

The matter was not allowed to rest there. When the Board convened again in October, it received a strong endorsement of the principle of compulsory Commons from the Readers and Lecturers. They were of the opinion that the meal should continue to be subsidised, and they also wanted non-residents, including women, to be admitted. 'We feel strongly', they said, 'that Commons is an integral part of the institutional life of the University and that it occupies an integral place in the educational development of students.' This was certainly the view of the majority of the academic staff, but the ideal was hard to maintain in the face of stricter budgeting and the five-day week. Students were also becoming less willing to be constrained by any compulsions other than the need to pass their annual examinations.

In November 1964 the Treasurer and Agent toured seven British universities, including Oxford and Cambridge, to study catering trends. This tour resulted in a long memorandum, submitted early in 1965 and containing detailed proposals on evening meals in College. The proposals were made against the background of increasing food costs, the difficulty of getting waiters, and the growing resentment of students at the Commons fund, which charged them for meals they did not consume and (in their view) subsidised a better standard at high table. The main outcome was a decision that, in Trinity term, resident students should be compelled to sign on for four nights only per week, and that every effort should be made to attract non-residents to dine. This was the first step towards the abolition of compulsory Commons, a measure that came into effect in 1972/73. The Student Union representatives assured the Board that they would continue to encourage voluntary dining, but the trend was against set meals, and over the next few years attendances declined greatly, with few except Scholars signing on.

Weekend Commons was discontinued in 1977/78, but, rather against the odds, the cutbacks ended there, and a single serving through the week from Monday to Friday has since been maintained. Non-residents, guests and graduates are welcome, and high table attendance has remained reasonably good. On the occasion of society meetings, staff often dine with their students in the body of the Hall. Successive Junior Deans have worked hard to attract more support, and a group rate for block bookings encourages clubs and societies to entertain visiting teams or speakers. But the Hall is rarely more than half full, except at the very popular Christmas dinners, when even Senior Fellows may be seen wearing paper hats and pulling crackers.

Notes

1. The department was renamed 'systems and data studies' in 1982/83. Frederic Gordon Foster, Professor of Statistics from 1968 to 1991, has the distinction of having devised the ISBN system now universally used in book cataloguing.
2. The totals look rather different if part-time (mostly diploma) students are added. There were only 36 of these in 1939, as against 353 in 1956.
3. Between them, these six Fellows held the key posts for most of McConnell's provostship. Mitchell was Registrar from 1952 to 1966. Moody was Senior Tutor from 1952 to 1958 and Senior Lecturer from 1958 to 1964. Ryan was Bursar from 1962 until his secondment to the Department of Finance for three years from March 1964. Wormell was Senior Lecturer from 1952 to 1958 and again from 1964 to 1967. Chubb was Bursar from 1957 to 1962 and again from 1964 to 1974. Howie was Registrar from 1966 to 1974.
4. When he accepted the provostship, it was a life appointment, but McConnell considered himself bound by the retirement age of seventy, introduced for Fellows in 1959.
5. McConnell remembered de Valera's concern at the isolated position of Trinity after 1921, and recalled how he 'often expressed to me his great admiration for the contribution that Trinity College had made to Irish scholarship and learning and his desire to help bring that isolation to an end.' See *Eamon de Valera*, a centenary brochure published by the Dublin Institute for Advanced Studies (1982), 26.
6. Bigger contributed an article on the design to *Trinity* 1, 1949, 23–25.
7. The history of the Endowment Fund down to 1950 is outlined by T. C. Kingsmill Moore in *Trinity* 2, 1950, 29–30. See also the informative account 'The T.C.D. Trust Funds, 1927–1982', compiled in booklet form by Dr Michael N. McKillen, and available for inspection in the Trust/Association office. McKillen was elected Treasurer in October

1979. His figures show that between 1955 and 1982 grants totalling £380,250 were made by the Trusts. In 1982 the market value of the Trusts' investments stood at £159,509. Substantial support was given to the Trinity Hall extension project in the 1970s. The Trusts set a target of £1 million as their contribution to the Quatercentenary Appeal.

8. See his account in *Trinity* 8, 1956, 22–23.
9. The reconstruction in geology led to the removal outdoors of the statue of Provost Salmon, which had stood in the entrance hall of the Museum Building. It was then displayed to much better advantage in front of the east pavilion of the Old Library, before being moved to its present fine position by the Campanile.
10. See G. F. Mitchell, 'The Kells Ingram farm', *Trinity* 9, 1957, 20–22.
11. French was a Lecturer in English, the editor of *Trinity*, and a noted composer of witty sketches for DU Players.
12. R. S. (Ronnie) Nesbitt, Louis Sher, Lyal Collen, James Walmsley, Rex Dick and John Sedgwick were particularly active members of the subcommittee.
13. *The Irish Times*, 10 January 1961.
14. The need for such a measure had been brought home to the Board some years before in the case of a Fellow in mathematics whose academic performance became highly erratic and unsatisfactory. It was not clear that the College had power to dismiss him, and he was eventually induced to resign, but only with much difficulty.
15. From 1967/68 onwards, professional students in subjects other than medicine and engineering were no longer permitted to take an optional course in general studies leading to a BA. In medicine and engineering the traditional link with Arts was so strongly valued that medical (and dental) students were permitted to have their BA conferred on completion of their third professional year, a sufficient Arts element being deemed to be comprised in their course. From 1970 onwards, engineering students also began to conform to this pattern, much emphasis being laid on the mathematical element in the course.
16. *Board Register*, Vol. 29, p. 133.
17. Proposals for professional auditing of the accounts by a firm of chartered accountants were first brought to the Board early in 1958 by two Senior Fellows, Joseph Johnston and George Duncan, and arrangements were in place by the following June. Johnston had succeeded Thrift as internal Auditor, and was the last Fellow to hold the post, which was abolished at the end of the academic year 1958/59.
18. *T.C.D.*, 31 January 1964.
19. Up to Trinity term 1966, there were regular Board Minutes approving the term's programme of debates submitted by the College Historical Society, but then the Board agreed that this procedure need no longer be followed.
20. As the recently elected Board representative of the Readers and Lecturers, Dr Skeffington took the initiative in securing the extension of women's rights here described (A. Sheehy-Skeffington in *Skeff* (Dublin, 1991), 209). The Board had assumed responsibility for the luncheon buffet in the Dining Hall from 1 May 1959. It had previously been run by the Co-operative Society. The Society made over a balance of £2500 to the Board, and it was agreed that a consultative committee, with student representatives, should be set up to advise on its management.
21. *Companion to the Register*, Vol. 10, 53.
22. *Companion to the Register*, Vol. 11, 22.

CHAPTER 14

The 'merger': background and aftermath

When Archbishop McQuaid's Lenten Regulations were published in early February 1967, they stressed that, contrary to popular belief, there had been no relaxation in the law concerning the attendance of Catholics at a non-Catholic school or university.[1] A few days later, on 12 February, the *Sunday Independent* reprinted McQuaid's 1961 Lenten Pastoral on the subject, with its chillingly vigorous defence of the 'ban' on Trinity. 'We are all obliged', he had written, 'to pray for the reunion of Christendom. We have all the duty of showing justice and charity to all members of the pluralist society in which we find ourselves. But very few are equipped to handle at close quarters the problem of the reunion of Christian dissidents'. McQuaid then demonstrated his own historical grasp of the problem by recalling how Elizabeth I took 'active and permanent measures to impose on us a university formation to which death was in conscience preferable', and declared that it was worth waiting another four hundred years, if necessary, for a fully Catholic university in Ireland.

Others were not prepared to be so patient. Provost McConnell at once issued a statement in which he said: 'With respect, I suggest that His Grace misjudges the circumstances and does a grave injustice to Trinity College and particularly to the Catholic students and staff of the college in holding that in this day and age it is not a fit place for Irish Catholics.' The Laurentian Society (which claimed to be speaking for the 880 Catholic students in Trinity) commented publicly on the good treatment they had received in their allocation of rent-free rooms and an annual grant, and pressed for the appointment of a resident chaplain, as offered by the College.[2] A statement signed by sixty-one Catholic members of staff was issued on 2 March, urging the hierarchy to reconsider its position. And when the first volume of the long-awaited Report of the Commission on Higher Education became available at the end of March, Garret FitzGerald discussed it in a thoughtful article in which he said that 'the evolution of opinion with regard to religious problems of the kind posed by the university situation in Dublin has been extraordinarily rapid in recent years under the influence of the second Vatican Council'.[3]

This evidence of a shift in public opinion was undoubtedly one of the factors influencing Donogh O'Malley, the Minister of Education, as he wrestled with the problems of university expansion and finance. Another was the important fact that the Commission's views had been published at last, if only in summary form. The radical nature of what O'Malley was soon to propose will become clearer if we look at the solution favoured by the Commissioners.

The Commission had been set up by Dr Patrick Hillery when Minister of Education in 1960. Its brief was to enquire into the general organisation and administration of Irish higher education, and the nature and extent of the provision to be made for it. Among its twenty-six members, under the chairmanship of the Chief Justice, Cearbhall Ó Dalaigh, was Professor T.W. Moody, Trinity's Senior Lecturer at the time, whose liberal and scholarly views were influential in shaping its conclusions. The Commission performed its work with exemplary thoroughness. It carried out an extensive programme of visits in Ireland, Britain, Western Europe, and the United States, received 245 written submissions, and interviewed 154 witnesses. Not surprisingly, the digesting and ordering of the evidence (2.7 million words) took a considerable time. By April 1964 it had reached decisions on most of the major issues, but a further two years were needed for the preparation of its report, which ran to over 400,000 words, exclusive of appendices.

The Commissioners adopted as their guiding principle the need to maintain academic standards in the face of the rapidly rising demand for higher education. Most of their thirty-seven recommendations stemmed from this laudable aim. They recommended a national minimum standard for university entry (Leaving Certificate with two honours), and a minimum length of four years for first degree courses. They affirmed that postgraduate study and research should be given a large place in all departments, that university teachers should have half their working year free for study and research, and that the staff/student ratio should be progressively and substantially improved to 1/12 by 1975. After proposing that the University Colleges in Dublin, Cork, and Galway should be elevated to independent university status, they went on to recommend that 'no additional university should now be established', and that the existing universities should reduce overcrowding and match student numbers with

cont. p183

37 *Ernest Thomas Sinton Walton (b. 1903) was elected to a fellowship in 1934, and appointed Professor of Natural and Experimental Philosophy in 1946. He graduated from the College in mathematics and experimental science (with gold medal) in 1926. As a research student in the Cavendish laboratory in the early 1930s, he designed (with J.D. Cockcroft) an accelerator that 'split the atom', work for which he was awarded a (joint) Nobel Prize in 1951.*

38 *Samuel Barclay Beckett (1906–89), Scholar of the House (1926), Class I Moderator (with gold medal) in French and Italian (1927), Assistant Lecturer in French (1930–31), recipient of the Nobel Prize for Literature (1968).*

39 *William Arthur Watts (b. 1930), Provost from 1981 to 1991, photographed in the foyer of the new O'Reilly Institute.*

40 *On left, Francis Stewart Leland Lyons, Provost from 1974 to 1981, with (on right) his former teacher Theodore William Moody, Professor of Modern History.*

41 *Thomas Noel Mitchell (b. 1939), the present Provost, with his sons (from left to right) Kevin, Seán and Noel, on the occasion of the conferring on him of the degree of Litt. D. on 11 November 1991.*

42 *Albert Joseph McConnell (b. 1903), Provost from 1952 to 1974.*

43 *William Bedell Stanford (1910–84) in his robes as Chancellor (elected 1982). He was Regius Professor of Greek (1940–80), and represented the University in the Senate (1948–69).*

44/45 *Old and new in student rooms: the sketch is taken from* Student Life in Trinity College Dublin *by H.A. Hinkson (Dublin, 1892); the photograph shows the lounge of a double set in House 47 of the Pearse Street Residences, brought into use in 1991.*

46 *Tourist visitors examine the sculpture* Sphere with Sphere *(1982/83) by Arnaldo Pomodoro.*

47 *A cricket match in College Park: in the background (from left to right) the Luce Sports Hall by Ronald Tallon (1982), the Botany School building, and the Physics building (both by William Marshall, 1904–07).*

48 (Opp.) *The Atrium, a reconstruction of the central portion of the Dining Hall complex, by Shane de Blacam and John Meagher (1985).*

49 *The Moyne Institute at the south-east corner of College Park, by Desmond FitzGerald (1953).*

50 *His Majesty the King of Spain listens as the Public Orator delivers the oration on the occasion of the King receiving the honorary degree of LL.D. on 1 July 1986.*

51 *The Pavilion, after refurbishment in 1989–90.*

52 *The Dining Hall after the fire of 13 July 1984, with Thomas Hudson's portrait of Frederick, Prince of Wales, still in position.*

53 *The O'Reilly Institute for Communication and Technology, by Ronald Tallon (1989).*

54 *Her Excellency Mary Robinson (née Bourke), seventh President of Ireland. Mrs Robinson is a former Scholar of Trinity, a graduate in law, and now an Honorary Fellow.*

cont. from p182

resources. To cope with the rising flood of applicants, they proposed the establishment of 'new colleges', which would offer degrees at pass level after a three-year course in arts, science or commerce. This proposal followed logically from their desire to promote the highest possible standards in the existing institutions, but was a majority recommendation only, being opposed in reservations entered by the powerful voices of Bishop Philbin, General Costello and Dr J.J. McElligott.

The idea of the 'new colleges' — two were proposed, one in Dublin and one in Limerick — was not well received, and with the lapse of this recommendation the heart went out of the Commission's proposals. Though admirable in theory, they were probably overambitious in relation to the country's resources. O'Malley's *démarche* also made the report a virtual dead letter by the time it appeared in full. The only major proposal to be acted upon was that for the establishment of a permanent commission for higher education. The Commissioners had pointed out that the state was providing more and more money for the institutions of higher education but failing to make any provision for the planning and co-ordination of their activities. The government recognised the force of this criticism, and met it by constituting a Higher Education Authority (the HEA), which operated on an *ad hoc* basis from September 1968 up to 15 May 1972, when it was formally established under the terms of an Act of 1971.[4] The legislation necessary to implement other recommendations, such as the revision of Trinity's constitution, was never brought forward.

In the section of their report dealing specifically with Trinity, the Commission was severely critical of the College's policy of admitting so many foreign students, particularly from Britain, and did not accept that this way of keeping up numbers was a valid reaction to the 'ban'.[5] The policy, they said, used limited finances for the benefit of wealthier countries, overstretched staff resources, and made it more difficult to realise the College's desire to be accepted as an Irish institution. However, they did recognise that the position had altered considerably in the four or five years since the College had first submitted its evidence. The non-Irish student population had fallen from 46 per cent of the total to 30 per cent, and the Provost's target of no more than 15 per cent by the early 1970s seemed attainable.

In general, however, the Commissioners spoke appreciatively of the place of the College in Irish higher education.

> Its reputation and its liberal tradition as a house of learning are a valuable part of the Irish inheritance; so too are its historic buildings

> and the treasures of its famous library; and so, above all, is the vigorous life of the College today. These are assets that Ireland cannot afford to neglect or diminish.

They accepted the sincerity of Trinity's desire for full acceptance and integration, which, of course, would require a lifting of the 'ban'. On this point they stated that they had neither sought nor received any submission from the hierarchy, but Bishop Philbin, as a member of the Commission, contributed an explanatory statement of the reasons underlying the regulations. His argument may be summed up as follows: the inculcation of (Catholic) moral and spiritual values is the supreme goal of education; the Colleges of the National University of Ireland (the NUI), though not an ideal milieu, were acceptable as substantially satisfying Catholic requirements; Trinity, by contrast, was a place where 'currents of opinion more radically opposed to Catholicism may exert considerable influence'; and he raised the bugbear that a Marxist might even be appointed to a chair if he or she was deemed to be academically the best qualified candidate. Trinity's attitude was well put by the Provost when he stated: 'I do not want Trinity College to be regarded as a Protestant institution for Protestant students; I want it to be a university for all Irishmen', and he undertook to do everything possible to cater for the moral and spiritual welfare of all its students.

As a body, the Commission took the view that the hierarchy's regulations for the attendance of Catholics were a 'matter of conscience', and its members did not propose to comment on them (though they had often discussed them). However, they went on to point out that the 'ban' was one of the factors creating undue pressure of numbers on UCD and that it tended to accentuate unhealthy rivalry between the two Dublin Colleges. Their remedy for these problems was, in effect, to 'hasten slowly'. They did not think it opportune to suggest any form of merger. Dublin was large enough to support two universities, and relationships would be improved if UCD had full university status. In his oral evidence, the Provost had stressed that relations were good at individual staff and department level, but 'not nearly as good at the top'.[6] The Commission hoped that the cordial personal relationships at lower levels could be translated into fruitful formal arrangements for the co-ordination of activity, particularly at postgraduate level.[7]

As he studied the report, Donogh O'Malley was aware that Trinity had publicly pledged co-operation in any integrated scheme that could be developed.[8] He knew that the introduction of his own measures for free secondary education would in time produce many more qualified applicants for the third-level sector. University numbers were already showing a major increase, and Trinity's decision (in January 1966) to raise its 'ceiling' from 3000 to 4000 had led to an application for a capital grant of nearly £2.5 million for new buildings and scientific equipment.[9] The financial needs and demands of UCD, not to mention the other colleges, were no less large and insistent.

It was against this background that on 18 April 1967, without any prior consultation, the Minister of Education made his dramatic 'merger' announcement, as the plan soon became known (he did not use the term himself).[10] O'Malley indicated that he had outlined his proposals to cabinet the previous December when he found himself faced with particularly large and competing claims from the two Dublin colleges. Ministers then thought he should await publication of the Commission's findings. Now that these had appeared without any specific recommendation for a TCD/UCD link, he felt that the public interest demanded a much more radical approach to the particular problem of university education in Dublin.

O'Malley described the division between the colleges as a 'most insidious form of partition on our own doorstep', a clear reference to the 'ban', He then declared his intention to create a single multi-denominational University of Dublin which would take both the existing institutions under its wing. O'Malley was not, however, proposing a total fusion, which he thought would be an 'appallingly bad decision'. The two colleges each would maintain its identity under its own managing body, but would be conjoined in a federal union under the superior authority of a new governing body or Senate. His plan, O'Malley said, had received enthusiastic and unanimous government approval at the end of March.

Provost McConnell at once issued a statement in which he said that he would 'look forward to co-operating with our friends in University College, and with the Minister, in making a success of this new and exciting development'. But the reaction from UCD was less compliant. The governing body stated its opinion that the problem would best be solved by the foundation of a single new institution, which would 'pool all the resources, intellectual, material, and financial' under a single authority.[11] Such an amalgamation could hardly be expected to appeal to the smaller unit. Nevertheless, there was little or no immediate sign of major opposition to the O'Malley initiative, and many members of staff in both colleges welcomed it.

People felt that the Minister's heart was in the right place, even if he had not perhaps thought through the full implications of the scheme. Indeed, in response to questions at a press conference, O'Malley admitted that he had not worked out the constitutional structure of the new university in any great detail, but he was optimistic enough to feel that, given goodwill, the task would present no insuperable problems. He said on television that the new arrangement would save millions of pounds over the next few decades. He saw the present situation as financially intolerable and culturally and nationally undesirable. The new University of Dublin would not be denominationally 'neutral', but multi-denominational. There would be provision for both Catholic and Protestant schools of divinity or theology, something not allowable to UCD under the 1908 Act. 'Trinity', he trumpeted, 'is not going to pass away. It will be merely taking the final step across the threshold of that great mansion to which it properly belongs, the Irish nation.'

Statistics prepared by the Commission indicated a rise in university numbers from 16,000 to 23,000 by 1975. O'Malley himself predicted that they would rise to 27,000. This was bound to put a severe strain on the education budget. He asked why the state should have to pay UCD £160,000 and TCD £86,000 annually for two faculties of veterinary medicine producing forty-five and ten graduates respectively. In the Arts faculties, need there be unnecessary duplication of staff, buildings and equipment? Would it not be more economical for all the science students to be taught 'under the one roof, so to speak'? The questions seemed to imply much more than the avoidance of expensive and unnecessary duplication in one or two faculties or small departments. O'Malley seemed to be suggesting a much more radical form of complementarity, under which all arts subjects, for example, might be taught in Trinity only, and all science subjects in UCD. Under questioning, he denied that this was his intention. Some 'necessary duplication' would have to remain, but clearly the colleges were entitled to some necessary clarification also.[12]

On 19 April *The Irish Times*'s first leader, aptly headed 'Mixed Marriage', opened with the statement 'some form of close association or amalgamation between UCD and TCD has for so long appeared not only rational, but necessary, that Mr O'Malley's sudden move should have had an air of inevitability.' Fine Gael welcomed the proposal, but criticised the Minister's statement for containing too many rhetorical questions — a fair comment — and for being ambiguous and obscure. The government's statement of intent was also welcomed by the Labour Party, and the student representative bodies of the two colleges put out a joint statement approving 'the move towards rationalisation'. Despite the legislative problems looming up, which would include a referendum to alter the Constitution's section on university representation, Fianna Fáil deputies also appeared very pleased with the plan. On 22 April Cardinal Conway, just arrived back from Rome, expressed cautious approval. In short, there was considerable satisfaction that the logjam of decades was to be broken up, but no one seemed to have any clear idea of where or how the logs were to be reassembled.

Senator Patrick Quinlan, a member of the governing body of UCD, was a lone critic initially when he pointed out that all university education was poorly financed and that the amalgamation of the Dublin colleges could not be expected to achieve substantial savings. The same point was made more brusquely by Basil Chubb, Trinity's Bursar, when in the course of a television discussion he told the Minister that he was 'talking through his hat' in claiming that he could save millions.

Trinity's Board issued a press statement on 27 April in which it welcomed the decision of the government and promised full co-operation, but stressed that it was essential for independence of thought and freedom of expression to continue to flourish in the new University of Dublin and its constituent colleges. Trinity's initial willingness to go along with the merger plan derived much of its impetus from the Provost's long-cherished desire to see the College more fully integrated into Irish life. It was also based on a realistic assessment by him and his officers of the relative weakness of Trinity, compared with UCD, in the matter of attracting Irish students, although this was not altogether Trinity's fault since the 'ban' was still in force. The merger seemed to offer an immediate way round this problem. In the longer term, it also seemed to promise the Irish universities some hope of keeping up with rising international standards if cut-throat competition for the available resources could be replaced by a sensible and agreed division of labour, particularly between the Dublin colleges.

Other responses were less favourable. Before the end of the month, an elderly Trinity graduate (James L. Wilson) had written to *The Irish Times* in sad and defiant vein, quoting Wordsworth on the extinction of the Venetian Republic, and urging a last ditch stand like the Spartans at Thermopylae. A junior member of staff, T.N.F. Murtagh, also warned: 'There is an undue enthusiasm in the air about the prospect of the merger which is not far from sheer naivety.' Families even split on the issue, with the redoubtable cousins Owen Sheehy-Skeffington and Conor Cruise O'Brien taking opposite sides in the columns of *The Irish Times*. For O'Brien, the merger was in line with Thomas Davis's aspirations for 'one nation'. Skeffington, who also spoke against the merger in the Senate, wittily headed his reply with the motto of the city of Paris: *Fluctuat nec mergitur* ('waved-tossed but not submerged').

Any initial euphoria in Trinity began to die away after O'Malley met the Board early in June to spell out his proposals in more detail. He floated the notion that arts and sciences might be taught at Belfield, with the social sciences and smaller professional faculties concentrated in Trinity. The non-Fellow Professors now stated they would not welcome the merger, and the Board began to view it as an economic necessity rather than as educationally desirable. It would consider giving up autonomous university status in the interests of the community, and would agree to some 'rationalisation' in smaller departments, but all larger departments would have to remain on both sites. It was strongly opposed to the Minister's suggestion that the existing properties and other assets of the College should be vested in the new University.[13]

Formal meetings between representatives of the two colleges under the chairmanship of T. Ó Raifeartaigh, Secretary of the Department of Education, began in the autumn of 1967, but the year ended with little or no progress towards agreement, though the discussions laid the basis for subsequent ministerial proposals on the distribution of faculties. When the progress of the negotiations was reviewed at a Board meeting towards the end of February 1968, it became clear that College opinion had moved against the Provost and officers, and a more broadly based committee, the Merger Committee, was formed to handle further discussions. It included Professor Dawson as chairman of the Academic Staff Association and the Faculty Deans.

Donogh O'Malley died suddenly on 10 March 1968 at the age of forty-seven, having served for less than two years as Minister of Education. He was an inspiring figure, who achieved major advances at secondary level, but he left the third-level sector in a ferment of indecision. On 5 July his successor, Brian Lenihan, announced what amounted to a government blueprint for further progress.[14] After stating that Cork and Galway would be constituted as separate universities (which as of 1991 has not happened), he went on to spell out the merger in greater detail. It was envisaged that St Patrick's College, Maynooth would become an associated college of the new University of Dublin, which would be incorporated as one indivisible whole, with the academic personnel of all constituent colleges as its employees. There was to be a common standard for entry to the University, and through it to the colleges. The colleges would retain their identity and present property, though the use of such property must be available to the whole university as required. They would be administered by councils under the overall authority of a new governing body on which each would have equal representation from the academic staffs of their colleges, together with some representatives of other appropriate interests. The colleges were to be multi-denominational and would be managed and conducted on Christian principles, but there would be no religious tests for staff or students, save as might be arranged in relation to divinity or theology. Lenihan envisaged that Maynooth would be in a position to play the fullest part in the teaching and study of theology (on a multi-denominational basis, no doubt!).

On the allocation of subjects, the new Minister said that medicine would be located entirely in Trinity, which would also become the main centre for biological science. Engineering in UCD would be complemented by Belfield becoming the main centre for physical science. (Among the benefits of the scheme, he mentioned that only one new engineering building, with its very expensive equipment, would be required.) Trinity would get veterinary science, dentistry and pharmacy. Agriculture and architecture would remain in UCD. Commerce and social science would go to UCD because of the greater numbers studying those subjects at Belfield. Law was to go to Trinity where it would be conveniently near the courts. Finally, on behalf of the government, Lenihan expressed the belief that 'the Irish people will warmly welcome the plan which removes the greatest obstacle to the proper development of our system of higher education'.

By this time staff and student opinion in Trinity had hardened against any form of merger, and this was also the majority view of university staff throughout the country. The Merger Committee in Trinity continued work on a possible constitution for the proposed new University of Dublin, but by the end of 1968 any immediate implementation of the Lenihan plan began to seem increasingly unlikely. The authorities in UCD were totally opposed to it, and opinion in the HEA began to favour the Commission's proposals for collaboration, rather than merger, as a better and more feasible solution to the problems of university development and finance.

In June 1969 McConnell wrote to Professor J.J. Hogan, the new President of UCD, suggesting the need for further consultation. This approach came after the HEA had requested the colleges to make submissions on their capital needs for the following decade, based on the allocation of subjects laid down in the Lenihan plan. In his reply, Hogan indicated that he would prefer any discussion to involve all the NUI colleges, and towards the end of the year the NUI Senate formally invited Trinity to nominate representatives to negotiate an alternative to the government's proposals. Discussions were held over the opening months of 1970, and certain 'agreed proposals' were announced in a joint UCD/TCD press release on 24 April.[15] The accord was generated by the strong opposition to the merger that now existed in both colleges. It was also known that the HEA was prepared to consider an alternative scheme, provided it allowed for the degree of rationalisation and co-ordination sought by the government.

The NUI/TCD Agreement envisaged four independent but co-operating universities with broadly similar constitutions. Within this framework the proposals focused on the allocation of subjects between the two universities in Dublin. It was agreed that the range of arts subjects existing in each should continue to be taught, but subjects attracting only a small number of students *might* be assigned to one only. In science each was to keep its existing spread of disciplines, with the main centre for the biological sciences in Trinity. In medicine there were to be separate pre-clinical schools with equal numbers, but a single joint clinical school. Veterinary medicine and dentistry were to go to Trinity. With regard to pharmacy, the Agreement stated that it should go to one of the universities, subject to the wishes of the Pharmaceutical Society.[16] Two schools of engineering were envisaged, with Trinity continuing to provide a more general course, and UCD offering options that were more specialised and needed more expensive equipment. Commerce and social science were both to go to UCD, with agriculture and architecture also continuing there only. Finally, 'TCD should become the main centre of legal studies in Dublin, and further development should take place on its campus'.

On 25 June 1970, just two months after the Agreement was made public, the Catholic bishops announced that they were seeking approval from Rome for the repeal of the statute prohibiting the attendance, without special permission, of Catholic students at Trinity College. It was subsequently suggested that there had been prior negotiation between the College and the hierarchy, but this was not the case. The first direct intimation of change came in a letter to the Provost from Archbishop McQuaid stating his intention to nominate a chaplain. Approval from Rome was duly secured by the beginning of September, and Cardinal Conway stated that the move was the culmination of a process of rethinking which had been going on among the bishops since 1965. So the 'ban', which had been supported in one form or another by the hierarchy since 1875, was finally lifted. The growth of ecumenism since Vatican II had rendered it increasingly untenable, and the hierarchy's reaction to the O'Malley plan had encouraged many more Catholics to enter the College in the belief that the 'ban' had in practice ceased to be enforced.[17] If the Agreement was implemented, there would be compelling educational grounds for its total abolition since at least two subjects in great demand by Catholics and Protestants alike would be available only in Trinity. Archbishop McQuaid's appointment, in November 1970, of the Reverend Brendan Heffernan, then junior chaplain in UCD, as the first Dean of Residence for Roman Catholic students, sealed the rapprochement.

Details have recently been published about the subsequent initiative taken by Archbishop Buchanan to modify the original terms of consecration of the College Chapel, which restricted it to Church of Ireland services. Buchanan wished to open it for wider use by the Christian community in the College. After consulting his House of Bishops, and taking legal advice, he achieved his ecumenical purpose by making a formal enabling declaration in the Chapel after morning service on 18 October 1973. The declaration was made with the approval of the College authorities, and since then the Chapel has been in regular use for services (including Mass) by all the main denominations.[18]

The NUI/TCD Agreement was quite well received by the staff of Trinity, and the Board decided to accept it as the best that could be reached in the circumstances. It was also largely endorsed by the HEA when it made its merger report to the Minister (now Padraig Faulkner) at the end of 1971. The report was published in July 1972, and contained an important new proviso that a conjoint board should be established 'to promote rationalisation and co-operation between the two institutions', UCD being in effect regarded as the other main party to the Agreement. When the report was considered by the Trinity faculties in the following Michaelmas term, opposition focused on the proposal for a conjoint board, and the Board agreed that such a body would only complicate decision-making and resource allocation. The Board's general attitude was that the government should make a clear decision about the subject allocation proposed in the report. Once that had been done, the two universities could co-operate voluntarily to implement the decision in consultation with the HEA. The Board stressed the need to end the uncertainty so that planned accommodation for the large increase in students could go ahead.

The Fianna Fáil government's intentions, however, soon became irrelevant. It fell from power in February 1973, and Richard Burke took over as Minister for Education in a Coalition administration led by Liam Cosgrave. UCD had always been less happy with the Agreement than

Trinity, and now began to lobby hard for its revision, particularly in regard to the provisions for science, law, medicine and veterinary medicine. Trinity submitted its rejection of these arguments, and there the matter rested until 16 December 1974 when Burke went public with a new scheme for a definitive resolution of the university question. He declared that its provisions were 'final decisions', though they had not yet been discussed with the universities themselves. 'Perhaps it has been my lot', he said, 'to pick up the pieces (after the O'Malley "thunderbolt") and to produce a coherent plan for the last quarter of this century.' UCD was to be separated from the NUI and given university status. The original proposal — to join UCD and TCD in a single university — was dropped, but the ghost of the merger remained in the form of a conjoint board to 'co-ordinate the two Dublin universities with a view to ensuring rationalisation of resources and mobility of staff and students between them'. The proposed allocation of subjects was distinctly less favourably to Trinity, with UCD retaining its law school, taking sole responsibility for veterinary medicine, and likely to dominate the proposed 'joint science faculty'. Perhaps the most important feature of the Burke scheme was its new proposals for the fuller integration of technological education into the third-level sector.

Leland Lyons had taken over the provostship from McConnell in October 1974 and he at once issued a statement highly critical of Burke's announcement. He regretted its departures from the 1972 HEA report and the 'Agreement' (though in fact he recognised that second thoughts in UCD had long since turned the latter into a dead letter). The new Provost felt that the announcement created fresh uncertainties through its vagueness on many crucial points, and he found those portions of it that related to his own College 'quite unacceptable'. The Heads of Colleges meeting soon afterwards also expressed their dissatisfaction with the proposed conjoint board, with the failure to grant university status to Cork and Galway, and with what they (with some reason) regarded as a further intrusion of ministerial and civil service influence into the internal affairs of the universities.

The situation had an all too familiar look. The government was again trying to impose its will by ministerial *diktat* without proper consultation, the Colleges were still fighting their own corners, and the mutual distrust and hostility between Trinity and UCD seemed as strong as ever. Faced with determined opposition, it was likely that the government would drag its feet on the legislation needed to solve the problems to its satisfaction, and this in fact was what happened.

The College rallied behind the Provost. The staff met on 14 January 1975 and resolved to oppose all the main points in the Minister's proposals; soon afterwards the Board issued a statement to the effect that the Burke plan, though clarified, remained unacceptable. Trinity was happy enough to see two law schools since this would allow for a valuable diversity of approach and would enable UCD to preserve its traditional links with the legal profession. But it felt, with reason, that similar arguments would justify the maintenance of business and social studies on both campuses. It thought that the numbers taking science were large enough to justify the retention of a separate faculty in the College, and it naturally disliked the idea of an engineering faculty without capital investment, even though the Minister, in a private interview, assured the Provost that the capital embargo would be temporary only.

In the end, the only change that Burke succeeded in making was the termination of Trinity's veterinary faculty, which took effect in 1977. The College fought hard to retain the subject, but its case was weakest at this point, given the high costs involved and the small number of students in comparison with those in UCD. There could also be seen to be some compensation for the loss in the gain of pharmacy and dentistry.

As one traces the course of the university question from O'Malley to Burke, it is all too easy to conclude that mountains of paper generated only this one particular mouse, though the severance was traumatic enough for those involved. More radical change was inhibited by two main factors: the reluctance of any college to give up any of its activities, and the seeming inability of successive Ministers of Education to keep the necessary legislation at the top of the political agenda, or even to produce a White Paper on the future of third-level education in Ireland.

But there was more progress than appeared on the surface. The HEA, with strong university representation, was proving its worth as a body for co-ordinating plans and allocating resources on a more rational and equitable basis. Its first major capital expenditure was in funding for the new Arts and Social Studies building in Trinity. The universities themselves were also beginning to realise that there was more to be gained by co-operation than by outright competition. Most importantly of all, Trinity had now been officially accepted into full and equal partnership in the third-level system. The voices that wished to exclude it had had their last say, and the 'ban' had been quietly buried in the welter of negotiation that followed O'Malley's initial announcement.

The desire to find allies in the fight against the Burke proposals also brought Trinity into significantly closer partnership with the City of

Dublin Vocational Educational Committee (the VEC). The VEC Colleges originally prepared students for the examinations of external bodies like the City and Guilds of London Institute. By the 1960s they had developed their own examinations and diplomas, which in many cases, and particularly in engineering, were accepted by external professional bodies for their registration requirements. Diploma-holders were also allowed to register for postgraduate work in Irish and British universities, and Trinity had been particularly accommodating in this respect. By the end of 1974, some fifty Engineering diploma-holders of the Bolton and Kevin Street Colleges had been admitted to postgraduate engineering courses in Trinity, and had gone on to take higher degrees.

The VEC Colleges were hoping to develop towards university status through the so-called 'Ballymun project', but these hopes were dashed early in 1975 when Dick Burke established the National Institute of Higher Education (Dublin) with its own governing body independent of the VEC. So the VEC began to look to Trinity for help in its aspirations, and at the same time Provost Lyons was disposed to bolster the College's position by its influential support. Professor Bill Wright, as head of Trinity's School of Engineering, was very much in favour of a TCD/VEC partnership. He saw his School under particular threat from the Burke plan, and, as a member of the governing body of Bolton Street, was well placed to judge the standard of VEC technological training. So, early in 1975, discussions about extended co-operation began between representatives of Trinity and the VEC. By May the Council had agreed to accept the Dublin Institute of Technology engineering courses as of honors degree standard, and this earnest of good faith led both bodies to decide to develop an operational framework for accrediting courses.

By the spring of the following year, co-operation has progressed to the point where it could be embodied in a formal partnership agreement, jointly signed by Provost Lyons and Patrick Donegan, chairman of the City of Dublin VEC, and published on 29 April 1976. The Agreement gave formal shape to consultation and co-operation 'on a basis of absolute parity', a phrase and concept due to Lyons himself. He reached it after a significant consultation with Lord Bowden, who told him that in his experience (in Manchester) the biggest obstacle to successful co-operation between universities and colleges of technology was the tendency of university staffs to think of and treat their opposite numbers as in some way of inferior status, an attitude embodied in terms like 'constituent college' or 'recognised college'. Lyons, the historian, took a broad humanistic view of the liberal and technical traditions, and realised that there would be opportunities for each to learn from the other.

The two parties pledged themselves to encourage co-operation in research (which has been successfully achieved in a number of disciplines), and to join in the design and development of courses (where examples may be seen in music education and dietetics). The agreement to 'make facilities and staff available to each other' has tended to operate more at student level, where Trinity fourth-year engineering students sometimes do projects at Bolton Street, while Trinity library tickets are issued to VEC students. The Agreement provided for a Liaison Council to promote and supervise the 'co-operative association', and rapid progress was made in the recognition of VEC diploma courses for Trinity degree awards. University standards are safeguarded by rigorous course evaluation and the monitoring of results by external examiners. By 1977 degree awards were available in architecture, construction economics, applied science, advanced business studies, advanced marketing and hotel and catering management (higher diploma). Recognition was given to human nutrition and dietetics (a joint Kevin Street-Trinity course) in 1982, to building services (Bolton Street) in 1983, to environmental health (Cathal Brugha Street) in 1984, and to music education (College of Music, in association with the Royal Irish Academy of Music) in 1985. The most recent courses to be recognised were management law (Rathmines) and medical laboratory sciences (Kevin Street). By 1989 the number of students from these various subjects annually eligible for degree awards had risen to over five hundred, a type of 'merger' very different from that originally envisaged, and sensibly based on consent, not coercion.[19]

Notes

1. The hardening of the hierarchy's attitude to Trinity in the 1940s and '50s is well documented by J.H. Whyte in *Church and State in Modern Ireland* (1971), 305-07. The current regulations derived from a Maynooth synodal statute passed in 1956, but phrased in somewhat archaic language — there was no mention of Catholic maidens — as follows: 'We forbid under pain of mortal sin: (1) Catholic youths to frequent the College; (2) Catholic parents or guardians to send to that College Catholic youths committed to their care; (3) Clerics and religious to recommend in any manner parents or guardians to send Catholic youths to that College or to lend counsel or help to such youths to frequent that College. Only the Archbishop of Dublin is competent to decide in accordance with the norms of the Holy See, in what circumstances and with what guarantees against perversion, attendance at that College may be tolerated.' This last clause had the effect of making Archbishop McQuaid the sole arbiter of requests for permission from all dioceses in the state. The statute came into force in 1960 and at once led to a reduction in Catholic admissions from 25 to 17 per cent, though they picked up later in the decade.
2. The inaugural meeting of the Laurentian Society was held on 30 November 1953 with Dr Donal O'Sullivan, Lecturer in International Affairs, as its president. The Society was then fully recognised by the Board and given rooms. Its object was to provide social, cultural and recreational facilities for Catholic students. Such students were not left wholly without religious ministration since the Archbishop normally assigned one of the priests attached to Westland Row parish to be responsible for their spiritual welfare. Shortly before the 'merger' announcement, three Catholic Fellows, David Thornley, Jim Lydon and Dermot Hourihane, went to see the Archbishop to ask for some further action in the matter of a resident chaplain. They were courteously received, but reported his reply as 'devastating'. He had not, however, stood totally aside from ecumenical trends, for at a public meeting in 1966 he had joined with the Protestant Archbishop of Dublin in a recital of the Lord's Prayer.
3. In *The Irish Times*, 5 April 1967.
4. Tarlach Ó Raifeartaigh, the Secretary of the Department of Education under O'Malley, became its first chairman, and was succeeded by Seán O'Connor in 1974/75. In its first full year of operation, 1973/74, it disbursed £11,751,078 in recurrent grants, and £1,756,609 in capital grants. Trinity's allocations were £3,063,100 and £358,441 respectively. By 1983, grants to Trinity had risen to £18,047,000 (current) and £1,856,963 (capital). In the 1970s, when funds flowed freely enough, the Authority became an effective 'third force' between departments of state and the third-level sector, assessing and co-ordinating development proposals submitted by the colleges, and helping to establish an equitable basis for the allocation of current and capital grants. When cutbacks became increasingly stringent in the 1980s, its independence was sapped, and the Colleges began to think that it operated only to pass on the bad news of successive retrenchments from the Departments of Finance and Education.
5. II *Report*, Vol. 1, chapter 16.
6. Dr Michael Tierney, then President of UCD, said in a written submission and in oral evidence that he viewed Trinity as a rival institution claiming parity with UCD and holding itself out as a university suitable for Catholics. But he considered it to be a 'foreign body' whose whole tradition 'is something that we can never assimilate into the national life'. He described the relationship as a 'truceless cold war' (p.446). The 'ideal solution' (though he hesitated to advocate it as a practical one) would be to 'close down Trinity College' and to found a new University of Dublin at Belfield. The only future he could see for Trinity was as an 'enclave for Protestants'. The only other substantial submissions on the position of Trinity came from the Catholic Headmasters Association and the University Research Group of Tuairim (Dublin branch). Neither of these bodies appeared unsympathetic to the idea that Trinity could and should be better integrated into the Irish university system. (II *Report*, Vol. 1, 438-39 and 446).

7. Here they specifically wanted to see a joint development of studies, with specialised fields mutually demarcated, specialist staff exchanged, and costly research equipment shared. As a basis for general co-operation, they suggested the need for a formal agreement that neither institution would engage in work not appropriate for a university, nor take on activities for which existing facilities were inadequate.
8. He could also have seen an *Irish Times* report (1/2/67) of a meeting of Trinity's Elizabethan Society (a society for woman students) at which Professor Denis Donoghue of UCD had expressed the opinion that the country could not afford to have in Dublin 'two fully-equipped universities each supplied with its own full range of university facilities at the highest international level'. Donoghue suggested that the 'university scandal', as well as the 'ban', could be terminated if TCD and UCD were to be incorporated as two colleges of the University of Dublin. The suggestion was welcomed by Professor Stanford, who was one of Trinity's Senate representatives at the time.
9. In 1965/66 there were 3327 students in Trinity: 2085 from Ireland (including 741 from the Six Counties); 947 from Britain; and 295 from elsewhere. O'Malley was piqued that the College had taken its decision without any prior sanction from the state, and at a time when it still had over 1200 non-Irish students, most of them from well-developed countries, and estimated to cost the taxpayer £170 a head per annum.
10. The full text of the Minister's statement is given in the HEA's *Report on University Reorganisation* (1972), 68-76.
11. Their opinion probably coincided with that of General Costello as presented in the Commission Report. The initial summary of Costello's position might have been taken to favour a merger in the statement: 'Our limited resources make it impossible for us to support more than three universities.... For this reason and to end the wasteful and otherwise undesirable competition between T.C.D. and U.C.D. I recommend the establishment of a new University of Dublin absorbing both of them....' (I *Report*, Vol. 2, 891-96). But the full statement of his Reservation (II *Report*, Vol. 2, 891-96) revealed strong antipathy to Trinity. He proposed a fresh start, with a new university at Belfield 'partaking of none of the traditions either of Trinity College or University College'. In such a situation, Trinity would have been abolished rather than absorbed, and Costello suggested that its historic buildings could be taken over for postgraduate use and to house the Dublin Institute for Advanced Studies.
12. Garret FitzGerald supplied this in a thoughtful analysis (*The Irish Times*, 26 April 1967). The options appeared to be: (1) a two-college system in one University with separate faculties where numbers justified it, and single faculties in one or other college where numbers were small; (2) a two-college system in which each would have a different but complementary range of schools and faculties; (3) a complete merger resulting in a single-college university. FitzGerald hinted that the colleges would be well advised to try to reach agreement among themselves on their preferred option, independently of the Minister's efforts.
13. The Board conveyed these views to the Minister in a memorandum dated 19 July 1967, in which it made a sensible first attempt to work out the constitutional and other implications of merging the colleges in a new university structure.
14. For the full text of the statement, see the HEA's 1972 *Report*, 77-82.
15. For the full text, see the HEA's 1972 *Report*, 83-92. The statement and other press comment made it clear that the NUI/TCD Agreement, as it came to be known, consisted of proposals agreed by representatives and not yet ratified by the respective governing bodies. It was still to be discussed by the staffs of the colleges, and the attitude of the government remained unknown. Some of the most important details of the plan — for example, those relating to medicine and law — still remained to be worked out.
16. The Society subsequently accepted a government proposal that pharmacy should be taught in TCD, and the Board was notified of this in January 1971.
17. In 1969/70 the *total* number of undergraduates stood at 3640, of whom 1241 (34 per cent) were Catholics. But in the first-year class (834 in all) they numbered 400 (48 per cent).

18. For details of Buchanan's initiative, see the important article by George Dawson in *The Irish Times* of 28 June 1991 (but his dating of the end of the ban to 1971 needs to be amended to 1970). The Blessed Sacrament Oratory in the gallery of the Chapel was opened on 22 February 1976.
19. As further proof of the very extensive network of relationships built up by Trinity in the third-level sector, one may record that the University also has teaching and degree-awarding relationships with the Church of Ireland College of Education in Rathmines, St Mary's College of Education at Marino, the Froebel College of Education at Sion Hill, Blackrock, the Irish School of Ecumenics, the Irish Management Institute, the Institute of Public Administration, and the Church of Ireland Theological College — the last being a new phase of a very old relationship.

CHAPTER 15

Student unrest from 1968 to 1980

In the mid-1960s, student protests and occupations became a feature of university life on a worldwide scale. 'Direct action', exacerbated by the Vietnam War, led to violent disruption on many campuses in the United States, and European universities began to experience the revolutionary fervour of hard-left politics. In 1966/67 the London School of Economics was thrown into turmoil over the appointment of a president with South African connections. It was not therefore surprising that Trinity should have had its first taste of politically motivated student disturbances in 1968, but it was somewhat ironic that the trouble broke out just at the moment when the Board was beginning to respond positively to student demands for a greater say in the running of the College.

On 1 May 1968 the Board approved a recommendation from a committee chaired by the Vice-Provost, Dr Herbert Parke, that students should be given representation on all School Committees, a practice already established in the schools of mathematics and business studies. Further recommendations for student participation soon followed, leading to the setting up, in Michaelmas term, of a Central Staff/Student Committee chaired by the Provost, with equal representation of staff and students. Five special committees were also established on similar lines to cover discipline, accommodation, catering, amenities and the capitation fee. The following year the Board showed its willingness to go much further down the democratic path. On 2 February 1969 Adrian Bourke, president of the Students' Representative Council, proposed that sabbatical years should be allowed to the president and deputy president during their term of office, and this was soon granted, together with a salary of £550 plus £100 for expenses. A further demand for student representation on the Board itself was also conceded on 2 April, it being understood that seats would be offered to the two sabbatical officers elected for the following academic year, provided the election was by direct franchise of all the students. The constitution of the SRC was revised to allow this to happen.[1]

These changes were just beginning to be made at the time of a Belgian royal visit to Ireland that included the two Dublin colleges in its itinerary. The visit to Belfield passed off without incident, and about noon on 15 May 1968 King Baudouin and Queen Fabiola arrived at the Front Gate of Trinity.[2] As their car was entering, a picket of five students stationed under the archway began to boo and wave a banner bearing the legend: *Lumumba tué par l'Imperialisme Belge.* The students belonged to the Action Group on Southern Africa, a subsidiary of the Trinity Maoist group known as the Internationalists.[3]

The focus of disturbance then shifted to the east end of the Old Library where a considerable crowd had gathered to see the royal couple go up to the Long Room. When the protesters reached the rear of the crowd at the gap by the Rubrics, they met with a hostile reaction from the majority of the students, one of whom tried to pull down their banner. The police in attendance then became apprehensive for the safety of the royal party and decided to break up the demonstration by force. Reinforcements were summoned, and Nick Miller, the chairman of the Internationalists, who was standing nearby, had his arm twisted by a Garda. Scuffles at once broke out, and a violent tug-of-war developed around the banner. Fists and boots were used on both sides, but no serious injury was caused.

After ten or fifteen minutes, Professor Stanford made his way through the mêlée and persuaded the police to allow the demonstrators to keep their banner. This cool-headed intervention quelled the trouble for the moment, but disturbances broke out again in Grafton Street when the King and Queen, who had been whisked away through the Fellows' Garden, made to leave the Provost's House. The Gardaí may again be thought to have over-reacted, using strong-arm tactics to move the students on, thus fuelling the allegations of 'police brutality' which were soon heard at an impromptu mass meeting by the Dining Hall steps. The Socialist Society (formerly the Fabian Society) strongly condemned the action of the Gardaí against 'peaceful demonstrators'. When the Internationalists spoke, they were heckled as 'communists'. The SRC, with Alan Matthews as its president, took the line that the majority of students had no objection to the royal visit, but deplored the forcible suppression of the demonstration.

Meanwhile the *Evening Herald* came out with a sensationalised report describing how uniformed Gardaí clashed head-on with 'hundreds of wildly demonstrating students chanting anti-Belgian slogans and waving banners'. The students were now further incensed by 'press misrepresentation', and later in the evening about a thousand of them marched to make a protest at the Independent Newspaper Group offices in Middle Abbey Street, and also at Pearse Street Garda Station.

No disciplinary action resulted from any of these incidents, but the College was thrown into a fever of meetings and a ferment of argument at the very moment when student 'revolt' was reaching state-threatening proportions in France and Germany. When tempers cooled, the consensus was that the police had probably shown some lack of discretion, but no brutality. The affair was very minor by continental standards, but it was a classic example of how quickly student feeling could be stirred up against 'authority' in general when a tiny but determined left-wing group made a specific political protest, and then helped to foment trouble on other issues. It was significant as the first manifestation of 'student power' on the Trinity campus, and as the prelude to more than a decade of organised demonstrations, occupations, boycotts, and harassment of visiting Ministers of State.

The 1970s opened with a student body much politicised by international events and the Northern crisis, and open to radical ideas emanating from various quarters. The hard-line Marxism of the Internationalists proved attractive to some, especially when propounded by what one student of the time remembers as the 'mesmerising brilliance' of David Vipond. 'Bloody Sunday' and the burning of the British embassy early in 1972 lent impetus to the republican movement on campus. In general there was a broad measure of sympathy for the 'left', reflected in support for the Workers' Party, the Republican Clubs, and Labour in general.

The move to the left led, in 1975, to the replacement of the SRC by a Students' Union. This was more than just a change of name. There was an extensive reorganisation based on smaller constituencies with the 'class' (e.g. first-year medical students, third-year engineers) as the unit electing council representatives. This reform led to more direct and sensitive contact between the sabbatical officers and the executive on the one side and the student body on the other. A third seat on the College Board was granted to the Education Officer, and Union representatives were also admitted to the University Council.

The growing commitment and self-assurance of student power was seen in a number of disruptive campaigns, including a short occupation of the Senior Common Room in 1973, an extended catering boycott of several weeks in 1975, and several overnight occupations of the Library. The more militant of the left-wingers took the view that such 'direct action' was justified as the culmination of any campaign of negotiation that failed to produce concessions on well-established grievances. These demonstrations were non-violent, but a serious threat to public order (in which the SRC was *not* directly involved) occurred on the occasion of the inaugural meeting of the College Historial Society in 1973. The invited speakers included Jonathan Guinness, chairman of the British Tories Monday Club, and the then Minister for Justice, Patrick Cooney. Under the slogan 'No free speech for fascists', Maoist and Republican sympathisers joined forces to prevent speakers and guests from entering the Examination Hall where the meeting was due to be held. When the venue was switched to the Dining Hall, fighting broke out between the protesters and those wishing to attend. Fortunately, no serious injuries were sustained by either side, but in the end the Senior Dean, George Dawson, had to call in the Gardaí to restore order.

The College made no move to discipline anyone after this fracas, but a more serious disturbance some years later had a different outcome. The occasion was the opening of the Bauhaus exhibition in the Douglas Hyde Gallery by James Tunney, Minister of State for Education, on 6 March 1979. It was known that the Union intended to place a picket in order to convey to the Minister their members' dissatisfaction with the incoherence of government policy on education, and Captain John Martin, the General Services Officer, claimed that the Union officers had been fully briefed beforehand about security measures to be taken by the College. Afterwards the Union officers claimed that the picket had been kept further back from the gallery entrance than they had been given to understand it would be. They also claimed that the large numbers of security staff on duty, the bringing in of the Minister by a side door, and the erection of steel barriers, all constituted a provocation. The Minister did speak to the picket over the barrier, but the demonstration then got out of control. The barriers were rushed, scuffling broke out between students and security staff, and some injury was caused, particularly to Michael Keogh, the superintendent of the Arts building, who was attacked by a woman student. An attempt was also made to prevent guests from entering the exhibition. After prolonged investigation and discussion, the Board decided that six students, identified by various witnesses as ringleaders in the disturbances, should be charged before the Disciplinary Committee. The hearing did not take place until the following October, when some fines and one three-month suspension were imposed, decisions which at once became the subject of an appeal to the Visitors.

The protracted nature of the proceedings caused a souring of relationships within College, and this estrangement was a significant factor in the most bitter and prolonged of all the student disputes, which occupied much of the academic year 1979/80 during the Union presidency of John Joseph ('Joe') Duffy. Duffy and his executive took issue with the Board over the catering services, and in particular over the subsidisation of Commons and the staff outlet known as the Upper Lunch Room. The root of the trouble went back to a 1977 Board decision to cut catering overheads by reforming accounting procedures and restricting all services to a five-day week. At a time when fees were increasing and grants lagging behind inflation, the students were particularly sensitive to any government or College decisions affecting their social or economic welfare. They felt, with some reason, that the financing of catering was being altered to their disadvantage. In particular, they objected to prices in the main outlets being adjusted to cover all direct costs while what they viewed as disproportionate subsidisation of staff meals continued. The financing of Commons was complicated by the statutory entitlement of Fellows and Scholars to free meals, and by the need to maintain the service at times of small demand. The Treasurer estimated the annual direct subsidy to be £7500, but pointed out that this cost was borne, not by other catering outlets, but by the *cista communis*. In the Upper Lunch Room the prices were double those in the cafeteria; but, because of the waiter service and other amenities, direct costs were not being met and there was an annual subsidy of £3500 (not more than was provided by many a firm for its employees). The facility was valued by the staff, especially for the entertainment of guests and extern examiners, and the Academic Staff Association regarded it as part of the conditions of employment. (In June 1978 the Board had decided to continue the service in 'more or less its present style' while effecting some modest economies.)

The Union campaign was initiated by a one-day boycott of catering on 22 November 1979, and the animus of the executive was further shown by an occupation of the Dining Hall complex that disrupted Commons and other catering services on 29 and 30 November. The Union claimed that the occupation was primarily its contribution to a National Day of (student) Protest against inadequate government support for higher education, but it was also designed to highlight the students' grievances with Trinity. In addition to their dissatisfaction with catering, the students felt badly treated in the provision of College venues for Union entertainment ventures (Ents). Concerts organised over the previous two years had led to much friction, not only with the Deans, but also with the staff who had to service them. There had been such a legacy of excessive noise, invasion by disorderly non-student elements from the city, and sheer mess, that the security staff and cleaners were becoming restive about Ents events, and early in November a disturbance in the buttery led the bar staff to refuse to service concerts there. In order to find some way out of this impasse, the Senior Dean had called a tripartite meeting between the Union, middle management, and trade union representatives shortly before the protest occurred. This meeting had produced an agreed code of practice for the notification and organisation of future gigs. The Union broke this agreement within days by running an unscheduled concert in the Dining Hall (an excluded venue) during the occupation, so the level of trust all round remained low during the Christmas vacation.

In January 1980 a series of Union class and council meetings indicated widespread dissatisfaction with a number of aspects of the catering service[4] and by the end of the month the council was calling for an all-out boycott if the Board refused to agree to Union demands. In addition to the issue of subsidies for staff meals (where a demand was formulated for their *transfer* to students outlets, rather than for their abolition), the Union wanted an improvement in the quantity of portions and in the nutritional value of the food served (though with prices remaining frozen), an extension of opening hours in the Arts Building servery, and better and cheaper provision of evening meals for students not dining on Commons.

On 7 February a Union Assembly held in the Edmund Burke Theatre endorsed the boycott. Armed with this support, the student representatives (Joe Duffy as president, Alex White as deputy president, Liam Hayes as education officer) put their case at a Board meeting a week later. The Treasurer had calculated the net subsidy on indirect catering costs for the current year at £61,000. This figure did not include an estimate of £31,000 for profits made by catering at special functions on a commercial basis, so the gross College subsidy to ordinary catering was £92,000, a not inconsiderable sum in relation to the total College budget. After hearing the students, the Board decided that the existing general policy on accounting, pricing and subsidies (which had flowed from a consultants' report and had been adopted after prolonged discussion the previous June) would continue unchanged for the current year, but offered to negotiate on any other aspects of catering. This decision effectively ruled out any immediate discussion on the students' main grievance, thus rendering an all-out boycott almost inevitable, and an Assembly meeting held after lunch on the Dining Hall steps duly mandated its commencement for the following day.[5]

The College authorities never questioned the right of the Union to mount a boycott, though they were much concerned about its effect on the morale of the catering staff, and about allegations of obstruction and intimidation by pickets. Some of the student officers, and the Union president in particular, believed in the 'propaganda of the deed'. This was the view that, in pursuit of a sincerely held objective, any action, no matter how outrageous or misguided, was better than none, and would prove self-justifying since it would provoke opposition and so lead to political movement. (The slogan 'Take over the city', dating from this period, is still faintly visible on a top-floor wall in the Arts Building). Accordingly, on 18 February, Duffy took over the Regent House, which since 1972 had been made available (within stated hours) to the Union as a Junior Common Room (the JCR), and announced the provision of an 'alternative catering service' there, including the operation of a bar. The bar had the unusual feature of advertising 'free' drinks, but an empty pint glass, for example, was priced at 49 pence. This subterfuge in no way mitigated the illegality of the operation since the Regent House was simply not licensed for the serving or consumption of alcohol. An attempt was made to block the importation of supplies, but this proved unsuccessful, and the superintendent of Pearse Street Garda station informed the College authorities that he would have to hold them responsible for any breach of the licensing laws on College premises. On Provost Lyons's instructions, the Senior Dean (J.V. Luce) wrote to Duffy on 21 February requiring the immediate termination of the bar service, but this order was disregarded. The Union was now not merely in dispute with the Board, but also in clear breach of College discipline and the law of the land.

A special Board meeting to consider the situation was held on 25 February. Duffy intimated that the decision to run a bar had been taken after proper consultation of the Union executive, a 'fact' subsequently challenged by at least one member of the executive,[6] and said that he would continue the service until the executive directed otherwise. He would bring the Senior Dean's letter to their notice, but did not think they would comply with it. He also complained that it had not been possible to negotiate any aspect of the catering demands because the Agent and the Catering Officer (Betty Pickering) had withdrawn from a meeting of the Catering Consultative Committee, and were not willing to attend while the boycott continued. Duffy and his officers crossed swords with the Junior Dean by persistent and unauthorised use of loud-hailers, and by breaches of the rules about posters; and Duffy compounded his defiance of authority by assuring the Board that similar action would continue as long as the boycott remained in operation.

Dr Lyons then asked the student representatives to withdraw, in accordance with normal procedure, so that their actions could be discussed in their absence. After hearing a representative of the College solicitors on the legal aspects of the situation, the Board decided that it must protect its interests by an ultimatum. The students were accordingly recalled to hear the Board's decision that if they did not accept a direction to close the bar by 11 p.m. that evening, steps would be taken to close the Regent House to students. Duffy and his colleagues interpreted this as an attempt to break the boycott by hitting at the 'alternative service', and his response was to sign for the keys of the Regent House at Front Gate, and refuse to surrender them.

In the High Court the following day, 26 February, the Board was granted an injunction restraining the Union executive, and all others, from selling alcohol in the JCR. An interim injunction was also granted against the unauthorised occupation of any College building. When the Senior Dean and Captain Martin went up to the JCR to try to enforce the injunctions, Duffy greeted them by saying 'You are not welcome here'. When the Senior Dean retorted: 'I could say the same about you', a faint smile appeared on Duffy's face, but he still refused to surrender the premises or close the bar until there had been negotiations on *all* the Union's stated demands.

The confrontation worsened at the next day's Board meeting when the Senior Dean reported on developments. The student representatives accepted his report as a fair statement, but refused to comment further. When again asked by the Provost to withdraw, they refused point-blank to do so. The Provost was forced to adjourn the meeting from the Board Room to his library, and the student members were not admitted when discussion resumed.

The authority of the Board and how to enforce it had now become the overriding issue. On the external front, the Board decided to take further legal steps to try to ensure compliance with the Court's order. This meant going back to Court on 5 March to seek an interlocutory injunction, with committal to prison looming for those persisting in contempt, though such an outcome was certainly not desired by the authorities. It was hoped that the week's breathing space would allow saner counsels to prevail.

On the internal front, the Board members found it intolerable that the students should claim the right to attend meetings while refusing to accept the directions of the Board and its chairman. Accordingly, it was decided that the representational privileges hitherto accorded to the students on the Board and its various subcommittees should be suspended until further notice. (This measure was felt by the Union executive to be deeply injurious to its interests, and turned out to be the most effective of all the sanctions that the Board imposed. Some left-wing members of staff thought it unacceptable.) The Board also confirmed its readiness to discuss all catering issues, except the matters of accounting and subsidy excluded at its meeting of 13 February, and showed good faith by nominating the Bursar (John Scott, an effective negotiator not unsympathetic to student demands) as its representative for this purpose. Finally, the Board instructed the Senior Dean to take appropriate action, under the statutes, to bring to the Board complaints relating to alleged serious offences by students of the College. The Board had primarily in mind the takeover of the Regent House and its use as a bar. To proceed thus against the elected representatives of the students was a serious step, but the Board could see no alternative if it was to assert its authority. Normally such charges would have been heard before the Disciplinary Committee, but the Union executive had given prior notice that it would not recognise this lower tribunal. The Board's invocation of its ultimate disciplinary powers was to become the chief *casus belli* in the weeks ahead.

All these decisions were notified to the Union, but there was no constructive response beyond a decision taken at an Assembly meeting on 28 February to close the bar the following day (which was the end of term). This move enabled Duffy to concentrate attention on the Union's retention of the JCR as a new and major issue, and to represent its continued occupation as a legitimate stand by the executive in defence of the Union's traditional privileges and facilities.

On 5 March the College was granted an interlocutory injunction restraining the Union from occupying or using any part of the College premises without permission. At 2 p.m. on that day the Union executive surrendered possession of the Regent House, and the Vice-Provost (Dr Howie) at once held preliminary discussions to arrange for the resumption of negotiations on the matters in dispute. Duffy probably hoped that he would get the premises back immediately, together with a promise of negotiation on all the Union's demands about catering. When it became clear that he could only expect a meeting with the Bursar the next day, at which a basis for the renewal of the JCR concession would have to be negotiated, and discussion of the subsidies would be ruled out, he decided to renew the struggle. Accordingly he and some supporters broke into the Regent House from No. 6 during the night and forcibly reoccupied it. Next morning a barricade of tables and chairs was found at the top of the stairs outside the main room.

This was a flagrant breach of the High Court order, and on 6 March Duffy was informed in writing of the College's intention to apply for its enforcement if the occupation continued. He replied in defiant vein: 'The Union firmly intends to continue the provision of food services in the Junior Common Room, and we shall therefore remain in occupation'. Duffy also described the use of a High Court order as 'nothing short of direct intimidation'. Over the next few days the legal process moved inexorably towards the arrest of the occupiers by the Gardaí, which happened on 10 March. Five students appeared in Court that afternoon before Mr Justice McWilliam to answer for their contravention of the injunction.[7]

Judge McWilliam directed them to appear before him again on 12 March, and expressed the hope that by that time they would have so ordered their affairs that he would not have to commit them to jail. This prudent stay of execution (represented by student propaganda as a triumphant 'release' and a judicial thwarting of the authorities' intentions) led to intensive discussions the following day between the Bursar and College Secretary for the College, and Duffy, White and Hogan for the Union. Agreement was reached to resume negotiations on catering on the basis that the Union would suspend the boycott for twelve days and end the occupation of Regent House. The College representatives agreed that the JCR could then be returned temporarily for Union use on the conditions on which it had originally been made available, and also agreed to ask the Court to postpone consideration of the committal application. At the hearing, the Judge accepted that the court order was now being observed, and further deferred the case until 27 March, when the College indicated that it did not wish to press the matter further. The case was not dismissed by the Court (as the Union was to allege) and the injunctions remained in force.

Negotiations on catering began on 13 March. The Union stated publicly that *all* their demands were being considered, but this was not in fact the case. The subsidy issue remained excluded, though the Union was allowed to table papers on its attitude to Commons and the Upper Lunch Room. Agreement on other matters was reached a week later. The main concessions secured by the Union were: a considerable extension of hours in the Arts Building coffee service, a temporary two pence reduction in the price of coffee, the provision of an evening hot food service in the West Dining Hall, and extended evening use of the JCR. Had the attempt been made, it is possible that improvements on this scale could have been obtained by consultation and discussion through normal channels without recourse to boycott or occupation.

Tension between the Board and the Union would now have eased if the Senior Dean had not remained obliged (by the Board decision of 27 February) to initiate disciplinary proceedings. It should be noted that the attitude of the High Court Judge was influenced by the College's intention, stated in Court, to bring the students before a domestic tribunal. The students later accused the authorities of failure to notify them that disciplinary proceedings were still pending, but they cannot have been unaware that this was the case, and it was also made clear to them that the question of disciplinary action was in no way linked to the agreement. The timing, however, was unfortunate, and it was all too easy for the Union executive and its sympathisers to represent the action as 'victimisation'[8] and a 'breach of the agreement'.

The Senior Dean took action on 13 March by letters addressed by name to twenty-six students (including the Union officers), setting out various complaints against them. On the basis of exculpatory responses from students and their tutors, the number of defendants was later reduced to seventeen. The complaints numbered eighteen in all, and the most serious of them related to the alleged sale of intoxicating liquor in the JCR and the subsequent break-in and occupation of the room. Alleged breaches of loudspeaker and poster regulations were also taken up. The complaints were made under disciplinary procedures long established by statute.[9] The Board hearing was initially fixed for 18 April but, at the request of the solicitors acting for the Union, was postponed to 2 May. That the Board should itself hear such charges was not, as alleged, 'totally unprecedented', but had become less usual with the setting up of a disciplinary committee. However, as noted above, the current Union executive had repudiated this committee soon after taking office. In fact, as soon became clear, the student leaders did not accept that the Board had any authority to call them to order when, as elected student representatives, they were pursuing policies or courses of action 'mandated' by student assemblies.

The hearing was scheduled for the Examination Hall, but was disrupted by student supporters, who forced an entry through the large windows at the end of the Hall. An adjournment to the Board Room fared no better, with students besieging the doors and hammering on the roof. The process eventually was concluded the following week under heavy security. The hearing was held in legal form with the due recital of complaints, the presentation of evidence, and the calling and cross-examination of witnesses on both sides. The Senior Dean, as chief 'prosecutor', withdrew after presenting his case, and was not present while the Board deliberated about guilt and fixed penalties. In the end, the Board made no finding on five complaints, and gave the Senior Dean permission to withdraw one. At least one of the more serious complaints was held to have been established against eight of the students charged, and at least three complaints against each of the Union officers. Six of the eight were members of the executive, and on 8 May 1980 all eight were notified of their penalty as follows:

> . . . immediate suspension from the College, lasting until midnight on 31 May 1981, during which period you may not enter upon or occupy any part of the College premises or grounds for any purpose whatsoever except with the prior written permission of the Provost or of a person authorised by him for this purpose or for the sole purpose of attending at such place and such times of examination as the Senior Lecturer may certify in writing to the Provost to be necessary for the keeping of your academic year.

The sentenced students had a right of appeal to the Visitors, but instead they decided to continue on a course of agitation and protest. In a broadsheet issued the same day, the Union claimed that 'for representing students, students are being expelled and suspended', and threatening that 'if one single student is either fined, suspended, or expelled on any one of these charges, this college will regret that decision for many a long day'. At issue was the question whether individual students should be arraigned for action taken on behalf of the Union. The situation was also inflamed by the fact that, in the end, only eight students were convicted, though several hundred claimed to have taken part in various stages of the occupation.

The Dublin University Employees' Representative Committee soon passed a motion deploring the fact that *after* the dispute between the College and the Students' Union had been concluded by an agreement, the representatives of the students were then tried by the Board. While 'not condoning some of the Union's actions', they expressed their belief that 'in the settlement of disputes with elected representatives there should be no subsequent disciplining of the representatives'. Furthermore, they stated their feeling that the sentences were too severe. Sympathy for the students was also voiced by twenty-seven members of the academic staff, who wrote to the Board expressing alarm at the 'worsening relationship between students and the college authorities', and calling for a revocation of the sentences 'in the interests of restoring the responsible behaviour on all sides which should characterise a university'.

Trinity now became the scene of disorders that verged on riot. Sessions of the Board had been twice violently broken up, administrative offices in West Chapel were occupied, two paintings in the Common Room (including that of Dr A.A. Luce) were sprayed with red paint, and Commons was disrupted by students using obscene language and shouting that they did not recognise the government of the College. The Junior Dean, J.C.A. Gaskin, was already used to hearing students tell him they did not recognise his authority when they felt they had a legitimate protest to make. Duffy addressed a meeting in College on the day on which his suspension took effect, and when the Board's barring order was reinforced by a Court injunction, he called a mass meeting outside the Front Gate, at which he referred to a 'purge' of the 'small working-class' element in the College. The situation was already an ugly 'crisis of authority', and now a hint of class-war overtones was being gratuitously raised by such utterances.

On 12 May Provost Lyons issued a statement in which he claimed that 'the root cause of the present controversy is the seemingly deliberate policy of the present Students' Union to repudiate the authority of the Board and to set itself up as an autonomous body within the College'. Many felt this to be an accurate diagnosis, although the student representatives would doubtless have claimed that they had been driven into rebellion by the Board's unwillingness to pay due attention to their grievances.

The Provost, who had acted throughout with firmness and moderation, also made clear that 'satisfactory assurances of normal behaviour would enable the Board to review the suspensions'. This was the olive-branch that enabled a leading trade unionist, Kieran Mulvey, to come forward with an offer to mediate. Mulvey had been secretary of the Irish Federation of University Teachers, and was asked to intervene by Tom Costello, president of the Union of Students in Ireland. By 19 May Mulvey had succeeded in calling a halt to the hostilities that were threatening to engulf the College in total anarchy. The basis of the truce was an agreement by the Board to suspend the suspensions in return for individual pledges of good conduct from the students concerned. The students also agreed to 'recognise unequivocally the legal authority of the Board in matters relating to the regulation of academic and adminstrative procedures' in the College. The Board reserved the right to reimpose their sentence on any individual who, in the opinion of the mediator, was found to be in breach of the agreement. The Board also gave an undertaking to the Union not to take any disciplinary action in relation to the disruptions that had occurred at and after the disciplinary hearing on 2 May. An agreed statement was also issued over the signatures of Joe Duffy and Eoin Scott (a co-operative and constructive president-elect) for the Union, and the Bursar, John Scott, for the Board. This was, in effect, a concordat under which student rights to representation on the Board and its committees were renewed in return for a Union undertaking to follow agreed procedures, and not to support or sanction disruptive behaviour by individuals or groups.

Thus, belatedly, both sides were enabled to draw back from the brink of irreconcilable confrontation. Lessons were learned. The Board's determination to maintain its authority was noted and not forgotten. Subsequent union executives have not felt bound to forego the weapon of occupation, but they have not since used it in such a defiant and provocative manner. The 'sit-in' has tended to become something of a 'ritual combat' prior to serious negotiation. The Board, for its part, began to listen harder when grievances were first aired. It also arranged to delegate its authority to hear charges about major offences to a panel of enquiry. The Board will not again be accused of being both judge and jury, but it still bears the responsibility for confirming recommended penalties and for seeing that they are enforced. On the whole, the Board probably emerged from a decade of trial and tribulation with its traditional prestige as the governing body still reasonably intact, and its control over College life and affairs not seriously impaired, at least by comparison with university administrations elsewhere in Europe.

Notes

1. There was precedent in Queen's University, Belfast (where there were four paid sabbatical officers and a paid administrator) and in UCD (where the student president alone was paid). But the Board was very progressive in its willingness to concede seats on the governing body.
2. The following account is based on a report to the Board by a committee of enquiry consisting of Basil Chubb and Jim Lydon (staff) and David Ford and Norman Glass (students).
3. The Internationalists were founded as a discussion group for the propagation of Marxist/Maoist views by H. L. Bains in 1965. See Michael Henry, 'Who are the Internationalists?' (*The Irish Times* 13 and 14 June 1968). Bains was a Canadian who had spent two years in the department of bacteriology as a deputy for W. S. L. Roberts (who was on study leave). The College was much saddened by Roberts's untimely death in 1985. Roberts was the first Trinity lecturer to make use of TV/video teaching aids (in 1971), and advised on their installation in the new Arts Building.
4. There was nothing new in such dissatisfaction. Under the date 2 April 1796, Elrington's *Board Note Books* (TCD MS 9721) refer to a complaint made by the fellow commoners that the quantity of Commons was deficient and the meat bad. They were promised redress.
5. A report on the meeting by Captain Martin, the General Services Officer, stated that the numbers attending never exceeded 200. When the motion for a boycott was put, there were about 150 present, of whom (by Martin's estimate) about 80 voted in favour and 70

against.

6. Martin Moloney, in a long and thoughtful letter to the Senior Dean received about 1 May. Moloney says the same about the subsequent forcible occupation of the JCR. He is predictably critical of the Board's attitude to the Union, which he views as unsympathetic to the point of hostility. He also argues that the move to discipline the Union's officers was impolitic and never likely to be effective. Moloney's letter throws valuable light on the state of student feeling at the time. It forms part of J. V. Luce's personal file on the boycott, now deposited in the Manuscript Room.
7. Their names, much publicised by the Student Union, were: Joe Duffy (President), Mary-Jane O'Brien (Editor of the *Union* newspaper), Brian Dowling (Community Action Officer), John Hogan (Catering Officer) and Paddy Little. All except Little (a Union council member) were members of the executive.
8. The tactic was nothing new, as a pamphlet of 1734, quoted by Stubbs (*History*, 159) makes clear: 'When the Board meets to inquire into a violation of the Statutes on the part of the Students, the young gentlemen who are conscious of their guilt assemble in the courts below; they have secured a number of their friends; they are surrounded by a great crowd of their brethren; how many they may have engaged to be of their party is not to be discovered, and they give, perhaps, plain intimations that they will not suffer them to be censured. Trusting in their numbers, they will not suffer any one man to be singled out for an example.'
9. *Consolidated Statutes*, Chapter IV, para. 35 and Chapter XII, para. 29.

CHAPTER 16

Approach to the quatercentenary: 1974–1991

Trinity's progress since the mid-1970s can hardly yet be assessed in anything like its true historical perspective. In this final chapter, the writer merely proposes to touch briefly on what seem to him to be some of the more significant events and developments not already mentioned. The chronology of the period will first be outlined in terms of its Provosts.

Provost McConnell's stated intention to retire in September 1974 afforded the College an unprecedented opportunity to discuss the terms of the next appointment well in advance of the vacancy. The agenda for change was set at a special meeting of the Fellows on 11 December 1972 at which two main issues were discussed: limitation on length of tenure, and the composition of the electorate. On tenure, the Fellows reached agreement that a ten-year term without the possibility of re-election was preferable to a seven-year term with that same possibility. On the electorate, they agreed that the conclave of Fellows and full-time Professors that had produced nominations for the previous three appointments should be enlarged by the admission of all full-time members of the academic staff with a certain (but as yet unspecified) length of service. In accepting these recommendations, the Board specified three years as the qualifying period for lecturers, and increased the electoral panel by the addition of the student members (for the time being) of the Board and Council. (By the 1981 election the qualifying period had been reduced to one year.)

This was the new and much extended constituency that met in the Public Theatre on 23 February 1974 for the provostship election. The government had asked for three names in order of preference. Over two hundred electors cast their vote for one of the nominated candidates in successive ballots, with elimination of the least favoured name at each stage. In the end Francis Stewart Leland Lyons (1923–83) received majority support in a close contest, ahead of D.I.D. Howie and G. W. P. Dawson, and the College's choice was soon ratified by Liam Cosgrave's cabinet.

Lyons's father was an Ulster Presbyterian, and on his mother's side he had southern and Church of Ireland connections. Through his mother, he was also descended from the Trinity classicist Thomas Leland.[1] In his undergraduate career in Trinity he achieved brilliant success, gaining scholarship in 1943 and a 'first' with gold medal in history and political science in 1945. He also excelled as a games player, being outstandingly good at squash rackets, where his tenacity and delicacy of touch gained him Irish representative honours. After spending four years as a lecturer at the University of Hull, Lyons was elected to a fellowship in history in 1951, and served the College in that position (and also as Senior Tutor 1962–64) until 1964, when he left to become a founder member of the University of Kent and its first Professor of Modern History.

During his time as Provost, Leland Lyons spearheaded an appeal for a research and development fund which raised approximately £2.5 million, took on the chairmanship of the British-Irish Association, and further enhanced his scholarly reputation by his biography of Parnell (1977) and by his Ford Lectures at Oxford in 1978.[2] But he found the competing claims of scholarship and administration increasingly hard to reconcile, particularly in respect of his commitment (contracted with the Oxford University Press in 1974) to write the official biography of W. B. Yeats. In the end Yeats won. In October 1980 Lyons informed the Board of his intention to retire the following September after completing only seven years of his ten-year term. To a mind as firm and cultured as his, the anarchy of the exceptionally bitter and protracted student disturbances of the spring of 1980 proved extremely distasteful, and were an added factor that helped to form his decision.

Still in his mid-fifties, he could look forward to many more productive years as Ireland's leading historian, and further distinctions to add to the six honorary doctorates he already held. Before he took office, it had been agreed that a Provost, on the expiry of his term, could either retire on pension or resume professorial duties. Lyons opted for a personal chair in history, and was in effect given two years' leave of absence, which he used to the full in gathering material for the Yeats biography. He began the writing of the work in his rooms in No. 38 on 1 June 1983, 'a wet, cold, dark Irish summer's day', as a note on the manuscript recorded. Less than four months later, to the amazement and grief of his College and country, he was dead. Until five weeks before the end he was still as active and apparently as fit as ever, and was actually running to catch a bus when, in mid-August, he was stricken by severe internal pains from the onset of acute pancreatitis, a comparatively rare condition that was not at first recognised as such. He died in a Dublin hospital on 21 September. A memorial tablet erected by his wife, Jennifer, in the cemetery by the College Chapel, records the deposit there of the ashes of one 'renowned as a scholar, esteemed as a teacher, and beloved as a man', an epitaph that he richly deserved.

The election to nominate Lyons's successor was held in the Public Theatre on 28 February 1981. The government again asked for three names with the College's preferred choice indicated, and the same voting procedure as before was followed. Professor T. D. Spearman, head of the department of mathematics, was eliminated on the penultimate ballot, and the final round was contested between the Professor of Irish, M. Ó Murchu, and W. A. Watts, with Watts emerging the winner by a substantial majority. Watts's name proved acceptable to the government, and he took up office at the beginning of the academic year 1981/82.

William Arthur Watts was born in Dublin's dockland on 26 May 1930, and educated at St Andrew's College. After winning an entrance scholarship to Trinity in 1948, he read modern languages (French and German), later combining this course with study in science (botany and geology), and gaining first-class moderatorships in both subjects in 1952 and 1953 respectively. His foundation scholarship in 1950 was in languages. After a short period as a lecturer in botany at the University of Hull, he returned to Trinity in 1955, was elected to fellowship in 1960, and was appointed to the chair of botany in 1965. He held the offices of Senior Lecturer (1970–74) and Dean of Science(1968–70 and 1976–80) and had just been made Professor of Quaternary Ecology (1980) when Lyons's retirement was announced. In the field of quaternary studies, Watts inherited the expertise and interests of Frank Mitchell, and gained an international reputation (and a professorial link with the University of Minnesota) for his work on vegetational history and climatic change. His eminence as a scholar was recognised by his election in 1982 for a three-year term as president of the Royal Irish Academy. He also served as chairman of the Federated Dublin Voluntary Hospitals from 1983 onwards.

Watts's provostship (1981–91) was particularly notable for the development of a building programme designed to mark the quatercentenary by extensive and permanent additions to College facilities. The first-fruits of the programme were seen when the O'Reilly Institute for

Communication and Technology, designed by Ronald Tallon of the Dublin architectural firm of Scott Tallon Walker, was opened early in 1989. A timely trip with the plans by the Provost to Pittsburgh in March 1987 had secured the munificent support of Dr A. J. F. ('Tony') O'Reilly for half the cost of the building.[3] The balance was raised by a public appeal. The same source provided funds for the other main elements in the first phase of the programme: the new residence blocks between Pearse Street and the rugby pitch, and the Samuel Beckett Centre for the Performing Arts in the same area.[4]

Before vacating office, Watts was also able to see work start on a project that will bring as much benefit to the life-sciences as the O'Reilly Institute has brought to computer science and physics. The Rowan Hamilton building will be located on the Parade Ground to the south of the O'Reilly Institute, and attached to it will be a biotechnology and applied sciences building. The project is estimated to cost approximately £10 million, of which a substantial portion will come from structural funding provided by the European Community. The balance will be made up by the government as part of its programme for student expansion which is expected to increase numbers in Trinity to 10,000 by 1995.

When a location fee of £100,000 accrued from the filming of *Educating Rita*, Watts persuaded the Board to invest the money in a special fund from which annual grants are now made to support the visual and performing arts in College. He also succeeded in realising an imaginative scheme for the redevelopment of the colonnades and east pavilion of the Old Library. The main object was to provide a treasury and exhibition area where the Book of Kells and other College treasures could be displayed to good advantage to the quarter of a million visitors who now come annually to Trinity, and also to rehouse the library shop. This project started in the summer of 1991, part-funded by a grant of £500,000 from the European Regional Development Fund.

Annual research funding secured by the College from outside sources went up from £1 million to £8 million during Watts's provostship. This surge of self-help came opportunely at a time when the annual government grant fell from 87 to 54 per cent of the total budget. There has been increased co-operation with Irish commerce and industry, and EC-funded programmes went up thirty-fold in the period. Outside links of this kind are seen as a beneficial stimulus to internal research, and the College, through its Innovation Centre, also provides advice and encouragement for the formation of campus companies, which now number twenty.

Thomas Noel Mitchell was nominated as Watts's successor at an election meeting on 2 March 1991, ahead of Vincent Joseph McBrierty, Professor of Polymer Physics, and David John McConnell, Professor of Genetics. A native of Mayo, Mitchell was born in Castlebar on 7 December 1939, and graduated with a 'first' in Latin and Greek at University College, Galway in 1961. He then pursued an academic career in the USA, gaining a doctorate from Cornell Univesity and climbing the promotional ladder at Swarthmore College, where he became Professor of Classics in 1978. He had spent a year in the College on a Mellon Foundation Research Fellowship in 1975/76, and in 1979 he succeeded Donald Wormell in the chair of Latin. With research interests centred in the history and politics of the late Roman Republic, Mitchell has won wide acclaim for his three books on the life and works of Cicero.[5] As senior Dean (1985–87) and Senior Lecturer (1988–90), he became well-known in College as an administrator with a humane and forthright style and a deftly innovative touch. As chairman of the Quatercentenary Committee, he supervised the development of an imaginative programme for the 1992 celebrations. If one excludes Michael Moore, who was put in to head the College in exceptional circumstances, Mitchell has already made history as the first Catholic to become Provost by normal process of election; but one must also make the point that religion has happily ceased to be an issue in Trinity politics.

Nearly all the building development during the 1970s and '80s had its roots in a series of studies undertaken by the Development Committee in consultation with Professor Myles Wright of the University of Liverpool in the late 1960s, forward planning in which the Bursar, Basil Chubb, also played a major role. The main elements considered were: an Arts building, a catering extension, the development of the East End, a sports hall, an administrative building, and a northern perimeter development, including a Fine Arts centre. All these elements, except the administrative building, have either been completed, or are nearing completion, at the time of writing.

The Arts and Social Sciences building, financed through the HEA, was the largest project ever undertaken by the College. The original intention was to accommodate the staff and teaching facilities for students in all the Arts-based subjects except Divinity, and this was largely achieved. One result was that much accommodation in the Front and New Squares was freed for student residence. The College's centre of gravity was also to some extent tilted away from these areas by the new pedestrian access from Nassau Street and the coffee and snack bar facilities provided in the new building.

Sited on the south side of what used to be the Fellows' Garden (now Fellows' Square), the building's total floor area of approximately 190,000 square feet makes it about six times as large as the recently completed O'Reilly Institute. Designed by Paul Koralek, the architect of the Berkeley Library, its horizontal lines and massively reticent structure provide a worthy counterpoise to the Old Library opposite. The architect's brief was agreed by the beginning of March 1970, and the formal opening by President Hillery took place on 11 December 1978. The building contract was won by John Sisk and Son Ltd at a tender price of just under £2.7 million. Included in the building were four large (and one very large) lecture theatres, an undergraduate library, an audio-visual centre, a conference room, an exhibition centre (named after Douglas Hyde), and offices for faculty administration in the wing projecting along the west side of the new square. The square itself, with its vista to the Provost's House and its eye-catching modern sculpture (*Cactus* by Alexander Calder), vies with the older courtyards in architectural interest. The happy blend of classical and modern outlines must have been a major factor in securing for the College campus the distinguished Vom Stein design award in May 1979.

The Arts Building had not been long in use when it became the scene of an extraordinary and disturbing incident. On the afternoon of 24 March 1981 a British Leyland executive, Geoffrey Armstrong, was addressing a seminar organised by the Dublin Junior Chamber of Commerce. The meeting, attended by about sixty persons, was taking place in Room 3074, when three men, two of them armed with hand-guns, burst in through a side-door near the platform. They were wearing combat jackets and balaclavas, and one of them shouted: 'This action is in support of the H-blocks.' (The hunger strike by Bobby Sands was in progress at the time.)[6] Three shots were then fired at Mr Armstrong, who was wounded in the leg, but not seriously. The attackers were thought to have made their getaway by the side-door opening on to College Park, and a decision to confine that access to staff with keys was taken in the subsequent review of security. Despite intense policy activity, which closed the College for some hours, no arrest was made. The IRA naturally came under suspicion, but they denied any involvement. There were no developments in the case until February 1983 when an Italian, Giovanni Mariotti, said to have had links with the Red Brigades in Italy, was convicted of the shooting by the Special Criminal Court on the basis of fingerprints found on the door of the room, and a previous confession (which he retracted in Court). He was jailed for twelve years. Newspaper reports at the time speculated about a connection with Revolutionary Struggle, a student organisation said to have been 'spawned' in Trinity in the mid-1970s, but nothing was ever proved.[7]

Out of numerous academic developments in the period, one in particular stands out for its historic interest. In 1978 entry to the courses leading to the award of the Divinity Testimonium was discontinued. This was the significant prelude to an epoch-making change in the status and organisation of the Divinity School. The changes had been foreshadowed in February 1968 when the Board received a letter from the Church of Ireland House of Bishops requesting a representative meeting to discuss the situation relating to the training of ordinands. In the light of the increasing disparity of numbers in the Divinity School and the Divinity Hostel, the Bishops indicated their willingness to move towards a situation where ordinand training would be centred in a Theological College in the Hostel under the direction of the Warden, with biblical and theological instruction supplied in the College through an interdenominational faculty of theology. The proposal envisaged a structural division between the academic and pastoral aspects of the training, and the Board, in reply, indicated its agreement with the general lines of the Bishops' letter.

Not surprisingly, the financial and other details of the reorganisation took a long time to work out, and the situation was complicated by the existence within the College of the two major Divinity chairs currently held by Fellows. It was noted, however, that Professor F. E. Vokes was due to retire from the Archbishop King's professorship in 1980, and Professor H. F. Woodhouse from the Regius professorship in 1982. The College undertook to suspend the chairs on their retirement, and in 1980 a new chair of theology was established. Nomination to this chair, as with the great majority of chairs in the College, was to be in the hands of the University Council and not the Divinity School Council. The appointment of Seán Vincent Freyne as from 1 January 1981 was made in this way.

So the beginning of the new decade saw an imaginative reconstruction of the College's traditional role as the main centre and focus for the training of ordinands for the Church of Ireland. No entry for the Divinity School as such appears in the 1981/82 and subsequent Calendars. Instead, an entry under the School of Hebrew, Biblical and Theological Studies directs those wishing to study the 'professional course in theology' to apply in the first instance to the Principal of the Church of Ireland Theological College (first so called in 1980) in Braemor Park. It is explained that the University provides teaching in the academic aspects of the course, while the Theological College (formerly the Divinity Hostel) undertakes the teaching of denominational aspects, together with the professional and practical skills. Students can gain their 'professional' qualifications by a three-year diploma course as well as by a four-year degree course, but all must be matriculated members of Dublin University.

On 13 July 1984, one of the hottest days of that summer, the Dining Hall went on fire at about 6 pm. The fire started high up in an attic at the south-west corner of the building. The cause was never determined. It could have been an electrical fault, but arson cannot be ruled out, particularly since the College had been plagued for some time by a rash of fire-settings, fortunately all detected before they could do extensive damage. The alarm was raised by George Dawson, a Fellow in residence, who was in the Common Room at the time. Dawson notified the security staff at the Front Gate, and the fire brigade was summoned. He also gathered a band of volunteers (staff and students, including the Students' Union Services Officer, Michael McCaughan) who succeeded in removing all the pictures and some other items from the Common Room before the fire took too firm a hold. Fire engines were soon in position with hoses playing on the roof and upper windows, but the water could not at first reach the fire which was raging through the roof space under the slates. After the roof beams collapsed and the roof fell in at about 10 pm, the flames were soon extinguished. Next morning, to everyone's amazement, all the large portraits could be seen still hanging on the walls of the smoking ruin, some quite badly damaged but others reasonably intact.

The College's Emergency Committee was soon in session, and acted with dispatch to appoint G. and T. Crampton as contractors to ensure the safety of the site and undertake salvage work under the direction of Ian Roberts and Nigel Jones from McDonnell and Dixon. The contractors moved in by mid-morning, together with the Dangerous Building Section of Dublin Corporation, whose supervisor declared unsafe the chimney stack serving the Common Room fireplace. He undertook to try to render it safe. Later in the afternoon the partially demolished stack crashed down through the floor into the buttery, doing considerable damage there. Fortunately, Cramptons had been able to use the Corporation's 'cherry-picker' to salvage Thomas Hudson's notable portrait of Frederick, Prince of Wales from the south wall before this happened. Later in the day they salvaged a further portait from the south-east corner of the Hall, and all the remaining portraits were rescued over the next two days. The Senior Dean, acting for the Provost (who was on holiday in Switzerland), appointed Dr Edward McParland to advise the contractors regading the salvage of the pictures, woodwork, and plaster fragments, and McParland supervised arrangements for the storage, safe custody, and immediate treatment of the salvaged items in the Examination Hall. He was assisted by David White, Tony Cains, and FitzMaurice Mills.

It was the unanimous wish of the College that the Hall should be restored as nearly as possible to its former condition, and this aim was triumphantly achieved under the direction of architects Shane de Blacam and John Meagher, and with the experienced assistance of Ian Roberts, who painstakingly compiled a detailed survey of the building and its fittings from the surviving fragments. Most of the oak wainscotting and other joinery was found to be not irreparably damaged, the pulpit was reconstituted, the original Portland stone floor replaced, and the portraits with their frames successfully restored and regilded. New furniture of Irish oak was fashioned in Navan and Kilbritten, and the Dublin firm of M. Creedon Ltd produced faithful reproductions of the original plasterwork. The Common Room was restored and refurnished at the same time. After a reopening ceremony on 14 October 1985, Commons was again served in the finished building from Michaelmas term onwards.[8]

The use of all parts of the catering complex had previously been under consideration by the Pearse Street Development Committee (chaired by Professor Holland and advised by de Blacam and Meagher). Underusage of the new dining hall and the cellars below it had given the building something of a 'dead heart', and outline plans for redevelopment were already in being. The fire afforded a golden opportunity for their speedy realisation, and the consulting architects devised the much-applauded concept of a central Atrium, day-lit from above. This imaginative development restored the high ceiling of the original eighteenth-century kitchen. Flanked by new accommodation for student societies, and containing two new 'private' dining rooms on its upper floors, the space at once became a popular focus for College receptions and entertainments. New kitchens and an elegant Food Hall completed the design. The architectual merit of the Atrium and its surrounds, together with the Dining Hall reconstruction, was honoured by a Europa Nostra award. The total cost of £2.7 million was covered by insurance.

In conclusion, the writer would like to draw attention to the striking fact that modern Ireland's seventh President, like her first, is a Trinity graduate. Douglas Hyde, a Protestant, was returned unopposed as a tribute to his life-long devotion to the Irish language and Irish culture. When Mary Robinson, a Catholic, triumphed in a hard-fought election in November 1990, it was on the basis of her proclaimed allegiance to an inclusive and pluralistic concept of Irish nationalism. The ideals of open-mindedness and tolerance, long cherished in the College, received a strong endorsement in her inauguration speech.[9] She had been a Scholar of the House, a part-time professor in the Law School, and a Trinity Senator (1969–88), and the College took her to its heart by electing her to honorary fellowship on Trinity Monday 1991. One could not but feel that the tide of Irish history was flowing Trinity's way.

In the past twenty-five years the country and the College have moved on convergent paths. When the jubilee of the Easter Rising was celebrated in 1966, the Board gave permission for an army artillery unit to fire a salute in College Park. At the same time the 1916 commemorative committee asked Professor T. W. Moody to give a public lecture on Thomas Davis. In retrospect, these gestures may be seen as significant symbols of mutual recognition and reconciliation. The hope must be that country and College will continue to draw increasing strength from each other. As it celebrates its four hundredth birthday, Trinity College will look forward as well as back, back over a long proud record of academic endeavour and achievement, and forward to new and wider opportunities in an evolving European Community.

The poet Yeats spoke of the 'ancient detonating impartiality' of the Anglo-Irish mind. Herein lies a strong and unpredictable force that has not seldom characterised the thoughts and actions of Trinity staff and Trinity graduates. As one looks back over the College's history, one senses this quality at work in the staunch conservatism that was needed for survival, in the surprising openness to new ideas that fostered progress, and, above all, in the spirited independence of judgment and versatility of achievement that has been the hallmark of the Trinity genius from Berkeley to Beckett.

Notes

1. For a penetrating account of Lyons's career and writings, see the appreciation by R. F. Foster in *Proceedings of the British Academy*, Vol. 70 (1984).
2. Published in 1979 as *Culture and Anarchy in Ireland, 1890–1939.*
3. Dr O'Reilly's father had attended Trinity as a King's Inns student, and he himself had received an honorary degree in 1978, partly in recognition of services rendered to Provost Lyons's Appeal. Attached to the Institute is an Innovation Centre, directed by Dr. Eoin O'Neill, and partially funded by the Industrial Development Authority.
4. These buildings represent phase one of the Pearse Street Development, designed by Dublin architects Shane de Blacam and John Meagher. Houses of Residence Nos. 47 to 52 (90 places), together with new accommodation for the Student Health Centre and the Day Nursery, came into use in the spring of 1991.
5. *Cicero, The Ascending Years* (1979), *Cicero: Verrines II.1* (1986), *Cicero, The Senior Statesman* (1990).

6. The political situation had become so tense by late April that Provost Lyons felt forced to take the very unpalatable step of cancelling a meeting arranged by the 'Phil' (with John Maxwell as president) at which General Sir John Hackett, former GOC of the British army in Northern Ireland, and Lord Chalfont, a former British cabinet minister, were due to speak. The debate was to have been on European security.
7. This account is based on reports in *The Irish Times* of 25 March 1981, 4 February 1983 and 17 February 1983.
8. For a detailed account of the restoration, see Ann Reihill, 'The Restoration of the Dining Hall, Trinity College', *Irish Arts Review*, Vol. 3, No. 1 (1986), 26–35.
9. 'The Ireland I will be representing is a new Ireland, open, tolerant, inclusive. Many of you who voted for me did so without sharing all of my views. This, I believe, is a significant signal of change, a sign, however modest, that we have clearly passed the threshold to a new pluralist Ireland.'

Appendix

Provosts of Trinity College Dublin

1592–94	Adam Loftus
1594–98	Walter Travers
1598–1601	*vacant*
1601–09	Henry Alvey
1609–27	William Temple
1627–29	William Bedell
1629–34	Robert Ussher
1634–40	William Chappell
1640–41	Richard Washington
1641–45	*vacant*
1645–50	Anthony Martin
1650–51	*vacant*
1651–60	Samuel Winter
1660–75	Thomas Seele
1675–78	Michael Ward
1679–83	Narcissus Marsh
1683–92	Robert Huntington
1692–95	St George Ashe
1695–99	George Browne
1699–1710	Peter Browne
1710–17	Benjamin Pratt
1717–58	Richard Baldwin
1758–74	Francis Andrews
1774–94	John Hely-Hutchinson
1795–99	Richard Murray
1799–1806	John Kearney
1806–11	George Hall
1811–20	Thomas Elrington
1820–31	Samuel Kyle
1831–37	Bartholomew Lloyd
1837–51	Franc Sadleir
1852–67	Richard McDonnell
1867–81	Humphrey Lloyd
1881–88	John Hewitt Jellett
1888–1904	George Salmon
1904–14	Anthony Traill
1914–19	John Pentland Mahaffy
1919–27	John Henry Bernard
1927–37	Edward John Gwynn
1937–42	William Edward Thrift
1942–52	Ernest Henry Alton
1952–74	Albert Joseph MacConnell
1974–81	Francis Stewart Leland Lyons
1981–91	William Arthur Watts
1991–	Thomas Noel Mitchell

Glossary of Trinity terminology

ad eundem (gradum)	'to the same (degree)'; a formula used of Trinity degrees conferable, without further academic exercises, on graduates of Oxford and Cambridge. The current regulations require such persons to be candidates for a Trinity higher degree, or members of the academic staff. The award is now confined to the degrees of BA and MA.
Annual officers	Fellows appointed annually by the Board, on the nomination of the Provost, to perform administrative and supervisory duties in relation to various aspects of College business. For historical reasons, particular prestige attaches to the office of Bursar, Registrar and Senior Lecturer (qq.v.). Much of the former workload of these officers is now carried by full-time professional administrators.
Botany Bay	The Square with two ranges of residences completed in 1817, lying to the north of Library Square.
Bursar	The annual officer (q.v.) concerned with the financial management of the College. By tradition he/she is also expected to take an interest in site development and maintenance, and in catering, e.g. Commons (q.v.)
cista communis	'the common chest'; the traditional name of the financial resources of the College, once kept in a strong-box, but now located in appropriate bank accounts.
Commencements	Degree conferring ceremony.
Commons	The main meal of the College, normally served with some ceremony in the old dining hall. The Provost, Fellows, Scholars, and Sizars (q.v.) are entitled to have their Commons at the charge of the College.
Fellow Commoner	A term now obsolete, but formerly used to designate a socially superior class of students who paid double fees, and were entitled to dine with the Fellows at high table.
Freshman	A generic term for undergraduate students in the first (Junior) and second (Senior) year of their course.

honor (courses, examinations)	Specialist undergraduate courses and examinations at a higher level than the ordinary (pass) course were first instituted under Provost Lloyd in the early 1830s, and grew into the system that is now the norm. The College still retains the Latinate designation for them, in preference to 'honour'.
Jurist	The Fellow (in the early College) charged with responsibility for teaching law.
Little-go	The Final Freshman (end of second year) examination in the undergraduate (pass) course.
Medicus	The Fellow (in the early College) charged with responsibility for teaching medicine.
Moderator	A candidate successful in the BA degree examination at honors level. He/she is said to have obtained a 'moderatorship'. This latter term is also applied to the various special courses leading to the award.
Pensioner	An earlier term for an undergraduate student paying standard fees.
Registrar	The annual officer (q.v.) responsible for recording the proceedings of the Board and the Senate.
Rubrics	The residential range on the east of Library Square.
Senior Lecturer	The annual officer (q.v.) responsible for the admission of duly qualified students, and for the supervision of their studies and examinations.
Sizar	Students of limited means holding entrance exhibitions (sizarships) entitling them to free Commons (q.v.)
Sophister	A generic term for undergraduate students in the third (Junior) and fourth (Senior) years of their course.

Select bibliography

A comprehensive listing of manuscript and printed sources will be found on pages 557–66 of R.B. McDowell and D.A. Webb's history of the College (*infra*).

Readers are also referred to the bibliographical essay by Charles Benson on pages 357–71 of the collection of essays on the College edited by C.H. Holland (*infra*).

For the convenience of the reader I list below the printed histories of the College, together with some other relevant items that appeared after the publication of McDowell and Webb's work.

Bailey, K.C., *A History of Trinity College Dublin, 1982–1945.* Dublin, 1947. A companion volume to Maxwell's history (*infra*). (cited as *History*)

Bennett, D., *The Silver Collection, Trinity College Dublin.* Dublin, 1988.

Coakley, D., *The Irish School of Medicine: Outstanding Practitioners of the 19th Century.* Dublin, 1988.

Crookshank, A. and D.A. Webb, *Paintings and Sculptures in Trinity College Dublin.* Dublin, 1990.

Dixon, W. Macneile, *Trinity College, Dublin.* London, 1902. (cited as *Trinity*)

Fox, P. (ed.), *Treasures of the Library, Trinity College Dublin.* Dublin, 1986.

Holland, C.H. (ed.), *Trinity College Dublin and The Idea of a University.* Dublin, 1991.

Luce, J.V., *Orationes Dublinienses Selectae.* Dublin, 1991.

Mahaffy, J.P., *An Epoch in Irish History: Trinity College Dublin, Its Foundation and Early Fortunes, 1591–1660.* London, 1903. Reprinted, Port Washington and London, 1970. (cited as *Epoch*)

Maxwell, C., *A History of Trinity College, Dublin 1591–1892.* Dublin, 1946. (cited as *History*)

McDowell, R.B. and D.A. Webb, *Trinity College Dublin, 1592–1952: An Academic History.* Cambridge, 1982. (cited as *History*)

McParland, E.J., *The Buildings of Trinity College, Dublin.* Dublin, 1977. Reprinted from *County Life* nos. 4114–16 and 4137–38 (1976).

Murphy, H.L. *A History of Trinity College Dublin from its Foundation to 1702.* Dublin, 1951. (cited as *History*)

Scott, D., *The Modern Art Collection: Trinity College Dublin.* Dublin, 1989.

Stubbs, J.L., *The History of the University of Dublin from its Foundations to the End of the Eighteenth Century.* Dublin, 1889. (cited as *History*)

Taylor, W.B.S., *History of the University of Dublin.* London, 1845.

Urwick, W., *The Early History of Trinity College Dublin, 1591–1660.* London and Dublin, 1892.

West, T.T., *The Bold Collegians: The Development of Sport in Trinity College Dublin.* Dublin, 1991.

Index

Note: 'n' before a figure in brackets denotes footnote reference

D

E

N

Other titles in the Trinity College Dublin Quatercentenary Series

No. 1 *The Silver Collection Trinity College Dublin* by Douglas Bennett

No. 2 *The Modern Art Collection Trinity College Dublin*
Compiled by David Scott

No. 3 *Trinity: One of the Great European Centres of Learning*

No. 4 *Paintings and Sculptures in Trinity College Dublin*
by Anne Crookshank and David Webb

No. 5 *Orationes Dublinienses Selectae* by John Victor Luce

No. 6 *Trinity College Dublin and the Idea of a University*
Edited by Charles Holland

No. 8 *Trinity College Dublin Record Volume 1991*
Compiled by D.A. Webb. Edited by J.R. Bartlett